Endorsements

"Stealing Fire from the Gods, a remarkably deep and subtle understanding of Buddhist meditation, is integrated with cutting edge insights into psychotherapy, developmental psychology, and contemporary spirituality. In this compelling account, the path to liberation involves complete embodiment, entering the fullness of our human incarnation, opening to its depths and all of its light and dark, and surrendering to the inherent, healing, self-transforming power within us. Buddhist meditation, in Rechtshaffer's description, is all about the deepest spiritual longing within each of us and how it opens the way to insight, freedom, and love, and enables us to find our own unique place within all the realms of being. This is a most extraordinary book, one that will inform, reassure, guide, and inspire anyone seeking to follow a spiritual way of life today."

~ **Reginald A. Ray, PhD, author of** *Touching Enlightenment*; *Indestructible Truth*; *Secret of the Vajra World*; *Buddhists Saints in India*; *In the Presence of Masters*; **former faculty member of Naropa University**

"Dr. Rechtshaffer draws upon many years of Buddhist practice and years of being a therapist to map a clear road through the confusions of life to lead to a more centered and peace-filled existence. He addresses both the powers and the potential blindspots of each tradition to let the reader see how they might navigate the challenges of meditation as well as those that life presents. The subtlety of his rendering of psychology and meditation is illuminated by his own experiences as a meditation teacher and draw anecdotes from his therapy practice. Underneath his straightforward common sense presentation is a scholarly understanding that doesn't interfere with the narrative, making his book very readable.

"Looking at the table of contents gives a sense of the breadth of the work and the intriguing way the author has created metaphors appropriate for his subjects. Having been in both disciplines for more than forty years, I appreciate the way the author explores themes so crucial to our survival and progress in a world that, at times, seems like it has gone crazy. If you have had a bit of therapy, done some meditation, or are just curious, this is a good book to read. There's much to learn here."

~ **Charlie Fisher, PhD, author and Emeritus Prof. Brandeis University**

"Stealing Fire from the Gods is a distillation of Ira Rechtshaffer's decades long experience as a practitioner and teacher of Buddhist dharma. With the heart and mind of one who deeply understands challenges of the crucible of self-transformation, he leads us on a hero's journey of self-discovery. In this book we sojourn through the dark places of our being, into the belly of the whale, and ultimately to an awakening of our authentic humanity. Read this book as an instruction manual for living a meaningful life in these challenging times."

~ **Reb Simcha Raphael, PhD, Founding and Spiritual Director DA'AT, Institute for Death Awareness, Advocacy and Training; author** *Jewish Views of the Afterlife*, **Rabbinic Pastor, Transpersonal Psychotherapist**

"While pursuing his own path of inner transformation, Ira Rechtshaffer has mastered many growth-related disciplines— including writing numerous books of heart and wisdom from which seeds of transformation burst forth simply in the reading. *Stealing Fire from the Gods* draws upon Ira's mastery of the essential Buddhist path, his many years as a psychotherapist, and his gift of the teacher's trusted voice—to help us infuse the path we take each day as Westerners with perennial Buddhist insight and wisdom. Reading his written word is much like having a conversation with a very wise, warm, and caring friend. Guidance for opening the gates of wisdom and for lifting veils of confusion is alive and very present through each of eight thresholds, that are identified along the path. As readers respond to the invitation to "steal fire from the gods," awareness is sparked and everyday reality is illuminated."

> ~ **Barbara L. Schultz, MA, Executive/Leadership Coach, InsightOut Coach, Leadership Coach, Change Leadership Strategist, Transformation Guide**

> "This is a very important, profound and life-changing book. It brings the height of esoteric wisdom in the Buddhist path down to the most ordinary aspects of our life, all in a very personal way. It goes beyond the religiosity of Buddhism and makes its wisdom available to all. It is both refreshing and a poignant call to action in life. Highly recommended to all spiritual seekers, regardless of religious affiliation."

> ~ **James Sacamano, MD, author of** *Getting Back to Wholeness, the Treasure of Inner Health and the Power of a Meaningful Life*

> "Ira Rechtshaffer has a gorgeous, sensual relationship to thoughts and words. His lifetime dedication to the path of psychospiritual development allows him to introduce gnarly issues in the simplest and most accessible of manners. He has done the work! This book will make yours easier!"

> ~ **Susan Aposhyan, author of** *Natural Intelligence: Human Development and Body-Mind Integration, Body-Mind Psychotherapy,* **and the forthcoming** *Heart Open, Body Awake: the Four Steps of Embodied Spirituality* **(Shambhala Publications, Spring 2020)**

"Stealing Fire from the Gods elucidates the spiraling spiritual journey of crossing through eight thresholds of development in becoming fully human and living up to our full potential. Drawing from Vajrayana Buddhism, Jungian psychology, a wealth of psychodynamic experience as a therapist, Ira Rechtshaffer weaves a solid and pithy framework of easy-to-identify experience markers on the path to realization. The result is an easy-to-read and entertaining guide to the heights and pitfalls of a Buddhist practitioner navigating everyday life."

~ **Melissa Moore, PhD, Executive Director of Karuna Training North America**

"For some spiritual aspirants, the writings of esoteric Buddhism can feel dry, heady, and disconnected from their daily living and very human struggles. Not so with Rechtshaffer's new book, *Stealing Fire from the Gods*. He writes, "The Buddhist path is about how to cultivate a love affair with our life. We do this by embracing ourselves wholly—both the good and the bad, the broken and beautiful, our wounds and our virtues." He brings ancient Buddhist wisdom to contemporary life, making it ever so relevant and useful to our living as ordinary human beings. Rechtshaffer illuminates how the embodied living of our human experience is where the spiritual "fire" is to be found. By embracing all that our human experience offers us, both in pain and in glory, we are delivered to the sublimity of our existence and to our very own Buddha nature.

"Blending his many years as a Buddhist practitioner with his training as a psychotherapist, Rechtshaffer provides the missing link in most spiritual and psychological texts—namely, that we are both holy and ordinary, and it is in embracing both our human ordinariness and our unique divinity that we are made whole. His model provides an wholistic approach to the task of spiritual awakening; one that tenderly advises us to meet ourselves with deeper and deeper levels of lovingkindness exactly where we are...where nothing is excluded and all is illuminated by the light of meditative awareness. Let this beautiful book be a steppingstone on your love affair with your own uniquely human and sacred life."

~ **Tina M. Benson, MA, author of** *A Woman Unto Herself: A Different Kind of Love Story,* **and** *Soul Whisperings: Erotic and Devotional Love Poems for an Outer or Inner Beloved*

"Ira Rechtshaffer is one of America's most sage, down-to-earth, and experienced therapist-authors on applying Buddhist principles and meditation practice to one's own daily life toward more balance, humanity and grace. *Stealing Fire from the Gods* reveals the practice of meditation as an adventurous and provocative journey of everyday life. I have known of his work since 1979 and it only gets better as the decades have rolled on. You can hear his tried-and-true confidence and kindness in every word he writes, as he guides you toward the wholeness that we all seek."

~ **Stuart Sovatsky, PhD, co-president emeritus, Association for Transpersonal Psychology, author,** *Advanced Spiritual Intimacy*

Stealing Fire from the Gods:

The Journey of Buddhist Meditation in Everyday Life

by

Ira Rechtshaffer

©Copyright 2020 by Ira Rechtshaffer Ph.D
Second Edition

All rights reserved. No part of this publication may be reproduced, stored in a retrieval system or transmitted in any form, or by any means (electronic, mechanical, photocopying, recording or otherwise) without the prior written permission of the author and the publisher.

Published by: Indra's Net
                San Rafael, California
Cover Design: Constance King Design

ISBN: 978-1-7359835-0-9

This book is dedicated to the many teachers from the various schools of Buddhism, who have transplanted the Buddhist teachings of liberation here in the West for the benefit of all.

Acknowledgements

I would like to offer appreciation to my editor, Laura Duggan, for providing helpful editorial suggestions and constructive criticism, and for her support and encouragement. I also want to extend my appreciation for the group of men and women who came together to form a sangha, a community of mindfulness practitioners, to whom these Dharma talks were given. This book could never have been written without having received the profound teachings of Buddhism from innumerable teachers over the past four decades. To them I offer a deep bow of gratitude. I also want to express gratitude for the many Western writers who have been integrating Eastern spirituality with Western psychology, establishing a developmental or evolutionary psychology, which has added richness and depth to the path of waking up and growing up.

TABLE OF CONTENTS

Preface vii

Introduction: Finding Your Own Light 1

First Threshold: The Wake-Up Call 7
  1. Disappointment as the First Threshold 9
  2. The Secret Gate 15
  3. Necessary Sacrifices 25

Second Threshold: The Siren's Call 37
  4. The Tricks We Play on Ourselves 39
  5. Ego's Footprints 45
  6. Cutting Through Ego is Only Half the Story 55
  7. Ego's Bureaucracy: Subpersonalities 65
  8. Buddha's Last Temptation: Facing Our Demons 73

Third Threshold: Journey into the Labyrinth 85
  9. Motivation, Desire, and Grasping 87
  10. Karmic Entrapment and Liberation 95
  11. The Karma of Personality 105
  12. Character and Meaningful Coincidence 113

Fourth Threshold: Belly of the Whale   **121**
  13. Trusting our Right to be Here   123
  14. The Method and Essence of Meditation   129
  15. Mindfulness and Awareness   135
  16. Being All There   141
  17. Meditation as a Way of Life   147

Fifth Threshold: The Journey of Descent   **159**
  18. The Wisdom of the Body   161
  19. Pleasure: Problem or Promise   169
  20. The Two Faces of Desire   175
  21. Fearless Love   181

Sixth Threshold: The Journey of Ascent   **191**
  22. The Life We've Been Missing   193
  23. The Mystery of Being   201
  24. Freedom   209
  25. Warriors of Virtue: The Bodhisattva Path   215

Seventh Threshold: Heaven, Earth, and Human   **233**
  26. Not Knowing   235
  27. Integrating the Horizontal and Vertical Paths   241
  28. Imagination: Bridge Between Heaven & Earth   251
  29. Soulfulness: Finding Heaven on Earth   259

30. The Web of Life: Earth Community & Culture 267

Eighth Threshold: Being Human **277**
   31. Redefining Leisure 279
   32. Celebrating Daily Life 287
   33. Loving What's Wild 295
   34. The Seasons of Life 301

Epilogue: Enlightenment Wherever You Are 311

About the Author 317

STEALING FIRE FROM THE GODS

Preface

This book is based on excerpts from transcribed talks that I gave to a Buddhist meditation group over the span of several years. My intention was to offer people a safe place to meditate and to articulate a map for how to walk the Buddhist spiritual path, regardless of one's beliefs or religious affiliations. Buddhism views the path of meditation as a developmental or evolutionary process, one that develops through stages, each building upon the previous stage.

The path of meditation described in this book developed out of the Buddhist nontheistic tradition. Nontheism is not a rejection of the divine, but regards the idea of God and the gods to be metaphors or symbols that inspire the mind to go beyond itself. Buddha was a human being, an historical embodiment of the Eastern traditional path of spiritual enlightenment and liberation.

Spirituality is the growing awareness that we are in relationship with an intelligent, living, and responsive universe of which we are an integral part. We are embedded in nature, and at the same time, nature animates every atom and molecule, every cell and organ of our body, and its intelligence radiates through every aspect of our mind. The spiritual path is a process of deepening this understanding and dissolving the false sense of separation between our mind and body, between self and other, and between ourselves and the natural world.

It's instructive that the word "spirit" comes from the Latin *spirare*, which means "to blow or breathe"—suggesting an animating or vital principle that gives life to all beings, as when God blew the breath of life into Adam, as described in Genesis. When we feel inspired (also from the root *spirare*) we feel enlivened, infused with energy, uplifted, moved, or guided by a vision. From this perspective, the spiritual process is about life and aliveness. We can connect with the deepest place within ourselves where this quality of aliveness is most available. It is the source of love, compassion, and understanding. Meditation is a time-honored and time-tested method for discovering our own light and aliveness.

I think it's safe to say that we all want an inspired and abundant life, one that affirms our heartfelt purpose and our unique significance. The great teachers of the past have taught that by tapping into our aliveness, we draw on the very same life force that animates all of life, and this is what permits us to manifest an inspired and abundant life. This energy or force is the "fire of the gods," but it exists within our own heart, at the core of our very being.

The Buddhist teachings go to the heart of what human beings want most—to be released from our sense of isolation, limitation, and suffering, and to discover a creative way to deepen our humanity. This book articulates a map for how you can access the fire of aliveness and how you can tend your fire so that it sheds illumination, warmth, and a fierce energy to accomplish your life.

I invite you to take a journey with me to discover your own fire.

Stealing Fire from the Gods:

The Journey of Buddhist Meditation in Everyday Life

STEALING FIRE FROM THE GODS

Introduction:
Finding Your Own Light

In the crack of huge granite boulder, a small crisp seed embeds itself in a sliver of dark earth. It waits patiently for the right moment, and without so much as a thought, a shoot magically springs forth, faithful to its genetic blueprints, and moves infallibly towards its fruition. Drawing sustenance from its meager surroundings, this tender shoot soon breaks the soil's surface and arches towards the light of the sun. Upon reaching the apex of its development, its vulnerable petals fearlessly spread open before the expanse of space. Before its demise, without fear of death or hope of immortality, it will ensure the continuity of the species, making a complete life cycle from seed to seed.

How perfectly simple. Birth, growth, completion, continuity—fulfillment. Life without ambiguity and death without struggle. Why couldn't we simply permit nature to move through us as it does through a plant, without the challenge of choice or the burden of indecision, without the consideration of consequences, or regret over the unanticipated results of our actions? For we humans, it's another matter altogether. We become fully human through our effort to find meaning, value, and purpose in our lives so that our passage from womb to tomb feels like it has a rightful place in the immense design of things.

When we truly engage our hunger to discover who we are at our depth and why we're here—*this* is the wake-up call, announcing that it's time for a fresh way of looking at our lives so that we can touch life deeply and be opened to its magic. This is the spark that initiates the stealing of the sacred fire.

The title for this book comes from the well-known myth of Prometheus and his fire theft from the gods, but the book draws its inspiration from the nontheistic tradition of Buddhism, which is more a path of liberation from anxiety and neurosis than what we in the West think of as religion. The Sanskrit term *Buddha* means "awakened one," indicating that a human being, and not a god, realized his ultimate nature. The nontheistic approach to spirituality teaches us that no cosmic entity will protect or guide us on our exploration into our own deepest nature. We each must contend with and answer the great existential questions of the human condition.

The Buddha's *Dharma* or teaching, is a 2,600-year-old map for how to live an abundant life, one of creativity and compassion, joy and peace. By walking this path we learn how to skillfully cut through our habit of obsessive thinking, soothe our emotional reactivity, and transform our distorted beliefs about ourselves and the world. In essence, the Buddhist path is a process of personal transformation enabling us to perceive a sacred world without reliance upon a cosmic deity. Meditation is the indispensable vehicle and trusted ally that guides us along the way.

For our human journey to continue evolving we must go up the mountain to the exalted place where the "gods" live (our

Introduction: Finding Your Own Light

own deep mind) and reclaim the sacred fire that is hoarded there. Fire is the luminous awareness of our innate wisdom. It is the luminosity of the spiritually awakened mind, the warmth of compassion, the energy of inspiration, the heat of primordial desire that magnetizers us to love the world. Fire is the image of hope, the flame of truth that ignites our innate wisdom. Like a brilliant bolt of lightning that sears the evening sky, fire also symbolizes communication between heaven and earth, between our unconscious psyche and our self-conscious mind.

The element of fire illuminates a way to go forward to continue our human journey. However, when we bring the divine fire down off the mountain top, it must be embodied within a well-integrated personality that has given equal attention to the development of mind and body, heart and soul. If the energy and force of fire is to shine through us without distortion and without causing destructive consequences, then we must transform ourselves to be worthy holders of the fire. For this integration to be successful, a map is very helpful to clarify the pitfalls, temptations, blind alleys, and "demons" that will inevitably confront us.

The particular emphasis of this book is that the practice of meditation is an evolutionary path of discrete stages, one building upon the next. I have envisioned the practice of meditation as a sequence of eight thresholds that we pass through on our way to discovering greater aliveness, awareness, and joy in everyday life. The first threshold, "Wake-Up Call," marks the initiation into the meditative state of mind. It begins by leaving home, as the Buddha did—leaving the status quo, the cocoon of our habitual and predictable lives.

The first threshold is followed by "The Siren's Call," which represents the perilous seductions and temptations that throw us off course, distracting and entertaining us into mindlessness. The threshold of the "Journey into the Labyrinth" describes the more subtle challenge of how to creatively work with the law of karmic cause-and-effect. We learn how our desires and motivations shape both of our thoughts and behaviors and the world in which we live, for better or worse. The "Belly of the Whale" is the sacred crucible of meditation itself, where we enter into more profound periods of incubation and reflection that deepen our awareness and that promote our personal transformation.

The complementary thresholds of "Journey of Descent" and "Journey of Ascent" challenge us with the more subtle problems and promises of both embodiment and transcendence. The threshold of "Reconciling Heaven, Earth, and Human" describes and explains how to integrate the contrary pulls of the horizontal and vertical paths—embodiment and transcendence, that is, growing up and waking up. And the last threshold, "Being Human," is the culmination of the meditative journey, where we can embody simplicity, freedom and joy in everyday life.

We cross one threshold after another where we meet the denied or unacknowledged aspects of our larger self—the elements of our own unlived life. Eventually through a series of challenges we discover what our true gift is to bring back to the world. Through this journey we discover that the enlightened energy and intelligence that we've attributed to our gods (God, guru, and grace) is the very same energy and intelligence that burns in each of our hearts. In the ordinary affairs of everyday

Introduction: Finding Your Own Light

life, the human and the divine, the sacred and secular, live side-by-side. When the lines of communication between the two are ruptured, the odyssey must be undertaken again to heal this rupture.

The main purpose of a genuine spiritual path is to initiate us into the depths of our own mind and heart, guiding us towards the realization of our true identity. But for this to be realized we must be able to trust ourselves and the world in which we live. This, in turn, is based on knowing *who* and *what* we are, and *why* we're here, so that we may discover our unique gift to offer to the world.

STEALING FIRE FROM THE GODS

First Threshold: The Wake-Up Call

The motivation to embark on a spiritual path usually comes from the experience of dissatisfaction. Plodding along day after day we might suddenly realize that we've been on a plateau without having experienced anything new, fresh, eventful, or uplifting for a long time. There's no longer a song in our heart, yet we feel compelled to keep the beat going, dutifully walking the tried and true way of many yesterdays, until one day we can no longer postpone the urgent need to cut the rope and be free.

The spiritual passage begins with questioning our cherished assumptions about who we are and whether the life we have chosen has been a conscious choice. By considering these questions, we retreat from the world into our depths where great challenges await. It is here, in this invisible domain, that we become more sensitive to our unmet longings, but also to our feelings of limitation and the pain of dissatisfaction. Yet, as we continue to communicate with our inner being in all of its manifold expressions, we eventually get to know the real longing of our heart.

Here in our interior world, we have the opportunity to re-claim a brilliant energy that can both liberate us from the tedium of merely surviving, and invigorate our lives. This timeless life force circulates through all of existence, and although it has never been lost, paradoxically, we must search for it in order to discover this forgotten dimension of ourselves.

STEALING FIRE FROM THE GODS

1.

Disappointment as the First Threshold

Samsara has been defined as wanting what you can't get and getting what you don't want. Disappointment sobers us up from wishful thinking and levels the playing field, inspiring us to seriously question our beliefs about ourselves and our life. Disappointment can provoke a spiritual quest.

Imagine that on a bright sunny day you visit a neighborhood park. Families are sitting on blankets, sharing food and drinks and enjoying each other's company. Young couples are playfully tossing a frisbee while their dog chases in mad pursuit. Brightly colored balloons strung to a family's picnic table are bobbing in the air amidst the joyous laughter and raucous shouts of children. All is well here. Feeling relaxed and at peace, you lie down on your blanket and fall asleep. You sleep soundly, but upon waking you discover that the park is deserted except for several men picking up trash. The temperature has dropped, and ominous clouds are rolling in. You wonder if you dreamt that idyllic scene of children laughing, frisbees spinning, and balloons dancing in the air. Unfamiliar feelings of vulnerability and disorientation now take hold of you.

Change can insinuate itself in our lives ever so slightly until one day it feels as if the entire atmosphere has changed, causing us to question how this happened. We didn't notice the subtle shifts taking place beneath the distracting business of everyday life. These disorienting moments are also precious because like a cosmic slap in the face, they wake us up and bring us face-to-face with the realization that we've been hiding from ourselves. When life has reshuffled our cards without consulting us, we have to make our way through feelings of "being at a loss." But getting what we weren't expecting can initiate a process of inquisitiveness. We might get to see who and what we've been holding onto to conceal life's unpredictable shadowy side.

After years of one kind of meditation or another, and even after years of psychotherapy, we're not immune from feeling distressed by life's capricious turns. A spouse becomes seriously ill and needs hospitalization; one of our children becomes addicted to drugs and refuses our intervention; a teenage daughter has become emotionally inaccessible, and we're at a loss for how to bridge the gap. We don't know how or when it happened, but like the fog creeping in, little by little, she gradually became remote and unrecognizable to us. Such events provoke us to question how we might have contributed to such painful outcomes.

Disappointment is not a very sexy topic. Yet, it's unavoidable in ordinary life and can initiate a spiritual quest. Disappointment could mean not achieving your goals or objectives, or not being able to either magnetize or maintain a loving relationship, or feeling defeated for not living up to your standards or ethical principles, or feeling helpless to protect your loved ones from danger. In a more general sense, no matter how careful or strategic you play it, it's the failure to get what you

First Threshold: The Wake-Up Call

want, or to avoid getting what you don't want. We can't always insulate ourselves from life's uncertain twists and turns. From time to time, even the best of us could find ourselves in free fall.

Few people begin or persist on a genuine spiritual path without experiencing a kind of disappointment that doesn't admit of a remedy. If we're going to wholeheartedly engage the spiritual process then we must be wary of the temptation to deny or rationalize the feeling of being burdened by something that's hard to name. Our life may bring us to the edge of our known world and invite us to step into uncharted territory. Finding ourselves not knowing how to go forward can leave us with a formless malaise.

There are many ways in which the feeling of disappointment creeps into our lives. Sometimes the bottom falls out abruptly and we're in the midst of a crisis. We might wake up one morning to realize that there's very little meaning either in our life or in our work. We could begin to feel that the life that we've been living is not the one we chose, and day by day we lose heart. "What did I do wrong?" we might muse to ourselves. We could find ourselves dealing with the pain of unexpected loneliness, finding ourselves without close friendships, and feeling confused how it came to this. We could be dealing with illness that saps our energy and compromises the quality of our life, limiting the things we can do. Or we suddenly recognize that we're in an older body, having diminished energy, suffering aches and pains that we never had before. It seems like just a short time ago we were enjoying downhill skiing and hiking, and now we need walking poles to walk a flat trail. It can all feel surrealistic and haunting.

Such disappointments drop us into places that we wouldn't go to voluntarily. Yet there's something valuable about being delivered to our depths, beyond ego's controlled and rational world. As spiritual practitioners we're encouraged to bring disappointments onto our path, so that we witness how we try to protect ourselves from the raw, rugged, and unpredictable aspects of life. The Buddhist practice is to develop complete openness to whatever life brings us, so that we experience all situations and the feelings they evoke, without reservations. This is a daring gesture, but the spiritual process is an *initiation*—one that can transform our disillusionments into a refreshing sense of openness and intimacy with life.

Many years ago I decided to live in a small cabin in rural Vermont in order to meditate and write. After several years I ran out of money and needed to resume working again, but I didn't know what to do. I was a veteran teacher with a Ph.D., but I wanted to work with human suffering in a deeper way than teaching permitted. So, I continued meditating and writing, dropping deeper into my condition, as emptiness stretched out and filled the margins of my life. In truth, I was at a loss and felt groundless.

One winter evening a friend telephoned me, sounding very shaky. He explained that his wife had just left him and that he had started drinking and smoking again, and was feeling really scared. I invited him to come over, knowing that the northern Vermont roads in the evening were mostly empty, and cautioned him to drive very safely. Forty minutes later, Benjamin arrived with his two dogs, a case of beer and a carton of cigarettes. He sat down and began talking from a place of deep hurt. I was just there with him listening deeply to his feelings of

First Threshold: The Wake-Up Call

loss and hurt. We stayed up all night talking about the pain of betrayal and abandonment, life and love, men and women, meaninglessness and the purpose-driven life. By about 5:00 a.m. I began preparing breakfast and made a pot of strong coffee.

After a silent breakfast, we sat quietly as the morning light filled the kitchen. At some point I looked at Benjamin and asked, "You okay?" to which he replied, "Yeah, I am actually." An hour or two later, after many cups of coffee, he stated that he felt safe to drive. He thanked me for being there for him, summoned his two dogs and started moving towards the door. With his body halfway out the door, he abruptly turned to me and said, "You should do this for a living!" At that moment, everything that was vague and uncertain in my life, crystallized on the spot into a direction. Within a month I applied to graduate school again, but this time to get a clinical degree so that I could become a psychotherapist—one who could integrate psychotherapy with spirituality. This event awakened in me a calling, a sincere wish to be there for others during their "dark night."

Prior to Benjamin's visit I was lost and confused about what to do with my life. My commitment to my spiritual path was to not deny my true condition, and so I remained in that unsettled feeling of having lost my way. I could not find the reassuring cord that connected one chapter of my life with the others, giving it a sense of coherence and continuity. The encounter with Benjamin was an initiation. Because my mind and heart had been ripened through so much disappointment, as the seed of possibility fell, it blossomed immediately. *All* of me was there in that vivid moment with Benjamin.

Although it seems counterintuitive, when we keep company with disappointment, especially during a dark night of the soul, something positively unexpected might come of it. At the same time, we mustn't forget to extend compassion and loving-kindness to ourselves, and not judge ourselves harshly when we're feeling bereft, confused, and lonely. It's important that we shine kindness, gentleness, and tenderness on ourselves so that we can remain intimately connected with our mind and body, heart and soul during such periods.

2.

The Secret Gate

A spiritual path invites us to step into the unknown, where we are confronted by a gate that either invites or restricts our passage. If we dare to step through, we meet our unlived life. This requires our willingness to be vulnerable. Meditation is like walking through a gate repeatedly.

The motivation to steal the "fire from the gods" usually begins with a change in personal atmosphere, a growing sensitivity to our inner world, and the recognition that all is not as well as we had previously thought. Although our lives may be successful in the conventional sense, in terms of work, family, and friendships, our dissatisfaction might be vague and unnameable, creeping in like a strange mist. We might feel that we want release from something that has us in its grip so that we can feel free.

Perhaps our life has stopped growing in meaningful ways. Although we may not be suffering grossly, we're not looking forward to anything either. We're getting through our days eating, sleeping, paying bills, going to work, and dying a little bit every day. This might be analogous to the Buddha's first noble truth of suffering. It's the first blessing on the path of self-discovery because it can provoke a question that burns in our heart.

Mythologist Joseph Campbell termed such a moment "The Call," an intuition to begin a journey that cuts a path beneath the surface of our everyday life. It might present itself as some innocent mishap or chance encounter that hints at an unsuspected world lying parallel to our everyday life. The story of the Buddha's early life is a poignant example of receiving and responding to such a call.

Siddhartha was the given name (Prince Siddhartha) of the man who would later be called the Buddha, (the awakened one). Just prior to his birth, his father, who was the king of a vast empire, consulted a fortune teller who predicted that Siddhartha would not inherit his kingdom. He would choose a radically different path and become a king—but not a worldly one. The king was determined to alter the predicted fate of his son so that he would inherit his kingdom and continue his lineage. Upon the birth of the prince, the king strategically designed the palace compound so that his son would find life in the palace irresistibly attractive, and not be tempted to consider any other alternative to his royal life. A staff of the king's subjects were appointed to go around the kingdom and beautify the numerous palatial environments, so that wherever the prince walked, flowers were spread out on his path. Very aged or visibly ill people were relocated so that the prince would not encounter them, and if there was a death in the kingdom, the prince was not made aware of it. He was kept insulated and immune from the harsh realities of life in order to dissuade him from setting out on his own path, as predicted by the fortuneteller.

First Threshold: The Wake-Up Call

Prince Siddhartha lived in a luxurious palace and had an aristocratically privileged life, but a sheltered one. One fateful day in his twenty-ninth year he requested his servants to prepare for an outing beyond the palace compound. Although the prince's adventure begins benignly—in a remarkable series of encounters—Siddhartha, for the first time in his life, meets a very aged man, followed by a group of diseased lepers, and then he happens upon a decomposing human body. A seemingly chance occasion reveals an unsuspected world.

The prince was both shocked and saddened. His cocoon-like world was ruptured by his confrontation with the existential realities of old age, sickness, and death. On the way back to the palace he encounters a slender shaven-headed man, wearing only a loin cloth and carrying a begging bowl. Having never seen anyone like this before, the prince inquired why this man was wandering without clothing or possessions. The yogi replied that he was a *sannyasin*, a seeker of truth. In that moment, the prince's life in the palace became a prison. This seemingly accidental encounter was an opening into his destiny.

Siddhartha recognized that the life that he was living, although utterly privileged, was a profound limitation. The old ideals and royal way of being no longer fit him. He had outgrown his privileged life. It was time for him to cross a threshold into the unknown. That evening the future Buddha left his family, dropped his status as a prince, and abandoned the inheritance of his father's kingdom. In his heart of hearts he knew it was time to step into a much deeper dimension of life. A *gate* opened and he walked through it.

For the next six years he practiced the spiritual methods and sacred technologies that were in vogue in 6th century BCE

India, none of which satisfied his yearning for truth, but which eventually led to his spiritual awakening years later under the famed *bodhi* tree.

Many of us have probably had moments when we stepped through a portal which became a passageway to the next chapter of our life—the next relationship, the next job, the next place to live. Or perhaps our status abruptly changed when we became a parent, a widow, a retiree, or a disabled person. At the moment a gate opened, which might have felt both fearful and inviting, fortuitous yet uncertain. We could hear the "call," but perhaps we resisted stepping through because this gesture threatened our safety and security, and our sense of control.

A gate has a paradoxical function. It both permits and restricts entrance. On one hand, we may not recognize that we're encountering an "opening" with its hint of invitation. Or having recognized a gate, a chance opening, we might back off from the invitation to explore new possibilities because of the sharp edge of uncertainty. If we dare to step beyond our familiar boundaries, into "foreign territory," we could feel excited but also unsure how to handle ourselves. We might not realize that we're not hearing, seeing, or feeling anything refreshingly new— *until* we inch up to the gate, and step through it. Once we step through a gate, like Prince Siddhartha, we're stepping into the unknown where our *unlived* life awaits us. The whole design of our existence can change abruptly.

We exercise control over many things in our lives until calamity hits and then suddenly we're left with very few choices. When we get sick, we only want to get well, or we only want the pain to stop. If we have the misfortune of being involved in a car accident or when someone whom we love leaves us, suddenly

First Threshold: The Wake-Up Call

everything narrows. Having few choices intensifies our attention, and that may not be a bad thing. There's something relieving about that. Life's mysteries seem to surface in the cracks where our familiar and predictable life begins to crumble. At such times we could suddenly become aware of a gate that has been closed for decades.

We might notice for the first time that our teenage daughter or son doesn't depend on us or consult with us any longer, but prefers the counsel of her or his peers. Although we appreciate their maturity and new-found freedom, we might also feel obsolete in our role as a parent. On the other hand, the gate door could swing open as we experience liberation from our parental role as we joyfully anticipate opportunities that we had postponed for many years.

While preparing breakfast one morning, a heaviness lingers in our heart, pressing downwards, as we're gripped by the tedium of getting through another day without anything bright or promising to look forward to. Yet, in the next moment our knife cuts through a Macintosh apple, piercing the early-morning stillness with a crisp *shhhhhhhhhhish.....* Just that, and nothing else. Suddenly the melodious song of a sparrow draws our attention to the window where a Japanese maple dances in the wind, reminding us that *this* moment is the best season of our lives. A gate opens.

I think that most of us would agree that we experience some fear when we step into an open situation without structure or agenda. We're not sure what to do next. For instance, you're with a friend or your partner and you're sitting at a table across from one another. Both of you suddenly find yourselves looking into one another's eyes, but instead of filling in the space with conversation, you allow the wordless, naked moment to linger. There's something utterly intimate, revealing, and yet terrifying about maintaining that tender-hearted, open-eyed contact. There's no telling what will happen next. You could laugh, shed a tear, hug the other person and say "I love you." Or you could pour another drink, put on the music and flee from the moment because such intimacy is too revealing. In that case, a gate closes and restricts further passage.

We might notice how fearful or reluctant we are to be totally transparent before another. We all wear social masks or personas that are suited to our various social roles and their predictable scripts. We "play" at being the protective spouse, or the cheerful, upbeat friend, or the helpful parent as we try to solve our children's problems. But on occasion we're thrown *beyond* our social roles. This can be both exciting and confusing. There's a real fear of social transparency, of being completely visible to ourselves. In an unguarded moment we might see ourselves as we really are, and not as we imagine ourselves to be. In that experience of vulnerability a gate opens.

When we enter into the deeper dimensions of our mind and our heart, we meet the uninspected portions of our life. Initially, this could feel like opening up the attic door of our home for the first time in several decades. We might be confronted by a tangle of disjointed thoughts, images, and impulses. Yet if we don't panic, things eventually get sorted out. A clearing might suddenly appear in the densely wooded forest of our mind. With a refreshed perspective we could discover what's next in our life, something we weren't counting on. A gate has opened.

First Threshold: The Wake-Up Call

The haunting truth is that wherever you go, there you are! There's no real escape from ourselves and so when we talk about freedom in a spiritual sense we're talking about freedom from the patterns that shape our thoughts, emotions, and behavior—patterns that make us predictable and that limit us. Recognizing our patterns, and gradually liberating ourselves from their grip, is what opens the gate. This is the invitation to spread our wings and fly into the uncharted territory of the life that's waiting for us.

Meditation is like walking through a gate repeatedly. It's the practice of sitting in stillness and silence, and observing the activity of our mind without judgment or reaction. We witness our thoughts, feelings, and bodily sensations, but instead of entertaining them, we immediately release them, which takes us back to square one—here and now.

The bareness of ongoing moments of silence and stillness challenges us with boredom and loneliness. Most people think of loneliness as the absence of other people, but our loneliness may be our distance from ourselves. We may be so preoccupied and our thought patterns so compulsive and compelling, that we're lost in inner space, removed from genuine presence. Boredom and loneliness can be huge obstacles on the spiritual path. We do all kinds of things to keep the atmosphere percolating, distracting and entertaining, but we may be closing the gate on a deep dialogue with loneliness and boredom.

What exactly are we trying to protect ourselves from? What are our defenses preventing us from seeing? Are there places that are off-limits, places in our mind or our life that are taboo? What happens when we bring our attention to those places? For some people anger is "off limits," while for others it's sexuality and intimacy. Some people find that reshuffling the deck and doing something really new is threatening. Off-limits could mean moving out of our head and into our heart, *feeling* through a situation, rather than thinking it through.

The *closed* gate is usually the place in our mind that has a big sign "Do not enter," but it might lead us to what has been forbidden by our parents since our childhood. Our unlived life may be waiting for us in the very place we've pushed away for many years. But of course, not all gates should be opened, especially if they will bring harm to ourselves or to others.

If we can hold the tension between invitation and threat, and not jump the gun, perhaps a gate spontaneously appears where we least expect it. Wherever we happen to find ourselves, whether with illness or good health, with family problems or livelihood difficulties, when we fully land in the moment we're already having, surprisingly, we might find ourselves at ease. It's the struggle to be *other* than where we are that keeps the gate closed. This is Buddha's second noble truth, the cause of suffering—the desire for more than what's already here.

When we experience discomfort or distress without attaching a catastrophic narrative to our discomfort, it can have inexplicable results. Sickness and medicine might come together as one. In the absence of struggle—the wish for things to be different than the way they already are—we might become more kind to our aging parent, or reach out to a distant friend, or be more accepting of eccentric people, immigrants, or the homeless. The gate opens when we do.

When all else fails in our life, when we feel a profound sense of absence or emptiness, when there seems to be nothing to support or encourage us, what remains? What holds us when

First Threshold: The Wake-Up Call

no one else seems to be there? We might suddenly be struck by the realization, "I'm still here." Momentarily refreshed by our own renewed presence, a gate swings wide open and we find ourselves moving through new territory, guided by that larger indefinable something that is our life.

STEALING FIRE FROM THE GODS

3.
Necessary Sacrifices

We can't keep ourselves nor the people we love immune from change. We're repeatedly challenged to relinquish our outdated beliefs, our youthful dreams of invincibility, and illusions of unlimited opportunities. Sacrifice is how we mature on our spiritual path, but it's also what we resist.

Having left the palace on his twenty-ninth year, Prince Siddhartha sought the best yogic teachers of the day in ancient India. He practiced rigorous asceticism to discover the meaning of life and death and the way out of suffering. Having gained mastery in these practices from a succession of teachers, he realized that after six years of punishing his body, hoping to find release from the ego-self, he was no closer to enlightenment. Neither his previous indulgent life in the palace nor his years of self-denying asceticism was the way.

Out of despair he took a seat beneath a sacred fig tree and with fierce intent the prince unraveled his mind to fully realize the ultimate human potential—spiritual enlightenment. He discovered a middle way, a secret gate that permitted entrance into the highest truth. He also saw that the brilliant light within his own heart also radiated in the hearts of every being. But he also realized that this secret gate could be easily missed. This realization was the basis of Buddha's path as the "the middle way"—the paradox of both having control and simultaneously letting go, crossing the vast ocean of samsara to arrive here and now.

One of the earliest teachings of the Buddha was the "three marks of existence," which begins with a contemplation on impermanence. The evanescence of our lives can deprive us of who and what we're holding onto dearly. When we think of loss we usually think of losing people we love. But we lose not only through death, but also by changing, letting go, and moving on with our lives. Loss includes relinquishing our outdated beliefs, our youthful dreams of invincibility, and illusions of power and freedom. As we come to terms with life's imperfections, we recognize that even in the most intimate human connections there are blemishes. As wise, creative or charismatic as we may be, we're powerless to prevent ourselves from aging and from keeping the people and things that we cherish, immune from change. These unavoidable sacrifices are part of what's demanded of us by life's impermanence. Sacrifice is how we grow, evolve, and mature—but it's also what we fiercely resist.

The Buddha laid the foundation of his profound and elegant path with a teaching on impermanence, a seemingly obvious fact of experience. Perhaps he felt the need to address change because he saw that everyone he met was trying to hold onto some version of permanence. Permanence, as taught in Buddhism, is our continuous effort to solidify our *idea* of ourselves by reinforcing an interior witness that feels convincingly real, and separate and different from our body.

First Threshold: The Wake-Up Call

Philosopher Gilbert Ryle referred to this invisible, intangible sense of self as "the ghost in the machine."

We all know that we will die, but in most cases this is a conceptual acknowledgment, not a deeply felt realization. Freud stated that most human beings know that *others* will die, but somehow in our own mind, we can't seriously accept that *we* will. To contemplate our necessary mortality, to feel this existential fact in a very deep way, can take the wind out of our sails. The usual way of dealing with the uncompromising reality of our perishability is to deny it. Denial in this case is the unconscious defense against actually *feeling* the implications of our inevitable death. Many people are resistant to truly contemplate their mortality because they fear that if they embraced this realization they would become paralyzed with either depression or anxiety.

Although continual change is very challenging, throughout our life we grow by giving up some of our deepest attachments to others, as well as cherished parts of ourselves. The practice of meditation helps us to release our grip on who and what we're attached to moment by moment. We learn to accept loss and to make peace with the truth of our temporary stay on earth. At the same time, our spiritual journey involves reconciling ourselves with the aspects of *ourselves* that are no longer vital, that have outlived their usefulness. We're challenged to grieve the loss of former versions of ourselves, or else we will spend the rest of our days trying to prop up and defend an outdated image.

It's important to reconsider the "roads not taken" and to abandon youthful dreams that no longer fit us as we presently are. We may have to grieve the disparity between who we dreamed we'd become, and who we actually are. There may be resentment and regret for the things we expected from life but didn't get. The contemplation of impermanence shocks us into the recognition that the present moment is all that we ever have, and that our life emerges from each succeeding moment, and not elsewhere.

We have such a short period of time to appreciate the stupendous quality of this world. Our necessary mortality can shock us so that we use our inevitable death as a continual reminder, taking nothing for granted. We become stunningly sober about the fact of our perishability. As deeply as we can love, opening our heart and soul to another, and as passionately committed we can be to meaningful projects, at some point, we will have to say goodbye to all of it. This is a poignant truth about our human condition.

If we ignore this challenge, or intentionally resist it, then we will be haunted by what we've not made peace with. This is the second of the three marks of existence—suffering. The suffering that the Buddha was addressing was not limited to the obvious physical and emotional pain of illness or injury, or the suffering we experience when an intimate dies or a friend rejects us. The suffering the Buddha was referring to is resistance to and struggle with the truth of change.

The word for suffering in Sanskrit is *duhkha*, which has innumerable translations, among which are dissatisfaction, disappointment, boredom, restlessness, disillusionment, stress, or generalized unhappiness. From a meditator's perspective, duhkha is not knowing how to rest in our own being. The resistance to being with ourselves gives rise to thirsting for something *other* than the moment we're presently experiencing.

First Threshold: The Wake-Up Call

Out of confusion, we impulsively reach for the next moment, hoping that it will be more entertaining or gratifying. This is an expression of our dissatisfaction with the moment from which we are fleeing. This is a subtle point and not commonly recognized, until we begin some form of meditation.

The suffering that Buddha was addressing is our resistance to be with "what is." To truly be open to and embrace what is here, now, cuts through our ingrained habit of dividing the world between acceptable and unacceptable, challenging us to begin opening to what we feel is unlovable. When Buddha sat under the bodhi tree with the unshakable resolve to awaken spiritually, he became an open channel through which the primordial energies of life surged, revealing to him that attachment to pleasure over pain, beauty over ugliness, nirvana over samsara is precisely what causes human anguish and what conceals the highest truth.

When we are confronted by changes that we weren't expecting, we can become insistent that the world should be different than the way it is. Ironically, it's our very motivation to make ourselves feel safe and secure and exempt from change, that causes our unnecessary suffering. In a private corner of our mind, we're fighting a life-and-death battle to protect ourselves from the realization that we can't hold onto anything, including ourselves.

All of us want one reference point that remains unchangeable, whether it's our marriage, our children, our money, our business, our health, or our one loyal friend whom we've known since grade school. In the midst of the sandstorm of change everything and everyone shifts in time, and we have to continually readjust ourselves. We may need to adapt to a different relationship with our children or our spouse, or adjust to the absence of a spouse, or learn to cope with loneliness or deteriorating health. Life demands that we sacrifice our former holding pattern and re-position ourselves, again and again. It is difficult to have to leave home continually.

From the Buddhist perspective, suffering is not mandatory. The fact of life's transiency is not bad news. We can use the fragility of our human life as a wakeup call to live with love, passion, and intensity, and to get on with what we really need to get on with. With no more dress rehearsals, our moment by moment life can be vibrant and refreshing. The good news is that at any moment in which we're wholly and completely *here*, with our head, heart and belly—we're not suffering.

A great deal of unnecessary suffering is caused by the habit of manipulating our experience, trying to reassure ourselves that everything is going to be okay, catastrophizing about what can go wrong, or harshly judging ourselves for real or imagined misdeeds. The Buddhist teaching is not about how to avoid pain, but rather how to avoid *suffering about the pain that is unavoidable*. The Buddha proclaimed, in one of his earliest teachings, that there is the pain of birth, old age, sickness and death. This kind of pain is unavoidable. On the other hand, neurotic or unnecessary suffering involves our dissatisfaction when life often presents us with what we don't want, and when we can't get who or what we do want.

There is a way to creatively work with suffering, the second mark of existence. There are continual openings when we finish one activity and *before* we are about to leap into the next, before we check our email or before we make the next phone call —when we could take a seat in the space of nowness. We could

First Threshold: The Wake-Up Call

appreciate the living moments of walking aimlessly through our city or town with our senses wide open. We could take notice of the storefront window decorations, nod to the passersby who return a smile, and taking a seat in the neighborhood park, we might find delight before the stone lions, upon whose heads pigeons have perched. When we allow these open moments, where we don't feel compelled to shape our experience, we have the possibility of enjoyment and freedom. This is how we wear out samsara.

Because of the evanescent quality of life each moment is utterly fresh, never again to be repeated. Each moment also reveals that everything and everyone is inexhaustible, in that we can't experience or know everything there is to experience or know about anything or anyone, including ourselves. There is no bottom, no final conclusion that we can make about anything, which is another way of saying that everything is *egolessness*, the third mark of existence.

The third mark of existence is a paradox. Things change, we suffer the maddening affair of changes, but *no one* suffers! This may sound like a clever Buddhist verbal puzzle, but it's the foundation of the whole Buddhist path. In Western psychological terms, the egoless condition is one of having insufficient psychological "structures" to support a sense of identity. Such an individual would have a poorly developed sense of self, faulty reality-testing, a compromised capacity to adapt to change, and impaired social and occupational functioning. From the Western psychological perspective, egolessness is a problem.

By contrast, in most Eastern spiritual traditions, the ego refers to the *image* or *idea* we hold of ourselves, our mind-made, socially constructed self-concept or autobiographical identity. Any experience beyond ego's frame is either not perceived at all, or perceived as "not-me" or "other." Once we divide the world this way, we either grasp who or what is desirable, reject or defend ourselves against who or what is undesirable, or ignore what falls into neither camp.

From the Buddhist perspective, egolessness (*anatman* in Sanskrit) is not a regression to a pre-egoic state, but the realization of a *trans-egoic* state. From this exalted state of awareness, we step beyond the boundaries of who we think we are, into the unexplored aspects of our being—and the larger world beyond our learned description of it. Egolessness is not something that we witness, but an expansive state of awareness that we *are*. Yet, from the point of view of our autobiographical self or ego, the egoless experience is confounding and can feel hollow, like a deficient emptiness, a taste of death.

If we take an honest inventory and inquire how much of the time we're actually present in our lives, it can be shocking to realize how little we spend here and now. As soon as we attempt to sit in silence and stillness, we usually begin to anticipate the many things we have to do, or we remember past events, and soon find ourselves journeying back-and-forth between past and future. Landing in the present moment of nowness can feel like we're dissolving with nothing to hold onto, which is exactly what triggers the immediate flight into past or future.

This sense of momentum, of moving backwards and forwards in time, is what reinforces our *idea* of ourselves, that inner sense of "I." It gives us the sense of having a long historical past, a promising or catastrophic future, and a dramatic present. In actuality we exist as an existential dot—*now*, in this moment

First Threshold: The Wake-Up Call

only. When we do land in the experience of nowness, it can be a delicious moment of peacefulness and the absence of struggle.

Egolessness, the third mark of existence, is the experience of what lies on the other side of our *known* life, the life that we've mapped out with our beliefs, assumptions, expectations and our social roles. It points to the deeper, far-reaching dimension of what a human being is, on all levels—-somatically, intellectually, emotionally, artistically, creatively. When we're wholehearted in our love, our passion, in our creative expression, and even in our sadness and grief, when we give in totally to this moment without the impulse to be elsewhere, we're present in our totality. *This* is a taste of egolessness. What will happen next is unknown.

You've Crossed the First Threshold When...

As you read and consider the highlights that characterize each threshold, please understand that the spiritual path is not linear, but cyclical. We only need to achieve a "good enough" level of development in order to evolve to the next threshold. On our journey through the various thresholds, we will meet our particular core issues, again and again, but we encounter them on progressively deeper levels of personal development and understanding, where they are no longer impenetrable roadblocks on our evolving journey.

The Wake-Up Call

You know that you've crossed the first threshold when....

You realize that there's an ongoing sense of struggle in the background of your life, regardless of the external circumstances. This subtle tension is not related to anything specific. You begin to suspect that you might be living only on the surface of your life, and that a deeper, more authentic dimension lies just beneath the comings and goings of your daily existence. Even though you might have a good life with loving relationships and satisfactory employment, you still feel a vague, unnameable dissatisfaction. Such disappointment becomes the impetus to find a way to end your personal suffering. This aspiration begins to take shape as an actual *path* that will support your search. You recognize that the practice of meditation as a method of self-discovery, is an essential component of a spiritual path.

First Threshold: The Wake-Up Call

Through the practice of meditation you witness how you defend yourself against open psychological space by filling it with continuous loops of tangential thoughts. This is very humbling and provokes you to question why silence and stillness should pose such a threat. You begin to recognize your continual subconscious chatter as a fear of nonexistence, your denial of death. You discover that prolonged periods of silence and stillness are suicidal for ego, the idea or image you hold of yourself. This inspires you to question your true identity and whether your way of being in the world is too narrow, limited, and circumscribed by your habitual patterns.

The hallmark of the first threshold is to recognize that your life could be lived as an actual journey of continual self-discovery. You also recognize that the spiritual path requires necessary sacrifices, giving up something in order to connect with something of greater value, something that will support your path. When you dare to enter into the deeper dimensions of your mind and heart, you meet the uninspected portions of your life. You step beyond your familiar boundaries, into "foreign territory" where a gate opens. In that clearing you notice that many possibilities exist that you didn't notice before. You cultivate confidence and courage to step through the gates that you meet on your path. Crossing the first threshold fills you with excitement and hope, but it's also somewhat naïve and idealistic.

In the next phase of your journey you will be challenged by the "siren's call," the perilous seductions and tantalizing temptations that promise pleasure and comfort, but which lure you off your path and sabotage your spiritual journey.

SECOND THRESHOLD: THE SIREN'S CALL
Perilous Seductions and Tantalizing Temptations

In mythological terms, the siren's call was the enchanting melody that no one could resist. It lured sailors off course and to their destruction. The siren's call is the enticing appeal of something irresistibly alluring, but potentially dangerous. It symbolizes the sidetracks, detours, or traps that take us off our spiritual path of self-discovery. Because the siren's songs are hypnotically seductive, they're often mistaken for the spiritual path itself.

Our resistance or refusal to respond to the "wake-up call" represents all the ways that we avoid listening to and aligning ourselves with the deep voice within the sanctuary of our heart. This call invites us to step into unfamiliar terrain that can threaten who we think we are, the subjective feeling of "me" that we've become so familiar with over the span of a lifetime.

On a spiritual path, if we refuse to respond to this call, a call from our own heart, our life loses its value, meaning, and purpose—its sense of aliveness. In Buddhist terms, our denial of the call represents all the ways we refuse to wake up to our enlightened nature. This denial is characterized by the sense of endless repetition where we might experience movement and change, but without the feeling of having truly arrived anywhere.

Each chapter in this section describes the many ways that we lose the thread of our spiritual journey, and also represents a challenge to be both mindful and understanding of how and why we get seduced to step off our path of self-discovery.

Yet, if we begin or persist in a meditation practice, we eventually connect with what is deepest within ourselves. We activate the forces and energies of our intuitive mind and heart which radically expands and deepens us. But we must resist the siren's call by continually remembering to protect our spiritual path and not our ego.

4.

The Tricks We Play on Ourselves

Self-consciousness is our uniquely human power that enables us to shape our lives and our environment. But our complete identification with our self-image disconnects us from our totality. To reconnect with the total being that we are, ego would have to assume a subservient role to our wholeness, but it will do everything imaginable to avoid surrendering its territory. This is ego's treacherous game.

The most primary force animating us is the thirst to live, to experience, to feel. Every animal, every sentient being, everything that lives is driven by the same ferocious force. It's the desire for the next sensation, feeling, thought, the next moment—wanting more life, more organismic pleasure. Remarkably, out of a crack in the pavement of a city sidewalk, a plant grows from a sliver of earth, getting minimal sunlight and in spite of thousands of people trampling over it. The heartiness of the force of life is stunning.

Plants arch upwards towards the sun, while their roots grow downwards into the dark soil for nourishment and stability. Rivers and streams flow effortlessly to the sea, bees pollinate, while flora and fauna are in a frenzy of mating during the spring. Autumn arrives infallibly on time, as fruits drop effortlessly from branches. Animals, plants, rivers, and the orderly progression of the seasons do not *witness* themselves, but *are* themselves. There's no part of their being that stands apart from their totality. They are complete as they are, weaved into their environments *without* self-consciousness, as far as we know.

This indomitable life force animates us in equal measure. The curious thing is that on a psychological level, our image or idea of ourselves, upon which our personal identity is based, is moved by the same compelling urge to survive. In our evolutionary history as a species we did something unprecedented—-we disconnected from our totality and separated a part of our mind to witness ourselves. We became not only self-conscious, but over time we began to identify *all* of ourselves with that fragmented self-conscious part.

Little by little, we lost our connection with our roots. This disconnected part of us became exiled from our sense of wholeness. We commonly refer to this aspect of ourselves as our ego, or "I" or "me." Because the ego suspects that it sits on top of an unfathomable depth and that it doesn't speak for our totality, it is innately insecure. This is where ego's game becomes treacherous.

Human beings are distinct from other species in that we're morbidly aware of our necessary mortality, but as previously discussed, this truth is largely repressed so that we can get on with the business of daily life without crippling anxiety. To compensate for this denial the ego co-opts the life force and uses it for its *own* purposes. Instead of promoting the continuity of the organism, ego uses the very same force to promote *itself*. It does this by creating a boundary between "me" on the inside, and the world of others on the outside. From this

Second Threshold: The Siren's Call

protected enclosure, ego convinces itself that it has always been there, seemingly immune from change and contradiction. This "game" is supported by our non-stop inner dialogue, which reinforces our sense of inner continuity.

The double problem is that we not only deny our mortality, but we also repress awareness of the total being that we are—otherwise known as Buddha nature. We have created a symbolic substitute, an interior subject in place of our authentic nature. In other words, because we're conscious that our lives come to an end, we pretend to transcend our mortal condition by identifying ourselves with an invisible, intangible inner self that doesn't seem to perish. This becomes a substitute for our Buddha nature.

Because the ego-self is our creation, we endlessly seek confirmation in the eyes of others that we're worthy and lovable, smart or successful, that we're good people doing the right thing, and that God and goodness is on our side. The ego uses feedback as a way of solidifying itself and expanding its empire, and yet continues to feel insecure. Consequently, the absence of feedback, whether internal or external, is suicidal for our self-concept.

When we're fully there with our experience, with head, heart, belly, but *without* the internal "watcher"—such experience is complete and satisfying. On the other hand, once we attempt to stand out and apart from, and witness our experience, we've broken the circle of fullness, dividing it between an inner witness and an external world of beings and things. According to Buddhism, we're now left to relate with those entities through the three poisons of passion, aggression, and ignorance—"I like it, or I dislike it, or I couldn't care less." Ignorance is the strategic avoidance of subtle or ambiguous situations that fall into neither liking or disliking camps.

Under the banner of ego, almost everything that we do is a misguided effort to get some kind of confirmation that our inner witness exists as a solid and continuous being. Think about how you spent your day today, and the various settings that you were in, and the numerous interactions you had with others. What was your mind doing when you were in each of those settings? Did you notice that you were talking to yourself in a little private bubble, a non-stop subconscious dialogue throughout the entire day. Like whirling a lit incense stick in circles in the dark, creating the visual illusion of an unbroken circle of light, by continuously spinning thoughts we create the illusion that a "thinker" really exists separate from our thoughts. This is how the ego creates a false division within the mind's natural openness—an openness which puts us into intimate contact with things as they truly are. The ego steals our life from us in its campaign to colonize the entirety of our mind, siphoning the energy of our life force for its *own* perpetuation.

From a Buddhist perspective, open psychological space is referred to as emptiness, or *shunyata* in Sanskrit. It's the absence of the assumptions, beliefs, expectations, judgments, and interpretations by which we define ourselves and others. Ego cannot survive in this neutral psychological space, and experiences it as a death. To directly perceive this is shocking. Such a realization might drop the bottom out so that we actually land in the experience we're already having. We could actually taste the cookie that we're chewing on, or genuinely see the person who's sitting across from us over lunch, taking notice of their facial features and expressions, and even feel their personal atmosphere. It would be like putting on new glasses and seeing the world with precision and clarity, free of our past associations and interpretations of it.

Meditation practice is a slice of death, but in the positive sense of the word. This is why it can be very threatening to many people. Meditation is the practice of giving up that inner drivenness to feed our "monkey mind" with a stream of stimulating ideas and images. Instead, we open ourselves to what's here *before* we fill in the space with distracting or entertaining thoughts, images and memories.

The real meaning of austerity or discipline in a meditator's life is the repeated act of conscious dying—letting go of our personal narrative which reinforces our idea or image of ourselves. We intentionally boycott ego's hunger for both reinforcement and distraction. The challenge of dying psychologically shows up in daily life when someone hurts us, either unintentionally or intentionally, and we feel highly reactive. Before the cascade of reactions and feelings begin, before the emotional roller coaster gathers momentum, we can cut it on the spot. This opens us up to naked experience, but it can also throw us into a "no-man's land" of uncertainty and heightened vulnerability.

We would like to divide the world between friends and enemies, between desirable and undesirable, so that we know where we stand. Meditation repeatedly cuts through the boundary that divides the world into polar opposites, bringing us into the immediacy of the present moment without armor. It's an extraordinary practice, allowing us to know in an experiential way what it means to practice dying while alive.

The edge or boundary that separates "me" from the "not-me" has been ego's game all along. When we lean into and step beyond ego's edge, we enter into the unknown, where self and other no longer have sharp boundaries. The "other" begins to feel less alien or foreign—and this opens up a surprising intimacy between ourselves and the world.

5.
Ego's Footprints

Trying to witness our ego directly is like a looking at the sun. It has a blinding effect. A more effective method for recognizing ego's strategic activities is to look indirectly—at ego's footprints.

Successful navigation on a spiritual path begins with realizing that the voice in your head is not you. Although your inner dialogue is happening in your mind, your true identity is not based upon those loops of rambling, tangential thought. Meditation practice is largely about having your own experience of this. Meditation offers us a safe space to recognize ego's bureaucracy. In so doing, we discover the deeper, more profound dimension of ourselves that has been suppressed largely because it threatens ego's territory.

The person we've been socially conditioned to believe we are has enlisted us in a full-time job. We have an image to maintain and an army of defense mechanisms to protect that image. We also have beliefs and assumptions that support our social identity, and characteristic emotional patterns and interpersonal strategies which help reinforce "me and my world."

This full-time effort to be "me" is both socially necessary and yet precarious on a spiritual path. Even when we're on vacation, chilling out, not engaged in fulfilling responsibilities or solving problems—just getting through a day as "me" becomes its own challenge. Without consulting us, our ego is subtly manipulating our encounters with the world, so that our experiences are shaped to fit our idea of ourselves. What doesn't fit within ego's frame is either not noticed or is reinterpreted to conform to its known world.

The ego-self is very hard to see directly because it doesn't show up as an object in our mind. Instead, it is the frame *through* which we see both ourselves and the world. One of the ways we learn how to recognize its *modus operandi* is by seeing its "footprints." We get to see what our mind is up to, moment by moment, when it has been hijacked by the ego.

We can glimpse ego's immediate footprints by recognizing our minimal tolerance to be in the "here and now." Moment by moment, we usually find ourselves someplace other than right here. Even when we intend to sit quietly and be present, there's something about the bareness of just *this* moment that feels unacceptable, as if there wasn't enough oxygen. The unwillingness or inability to rest in simple *being* is based on a feeling of deficiency. Even if we have a Ph.D, are financially successful, have a community of friends, enjoy a happy marriage and have high achieving children—remarkably, when the sitting in silence and stillness, we're either percolating with restlessness, fantasizing about all kinds of things, or we're on the verge of falling asleep. The invitation to relax into basic *being* feels oddly threatening, and triggers a reflex for distraction.

Second Threshold: The Siren's Call

Like walking through a mall and having our senses titillated, we're eager to feast on stimulating images, thoughts, and sensations as a means of defending ourselves from the openness of psychological space. Our mind is very fickle, and sensory phenomena are very seductive. Resting in basic being poses a double threat to ego. It dissolves the sense of *before* and *after* which ego depends upon to convince itself of its own continuity. By continually returning our attention to the present moment, we discover that the so-called past and future are actually happening *now*, again and again. The present moment is not merely a point instant in time, but expansive and vast, stretching us beyond where we're holding on.

A second threat of resting in basic being, is that it dissolves the boundary between "me" and the world. As our mind and body become synchronized, in the same place at the same time, the boundary between inside and outside becomes fuzzy. In other words, it's hard to exactly pinpoint where the fragrance of the incense is located, or where the taste of coffee or the melody of music originates from, here or there, or some place in between. If we persist in doing such contemplative exercises they reveal the flexible open-ended nature of experience. Over time our experience of the world begins to feel more like a field of sensitivity rather than supporting the assumption of "me" in here, and the world out there. This undermines ego's effort to control the unfolding of situations in our life.

Another of ego's footprints is related to our resistance to letting go. Ego's habit is to tenaciously hold onto its presumed territory. One of the hallmarks of meditation is the practice of letting go. This is how we maintain the freshness of a beginner's mind. We can cherish those whom we love and cultivate those things that are precious to us, but at the same time, we hold them lightly so they can breathe and move freely beyond our grasp. We're more likely to move in alignment with changing circumstances, which promotes more ease and harmony, but also more vulnerability. This is a subtle practice that's difficult to express in words.

The problem for all of us is that the world is ungraspable because it's always changing. As the poet David Whyte states, "I want to know if you are prepared to live in the world with its harsh need to change you..." Our effort to satisfy a particular desire or ambition may be successful, but by the time we have achieved this goal, we might discover that it falls short of our expectation. We try to catch the water of life but it seems to slip through our net of ideas and conceptual categories. Through the practice of letting go, easing our grip on those we would like to emotionally possess, and not making people our personal territory, we could discover that everything we need is already here.

In meditation when a thought comes up, we touch it with awareness and then let it go. A memory comes up, and we notice it for a brief moment and let it go. The letting go is one of the secrets not only of meditation, but also of life and love. In the post meditation state we try to practice this as often as possible. In the gesture of letting go we open up to a wide range of possibilities. When we're holding onto our life or our lover or our success, or the way our children should be—that gesture limits the spontaneous movement of who or what we're holding in our grasp. When we're able to hold tenderly and let go lightly, the letting go might invite some kind of unanticipated possibility, and that's not a bad thing.

Second Threshold: The Siren's Call

Many years ago I heard a story about Shunryu Suzuki Roshi, the Japanese zen master who founded the San Francisco zen center, and Tassajara and Green Gulch zen centers. The incident was told to me by one of his dharma heirs. Roshi had a beautiful parrot or cockatoo that he loved very much. He kept this bird in a large cage. One day one of his students paid him a visit and noticed the caged bird. The student commented that Roshi often talked about the cage of mind, and how important it was for practitioners to be free of any self-imposed imprisonment. He then asked, "Why do you keep that bird in a cage?" Roshi spontaneously walked up to the cage, lifted the metal door, and then opened the window of his San Francisco apartment, and allowed his beloved bird to fly free. Just like that. He loved that bird, but in one moment he realized that he was imprisoning his beloved animal companion. I was very touched when I heard that story.

Another of ego's footprints is its need for continual reinforcement, largely because it doubts its own existence. As we discussed earlier in this chapter, ego is a social construction, formed when we were children seeking membership within our family and culture. Ego does not speak for the totality of who we are, but it gives us a handy icon for self-reference. Ego, in this sense, is a representation, an image of ourselves that permits us to negotiate socially, but which also traps us into believing that it is *all* that we are.

Suffering from a feeling of deficiency, ego always feels that it's lacking in substance or worth. One version of that unquenchable hunger to feel more substantial is the need to inflate ourselves, to overcompensate by becoming larger than we really are. We cultivate a desire to become famous, wildly successful, to achieve symbolic immortality, to create something that shows the world that we matter in the big scheme of things. This inflated mentality leads to either a relentless campaign to rack up one success after another to demonstrate our exalted status, or to surround ourselves with "yes" people who continually reaffirm our worth. This should not be misunderstood to mean that we shouldn't launch our ambition to make an abundant life for ourselves by being creative and industrious.

Another version of the desire to feel more substantial is to foster a belief in victimhood, that we didn't have a good childhood, or rich parents, or a good education, that we didn't go to the right schools, that we married the wrong person, or wound up with unremarkable children. It's the feeling that we got a raw deal in life. This poverty mentality often leads to either depression or an angry, aggressive posture towards the world, as if wanting to be compensated for past injustices.

The more subtle form of reinforcement is the default position of feeling that life is too complicated and the effort to connect the dots in order to make sense of our life—is just too much. Consequently, we content ourselves to chew off only a few crumbs of life, succumbing to distraction, half heartedly going from one thing to another, taking refuge in the attitude that life is a mystery that can never be understood, so what's the point anyway? This can lead to an underlying mood of regret, complaint, and apathy, which can be softened by indulgence in creature comforts and pleasure.

Striving to be either a somebody or a nobody, ego achieves a convincing identity which it reinforces with a self-serving narrative. The challenge for meditators is to try to

Second Threshold: The Siren's Call

objectively see what ego is up to under all circumstances. We do this by bringing awareness to our personal narrative, to our emotional patterns, and our interpersonal strategies—to discover how they reflect and reinforce a particular idea we have ourselves. The gift of meditation is to make us transparent to ourselves.

Another footprint of the ego-self is the compulsion to always be on our way towards a destination. Rarely do we do something for its own sake. We're very purposeful and strategic, and usually do things to achieve an outcome, a result to reassure ourselves of having control to bring about desirable circumstances. This reflects a mistrust of our own natural self-direction, which emerges from our deepest nature. Perhaps, our deepest nature has its own unique design that unfurls creatively when it's not subjected to ego's agenda. We are called to recognize what is most unique in us, the ultimate significance of our individual lives. In the words of Picasso, "My mother told me, if you become a soldier you will be a general. If you become a monk you will end up as a pope. Instead, I became a painter and I wound up as Picasso. Is this not a lovely thought—to wind-up as yourself—in all your absolute and unique divinity?"

One of the ways we liberate ourselves from ego's agenda is to do something purely for the sake of itself, and not as a means to an end. You can experiment by doing a simple activity without expecting a positive or negative result, but just for the sheer pleasure, the shameless enjoyment of doing that something. Meeting with a friend at a favorite cafe, and taking delight in simple conversation over coffee, just because you enjoy his or her company. It could be dancing alone in your living room to a favorite piece of music, or crawling around on the floor with your dog, or working in the garden, enjoying the fragrance of the wet earth and the feel of its gritty texture.

It is deceptively challenging to give your full attention to someone or something. A neighbor could be speaking with you, yet the momentum of your speedy mind propels you ten miles down the road, as you begin to think about what you're going to prepare for dinner and the phone calls you have to make before the day is up. When we give our full attention to anything, we invoke an expansive atmosphere, an invisible, formless dimension, which might reveal gifts we weren't expecting. Our presence mysteriously invokes the presence of the world.

Another of ego's signatures is the tendency to reaffirm its identity by distinguishing what its *not*. In other words, ego's secret agenda is to draw an indelible line in the sand between polar opposites—friend and foe, virtue and sin, praise and blame, gain and loss. This is also ego's complicity in creating adversarial conditions or enemies, so that it can define itself as separate and different from what it judges as negative and unwanted. As we cultivate a meditative state of mind, we learn to make friends with the good, the bad, the ugly, and the beautiful. By making friends with what life presents to us we undermine ego's strategy to define itself by creating opposition and conflict.

Peaceful coexistence with the unacceptable aspects of both ourselves and of life is a big part of the spiritual journey of self-discovery. We get to witness ego's insecurity and its strategies of avoidance, which is what makes us susceptible to the call of the sirens. Establishing communication with the unacceptable aspects of ourselves clarifies the relationship between the ego and our immeasurable depth. This is a

Second Threshold: The Siren's Call

preparation for the ego to eventually abandon its psychological primacy. As we recognize the ego as a caricature of ourselves, we might begin to feel some sympathy for it and make friends with it also. We could even lose interest in having to prop ourselves up to be "me," shaping ourselves to be a certain way in the eyes of others in order to justify our lives. This does not indicate a loss of self, but rather a loss of the inauthentic self.

As our meditation practice matures we might notice that we're animated by an immeasurable awareness that's impossible to conceptualize or capture. This radiant field of awareness and energy is our true identity beneath and beyond our ego. It is the core of our human nature, often experienced as an undramatic sense of peacefulness and well-being. Inconceivable as it may seem, each one of us *is* that formless awareness, which is always already free from the call of the sirens.

6.

Cutting Through Ego is Only Half the Story

Meditation is largely about increasing our awareness so that we recognize the cause of our suffering and the way out of suffering. But we will resist recognizing and understanding what we don't want to see. The shadow is the subconscious part of us that feels like a dark stranger, an inferior self, which our ego tries to defend us from seeing.

Buddha walked for more than four decades throughout ancient India clarifying the causes of unnecessary suffering and the path leading to its end. He gave the world a brilliant map of the confused or *samsaric* mind, and a detailed path for how to end unnecessary suffering. However, the path that he articulated is now 2600 years old and we have an understanding of the human mind in the twenty-first century that wasn't available in ancient India. This doesn't negate anything in the original teachings, but we can supplement those original teachings with the discoveries of modern psychology, making the *Dharma* (the way or truth) more meaningful and effective for our Western culture and for our historical time. In this way we can better understand how we get trapped in patterns that make us tone deaf to what's needed on our path to wake up.

The shadow is one such insight from modern psychology that was neither fully understood nor made explicit in Buddha's time. This term coined by Swiss psychologist C.G. Jung, refers to our "inferior" aspects that we keep hidden from ourselves through various defense mechanisms. Denying these negative qualities in ourselves, we unconsciously project them onto others who appear to genuinely embody our disowned "dark" side. When we find ourselves reacting in an irrational, emotionally over-the-top manner to particular people or situations, we are probably in shadowland.

The shadow side of our personality has its own thoughts and feelings, desires and patterns of behavior. Like a silent underground stream that runs through the city at night, the shadow lives beneath our everyday facade of respectability and normalcy. This subterranean personality is the part of us that we unconsciously deny. It's emotionally charged because it's antithetical to who we believe we are. The shadow goes against the grain, and so the ego deploys guardians at the gates of our consciousness to protect us from becoming aware of this disowned darker side.

The shadow makes its debut early in our personal development. In order for a child to gain membership in her family and culture, she must respond positively to the social cues given by her mother and father (and by extension, other significant people such as extended family members). By making the appropriate responses, the child receives attention, affection, and positive regard, thus qualifying her for acceptance into the family— and eventually into the clan, organization, or society. It's as if young children were saying, "If I'm just like you, Mom or Dad, now will you love me?"

Second Threshold: The Siren's Call

Without knowing it, the child learns to be a sophisticated actor or actress so that she can smoothly fit within her family and eventually be weaved into the fabric of her culture. This is part of normal development and acculturation, but in so doing, she abandons significant parts of herself. In order to survive socially, every child learns to adapt by developing an idea of who he or she is *supposed* to be in order to earn membership, but she simultaneously suppresses the "me" she's *not* supposed to be. Any aspect of ourselves that was not mirrored by our parents or society will eventually split off from our awareness and go underground to become part of our shadow.

The importance of understanding the phenomena of the shadow is that what went underground, didn't go to sleep. What we swept under the rug has remained psychologically alive and impactful, but in unseen ways. Buddhist meditation is largely about making the ego-self transparent, but that is only half the story. If we don't acknowledge and communicate with our "dark twin" or personal shadow, we then live with a part of ourselves that feels alien, an aspect that doesn't feel like "me." This foreign "other" has the power to shape our feelings, moods, motivations, and our behaviors.

Our meditation practice should illuminate *all* of ourselves, but many of us tend to leave the parts of ourself that contradict our self-image, in the dark. We will not notice what we're not willing to see about ourselves. We could meditate for decades and yet still be addicted to substance, still behave in a sexist manner, or still be blindly driven by a hunger for power, as we fight our way up the hierarchy of our secular or spiritual organization. We may still be compulsively enacting juvenile behavioral patterns that contradict the image that we present to the world.

Few of us have been given education for how to recognize and work with our shadow. As a result many of us live with the conflict between who we take ourselves to be and who we're secretly striving *not* to be. We're fighting a psychological jihad, trying to preserve the "me" that we hope we are, while denying the "me" that we suspect we might be. This is mostly under the radar of our awareness.

The ego serves as a kind of psychic immune system. Our biochemical immune system distinguishes what is proper to our body from any foreign entities such as bacteria or viruses that may threaten our health. By detecting what it perceives as alien, the immune system preserves the integrity of our body by fighting off any invading bacteria or viruses. Our ego has the same function, but it is psychological, distinguishing itself from what it perceives as other than itself. Ego's agenda is to divide our world between self and not-self, the latter often possessing qualities that might feel alien to who we think we are.

Any unwanted aspects of ourselves that are not made conscious are often projected onto others, who then become our "shadow holders" or scapegoats. Such targeted people or groups have some "hook," some quality, characteristic or quirk that makes them a perfect caricature for our projections. They could be the Mexicans who we think are trying to get into our country and steal our jobs, or Muslim terrorists who we think are trying to infiltrate sharia law into the America legal system, or those gay people who we think are subverting our Judeo-Christian idea of marriage. We make a whole category or a class of people

Second Threshold: The Siren's Call

the target of our own unwanted qualities that we attribute to them.

Psychological projection externalizes our psychic poisons so that we no longer feel contaminated by them, but it enables us to remain unaware of them. Due to the blindness of projection, our shadow confronts us in the form of external others who take on the appearance of enemies or as adversarial situations. At worst, they become scapegoats for our aggression and hostility. We also project positive shadow qualities onto our beloved other or our guru, qualities that we feel unworthy to own.

We can't embrace our intrinsic wholeness or Buddha nature if we are concealing something within ourselves that feels either unacceptable or if there are positive qualities for which we feel undeserving. When we shine a light into our own darkness, and extend our understanding and compassion to those parts, much to our surprise, we discover that our shadow could be quite infantile or adolescent, a product of early conditioning and memory traces of experiences that we didn't fully understand at the time.

The shadow is gold because it holds incredible potential to complete us. It represents our unexamined and unlived life. There is a body of methods that help us to explore the territory of our shadow that can be used to supplement our meditation practice. One method focuses on the body. We choose a time and place when we feel settled, and we recall a "hot button" problem, a conflictual relationship or situation that remains unresolved— and we allow it to take hold of us. We then tune into our body and try to be as sensitive as we can to its inner rhythms and energetic currents in order to get a *felt sense* of how we might be bodily armoring ourselves. We try to become aware of how we might be physically contracting our musculature to close down awareness to prevent ourselves from experiencing feelings that threaten our idea of ourselves.

For instance, we might feel anger towards ourselves or a particular person or situation. As a spiritual practitioner we could feel that we should've gotten beyond this by now, and so we don't permit ourselves to experience that anger. By not allowing the energy of anger to circulate so that it might express itself in the light of awareness, it congeals in certain parts of our body forming an energy knot, much like crimping a garden hose. As a result, our neck or back goes out, or we have gastrointestinal problems, or we develop fibromyalgia, or have continual migraine headaches. The shadow has camouflaged itself, and so we fail to understand our symptoms as a product internal division.

Because the shadow is mostly unconscious we can use various *projective* techniques to make it visible and understandable. One such method can be done with a trusted friend or by journaling. Invite one of your inferior parts into a dialogue. It could be the part of you that's selfish or indulgent, or promiscuous or narcissistic, or vindictive or power-hungry, or perhaps the part of you that lacks courage to step into life. It's important that you morph into that aspect of yourself in order to do this effectively. This won't work optimally if it only remains as a narrative in the head. It has to go deeper than our usual internal dialogue. Try to feel this aspect of yourself and relate to it as an actual character. Encourage it to find its voice and to speak to you from its *own* point of view. And after it has expressed itself, you respond by carrying on a genuine dialogue.

Second Threshold: The Siren's Call

Learn what you can from your hidden side by validating its complaints and wishes, hopes and fears.

For example, you're disappointed in the part of you that lacks courage. You initiate a dialogue with the "coward" that lives within you by imagining what it looks like, its age, its bodily posture and facial expressions.

You: I wish you'd grow up and stop being so childish, getting me to feel incapable of confronting challenges. I'm very disappointed in you.

Coward: You've been judging me ruthlessly and have never given me attention or understanding, let alone sympathy for how I got stuck in this place. Why can't you extend some understanding and compassion for my feelings of fear and powerlessness?

You: I never thought of trying to feel compassion for fear. It feels so unacceptable and makes me feel very small and immature. The closer I get to my fear, I feel tremendous resistance.

Coward: Can you recall the earliest memories you have of feeling small and powerless? Even then, you felt such shame as a boy to admit that you were feeling vulnerable and weak, and in need of your daddy's protection. These are such human qualities, but I'm the one holding them for you. What would make it easier for you to acknowledge your fear and gradually let yourself feel it as the truth of what you're really feeling?

You: I do feel less ashamed by my fear and don't feel that I'm a coward, but just stuck in an old emotional pattern. Yes, I'm beginning to feel the energy of my fear and when I don't judge myself, it seems that I can do this.

Another projective method involves your family of origin. What was unspoken in your family? What was the elephant in the room, the family taboo? In some families there's a conspicuous absence of conversation, perhaps about sexuality, or death, or money. Or there may be conversation, but mostly about fear and failure, and how hard life is, with very little discussion about personal achievement, success and fulfillment. This would be the family shadow. Try to identify what your family shadow was, and invite it into a dialogue by imagining it as an actual character.

A common example of such a psychic hole is a family with an angry father, who holds a rigid, black-and-white religious or political ideology. Neither the mother nor the children ever discuss his intolerance of other points of view because that's taboo. Instead, the children are expected to be compliant, and not raise political or religious perspectives that go against father's cherished belief system. Everyone in the family accepts compliance as the price to pay to prevent Dad from getting out of control and becoming rageful.

Alternatively, one of our parents may have been having a secret romantic-sexual affair that no one dares to speak about. It becomes another black hole, but at the same time, it normalizes breaking promises, not telling the truth, keeping secrets, and perhaps encourages the thrill of illicit behavior. Through a process of inquiry and contemplation, we might

Second Threshold: The Siren's Call

begin to understand how *we* repeatedly fall into this hole whenever we encounter a difference of opinions between people. Given our family background, divergent perspectives can feel like a frightening clash of ideas, a confrontation, causing us to either shut down or try to make a peaceful reconciliation between others. This is how we dramatize the family shadow without knowing what we're doing.

Through meditation practice we can inhibit particular impulses and behaviors that we recognize as dysfunctional or immature, but we may not understand why they continue to dog us in spite of years of meditation. We might naively believe that if we communicate with our shadow, we'll become contaminated with its inferior qualities. But by allowing these qualities to arise in the light of awareness and engaging them in dialogue we gain insight into their origin, what they mean, and what they're protecting us from seeing about ourselves. This kind of contemplation should *not* be done while we're meditating, but rather as a form of contemplative practice.

We see our shadow indirectly in the qualities and behaviors that we project onto others: in our disgust with gays due to our disowned homosexuality, or in falling in love with a new mysterious other, or in projecting our disowned soulful qualities onto a guru, we have a golden opportunity to witness the trickster-like machinations of our shadow—and take back what belongs to us! By shining a light into our own darkness we're less likely to disown significant aspects of ourselves or scapegoating others with our negative projections.

If we don't take account of our shadow it becomes like a primitive tail that we drag along with us, a product of our early stages of arrested development. On our spiritual path we eventually learn to not identify with either our persona or social face, or our shadow, for neither speaks for our totality. The gift of working with our shadow involves engaging it and gradually assimilating its contents into an enlarged sense of self.

7.
Ego's Bureaucracy: Subpersonalities

The Western psychological concept of subpersonalities, in some sense, reinforces the Buddhist teachings on selflessness. Our many subpersonalities or differing ego states, reveal that we are not as unified or singular as we may think, but we are more of a society of selves.

With all good intentions, we try to change our negative patterns into positive ones, but we often find ourselves reverting to our old ways. Whether attempting losing weight, minimizing our drinking, improving our diet, regularly exercising, listening to dharma talks on YouTube, meditating regularly, or visiting museums and art galleries more often—even under the best of circumstances, our intentions to make lasting change seems to get sabotaged.

Usually, when we decide to transform aspects of ourselves, our motivation comes from a place of frustration or disappointment. We're either unhappy about a personal quirk or habit or we want to cultivate a particular quality that would make us feel better about ourselves. The problem is that this intention is usually made from *within* our personality's bureaucracy, and not from the total being that we are.

Although most of us feel that we're one undivided person, one unified individual, if we look objectively within ourselves we might notice that we're more of a society of selves, many of which are beneath the threshold of everyday awareness.

One of the major "subpersonalities" is the shadow which was discussed in the previous chapter. We could think of the shadow as the unknown aspect of any of our subpersonalities of which there are many—the protector, the wise old woman or man, the muse, the mistress, the adventurer, the hero or heroine. These subpersonalities are like a crew of servants running around with their own agendas, each clamoring to be the master or mistress of our house. These subpersonalities are often at different levels of maturity, and so their hopes and fears, ambitions and obsessions, are often in contradiction with each other.

Each of our subpersonalities tends to get triggered by specific situations or interactions with others. Perhaps while visiting your parents for the holidays, your mother or father asks you any one of the following questions: "Have you met anyone yet on that dating site?" "So, when are you going to get a decent job with a respectable salary?" or "By the way, don't you think it's time to start a family?" or "You know, it wouldn't hurt you to pick up a phone and call your sister. She'd really love to hear from you." Although these questions are entirely predictable, you could find yourself reacting emotionally, irresistibly drawn into a heated and repetitious conversation that you promised yourself you would never engage in with your parents.

In spite of how much meditation we've done, we may find ourselves unconsciously acting out a *child* role with a predictable script, linked with a particular self-image and often with a characteristic posture, physical gestures, and facial expressions. Later in the evening when we're back home with our own kids, we enact our *parent* subpersonality. When we're alone with our significant other, we play the part of being a husband or wife. We could be a submissive and compliant lover,

Second Threshold: The Siren's Call

or a dominant, controlling partner, or we may enact varying degrees of codependency, but either way, we are in some variation of our *adult* role.

The danger of our sub-personalities is that they're semi-autonomous. They are like little psychological satellites that circulate within us, but under our radar. Any one of them could sabotage our commitment to not raise our voice with our children, or to not compete with one of our siblings, or not assume a compliant, one-down role when speaking with our boss. Hidden from our awareness, any one of our subpersonalities could derail us repeatedly, undermining our best intentions. The call of the sirens represents anything that diminishes our awareness, and leads us to mechanical behaviors that take us off our spiritual path.

If we think of ourselves as one unified monolithic entity, as an "I" or "me," we don't understand why we occasionally find ourselves out of character, acting out like children, rebellious teens, misunderstood victims, submissive wives, or seductive playboys. We didn't recognize that we were kidnapped by one of our subpersonalities or differing ego states. We were blindly enacting a role, unaware of what we were doing.

According to current research most of us have about ten or twelve subpersonalities and each of these personalities is associated with a self-image, a belief system, an emotional pattern, and a behavioral strategy. These roles got established when we were children, when there were social situations that left us feeling vulnerable and defenseless. From a place of powerlessness we developed a survival package, a way of psychologically surviving in difficult social situations by creating an alternate personality—a subpersonality.

Children are so tender and vulnerable, so full of wants and needs, but what is a child to do when she has needs that are not being met by her parents? Every child is a little creative genius for how to survive psychologically and emotionally. We learn to enact a particular role to get a specific need met from our parents. If a child is raised with an alcoholic father who is emotionally distant and ill-tempered, that little child learns to bring him his bottle of vodka and glass because that's the only time when her father smiles at her, giving her attention and affection. The little girl knows how to get daddy's love for a few minutes, but she inadvertently creates an enabling subpersonality. Thereafter, she may interpret all similar experiences of others' emotional distance as a cue to activate her enabling subpersonality, so that she can feel loved and accepted. That enabling function camouflages the *original* childhood pain of emotional abandonment by her father, which still remains unknown to her.

If a child's mother is very depressed and emotionally unavailable to him, in order to secure mommy's love and attention, this little boy might have to entertain her in order to get her attention. He tells her jokes, and uses his imagination to make up fantastic stories. "Hey mom, guess what? You'll never guess who I saw at school today! I saw Elvis's ghost. I swear to God." His mother opens her eyes wide, shakes her head and replies in disbelief, "What on earth are you talking about?" She begins to smile and for a few short moments she comes alive, and that little boy feels a ray of maternal love brightening his

Second Threshold: The Siren's Call

world and warming his heart. He's succeeded in engaging her to meet his need for maternal care.

That little boy knows how to get mom's love, if only momentarily, but he unconsciously might flip into that role thereafter whenever he feels lonely, insecure, and alienated, needing love and attention from others. He automatically goes back to that original template of entertaining others, playing the clown—but he does so unknowingly. His behavioral strategy is compulsive because he doesn't understand his motivation and therefore doesn't see alternatives.

Our early interactions with our parents and our environment helped to create templates for how to negotiate the challenges of being a vulnerable child in a world of big others. They enabled us to adapt to and gain membership in our family and culture. The problem is that these functional templates became subpersonalities with their *own* agendas, many of which have been largely unconscious to us. When we are identified with one of our subpersonality's roles, it can undermine the best laid plans because the master or mistress of the house is nowhere to be found.   In other words, when we get lost in one of our roles, we forget who we really are, and our choices become narrow, confined to the limits of a specific role. Playing the role of father, we're temporarily oblivious to our child's need for us to be a friend; Or by assuming a child's role, as an adult with our aging parent, we fail to assume responsibility for them, and neglect to make decisions on their behalf when they are unable to do so. Or enacting the role of the family protector we are defended against experiencing our vulnerability and our tender feelings.

In the midst of a perfectly normal day where everything's going smoothly, without any obvious precursor we could suddenly feel that our whole life is at a dead-end—our business, our marriage, our spiritual practice—all feels stale, tired and uneventful, not worth the effort. At that moment, where did we just go? What just arose? This requires sustained attention and an inquisitive spirit. Perhaps we get an image of our father, who, having just come home from work, sinks into a chair, looking down and dejected. At four years old, we imprinted that image of our dad as a defeated human being. That poignant moment became linked with the muted late afternoon light, a somber atmosphere where nothing seemed to move, and our innocent hope for good things to come seemed like a betrayal of our father.

The memory of our father became a complete statement about life. We remember hearing him say, "Never had a good day in my life." He suddenly notices us and immediately puts on a cheerful face and briskly walks into the kitchen to help our mom make dinner. Father's "dark cloud" is never discussed and is forgotten. That moment creates a lasting template and maybe that's the emotional place we drop into whenever we begin to feel happy or successful. Inexplicably, the wind suddenly goes out of our sails. Out of blind loyalty to our father, we unconsciously sacrifice our happiness or success because we don't want to transcend him, to ever be better than him. That's how the little boy thought he could stay connected to his dad.

Our blind identification with our subpersonalities transforms them into actual *subjects*, an assortment of little "I's" that have temporarily become masters or mistresses of our house. Once they're triggered, we find ourselves doing their bidding, which often take us to destinations not of our own choosing. They can openly resist our best intentions and act like an alien force with their own will and strategy.

The good news is that once we learn to be mindful of our sub-personalities and no longer identify ourselves with them, we can engage them in dialogue. By communicating with them they can lead us to the unresolved pain from our past which is crying out to be recognized and healed. By having the courage to be intimate with our subpersonalities, we can recognize them as reflections of ourselves at a certain time of our life. We can see how they function by trying to relieve anxiety or depression, loneliness or boredom—but in developmentally immature ways.

If we try to understand what triggered the formation of our subpersonalities, then we can dialogue with them when they try to usurp our attention and enact their pattern. We sit with that forgotten aspect of ourselves and talk to it, and let it talk back to us, encouraging it to express its concern or complaint, its problem or preoccupation. This goes against the grain because we're attempting to communicate with the original wound beneath the protective scab that conceals our pain.

Interestingly, in the Tibetan Buddhist tradition there is a practice of "feeding the demons." Here we envision our obstacles, conflicts, and stuck places as entities and we ask these "demons" what would satisfy them, what would appease their hunger. After the demons reply, we feed them by giving these aspects of ourselves that they want—an acknowledgment of our unprocessed, disowned parts.

Such dialogue is necessary because that's how we entice that invisible part of us to open up to us and share its secrets. We have to honor, speak to, and feel every part of ourselves or else we will not be able to completely heal ourselves from past hurts that continue to linger. The basic idea is to recognize our subpersonalities as satellites, as objects and not little subjects. We no longer experience them as an "I" but rather as an "it."

Once they are properly identified and we become aware of how they function, we transform what has been unconscious to what is now conscious. Although subpersonalities can thwart our best intentions, they can also be a healthy feature of our total personality. When we recognize them as aspects of ourselves, each can articulate and magnify parts of our psychic universe.

Getting to know our inner family gives us gives us more choices about how we react to problematic situations and how we relate with people who press our buttons. It allows us to recognize what drives us and to identify the sources of our wants and needs. This openness isn't another subpersonality, nor is it part of the personality system as a whole, but rather a taste of our egolessness totality.

8.

Buddha's Last Temptation: Facing Our Demons

Like Jesus, the Buddha-to-be was confronted by perilous temptations that threatened to undermine his spiritual realization. The four Maras are aspects of our own mind that tempt us with gratifications that cause us to lose our way. If we are determined to wake up from the sleep of samsara, we must choose whatever furthers our path of awakening and not what reinforces our ego-self and its limitations.

In one account of the Buddha-to-be, after six grueling years of ascetic practice, he came to the conclusion that he was no closer to realizing his essential nature. At that point he gave up all of the esoteric techniques that he had been practicing, and in a state of complete surrender, he took a seat under the famed bodhi tree and made a commitment to not move until he understood the nature of his human life. Having taken his immovable spot under the bodhi tree, he was confronted by Mara, the dragon-tyrant-monster of myth. Mara tempted him to give up his resolve to spiritually awaken and instead to return to ordinary life—parallel to the last temptation of Christ. Prince Siddhartha was tempted with sensual desire, tantalizing pleasures, power and success, and then its opposite—the threat of death. He was challenged by scenarios designed to trigger his emotional reactivity, and then tempted to rise above it all, immune from the world's suffering.

This encounter with the many forms of Mara symbolizes the primary temptations that seduce all of us to create *samsara* or collective neurosis, that the prince had to transcend in order to awaken as the Buddha. Prince Siddhartha maintained his unshakable resolve, represented by the immovable spot under the bodhi tree. This spot is the umbilical point through which the force of life breaks into the body of the world, which we interpret as pleasure or pain, friend or enemy, the sublime or the grotesque. This triggers our reactions of attachment or aversion, and hope or fear, binding us to the wheel of samsara. The Buddha-to-be embraced the brilliant force of life surging through him and transmuted Mara's temptations through his realization that all polar opposites emerge from the same common ground.

From this mythic narrative, the Buddhist tradition offers us a practical teaching to help us identify and work through four universal obstacles on the spiritual path: inflation, emotional reactivity, the solidification of the ego-self, and the terror of death. The four Maras kidnap our attention so that we become absorbed in the struggle to survive psychologically. Not knowing when we're going to die, we live with constant uncertainty. We hope that we will continue to survive and fear that we won't. Our body continually reminds us of how fragile and vulnerable our life and the life of our loved ones is. Most of us are not aware of how much of our lives are an effort to perpetuate ourselves in time. *Samsara* is the futile effort to secure ourselves so that we and our world feel reassuringly solid and continuous, safe and certain.

Devaputra-mara: False Transcendence

Devaputra-mara tempts us with gratification, either in the form of personal accomplishment, worldly or spiritual, or in the form of everlasting pleasure and comfort. This Mara seduces us with feelings of personal inflation, deflecting our attention away from our necessary mortality. We could misuse meditation or our spiritual path to transcend our body by channeling our attention inwards where the pleasures, pains, and limitations of the body are barely felt. This phenomenon is a trap, and represents spiritual by-passing. This becomes a subtle way of not dealing with our fear of death, sexual desire, anger, jealousy or loneliness. We create an spiritual cocoon, insulating us from authentic living.

Devaputra-mara could take the form of the expansive feeling "I've made it," perhaps as a popular spiritual or yoga teacher, a psychotherapist with a large following, an accomplished musician, a creative artist, or a highly successful businessman or woman. It could also be the self-congratulatory feeling that we have a great marriage, healthy children, a secure job, and a beautiful home. What puts these situations into Mara's camp is that we manipulate our attention so that we avoid noticing the "dark" side of these things. We deny anything shadowy or troubling about our partner, our family, our health, or our livelihood. It's a defense against seeing the full picture, which would amount to recognizing the possible negative or ambiguous aspects about ourselves and our world.

This Mara could tempt us to use psychological and spiritual methods to convince ourselves that we've transcended issues around money, sexuality, food or substance, or the existential challenges of loneliness, loss, aging, and death. Such spiritual bypassing does not change these issues, but leaves them uncooked, lying dormant within us where they can trigger a sudden upsurge of emotion without warning. In the Buddhist tradition there are many warnings about using meditation or spirituality as a way of becoming merely peaceful, while not dealing with the raw, rugged, and unpredictable dimension of human existence. From any inflated self-appraisal we might not believe that we need to work on ourselves any longer.

Eventually something gets through to us and just when we thought we had transcended the pedestrian problems and conflicts of ordinary life, we're dropped out of our cloud of self-inflation and find ourselves rapidly descending to earth. We might discover that we're actually angry with our partner, or jealous of our friends' successes, or filled with sadness and grief because of unfulfilled dreams, all of which have been suppressed. Self-doubt infiltrates our cocoon as we now suspect that we may have manufactured "heaven."

We begin to connect with the truth of impermanence and human suffering, which awakens us from complacency. Realizing the unique occasion of human birth we begin communicating with the shadow side of life. We take possession of Devaputra-mara's fierce energy and in a state of openness, we allow feelings of sadness and joy, anger and equanimity to coexist. With this openness we discover that beneath our struggle to defend ourselves from suffering, our true nature has a natural strength and resilience, and is unconditionally awake.

Second Threshold: The Siren's Call

Klesha-mara: **The Agony and Ecstasy of Emotional Reactivity**

If we don't cultivate openness and a benign acceptance of what life brings us, then we're easily seduced by *Klesha-mara*. *Klesha* in Sanskrit means conflicting or reactive emotionality. As human beings our emotions can get easily triggered, and this Mara can send us from heaven to hell at the drop of a hat. Someone driving a brand new BMW cuts in front of you on the highway, while you happen to be driving a Ford Falcon that you're still making payments on. In a flash, your mercury rises to the top of the thermometer!

Or you happen to run into your ex who's now with a very successful, good-looking and younger partner, and he or she is glowing with joy and confidence, qualities that were rarely displayed in their relationship with you. You walk away from this encounter feeling diminished by the thought that the new partner has something that you lack. Comparisons between ourselves and others and the negative judgments that follow are almost unavoidable. We could be angry or depressed for hours afterwards, unwittingly infecting everyone with whom we come into contact.

When we do become emotionally reactive with some person who said or did something that we disapprove of, there is something satisfying about the intensity of our dislike. Although such emotionality hurts, it can make us feel strangely pleased to call out this person as an "adversary," thus dividing an otherwise uncertain world into the reassuring categories of friend and enemy. There's something juicy and reinforcing about these negative thoughts and feelings. On one hand, they trigger the most wretched states of mind, and yet in spite of knowing that, we still give in to them because their intensity makes us feel more alive. (Can you hear the sirens calling?)

Irritated by the successes and imagined sleights of others, we could indulge in conflicting emotions for days or weeks. Our anger and resentment can get stirred up around people who we imagine are more successful, healthy or fortunate than ourselves. We might become obsessed with our children's safety, doubts about our spouse's fidelity, or chronic worry about not being able to keep up with the demands of daily life. Without noticing what we're actually doing, we make a lifestyle out of being disturbed, as we struggle to resolve problems that seem to continually multiply.

Finding ourselves wanting what we can't get, getting what we don't want, and occasionally getting what we thought we wanted, only to discover, to our dismay, that we're still dissatisfied—we lubricate the neurotic wheel of samsara. The key point is that such emotional reactivity kidnaps our attention away from our primary quest to discover who we really are and what we're here for.

The way to work with Klesha-mara is to realize that negativity and suffering are a part of life, as is the maddening alternations of success and failure, gain and loss, and praise and blame. By regarding conflicting emotions as bandits that can rob us of our mindfulness and dignity, we gradually learn to *disidentify* from the problematic story we attach to them, and instead relate with their *energy*. Feeling the fierceness of our gnarly emotions and moving along with their energy, opens the possibility of neutralizing their intensity. We begin to understand how they have us in their grip, and what they prevent us from seeing. This is how we skillfully work with the temptation of Klesha-mara.

Skandha-Mara: "Me, My, Mine"

According to Buddhist psychology one metaphor for the ego is the concentric skins of an onion. Onion skins are analogous to the layers of thoughts, feelings, perceptions, and the endless narratives that reinforce our autobiographical self. We tend to spin the same self-centered thoughts about ourselves and our world—our preoccupation with relationships or lack of relationships, our loneliness, our financial situation, our health, as well as promising opportunities for pleasure and success. We might muse, "Maybe I'm getting old and out of shape..... I think I'll dye my hair red, or maybe I should go on a diet and join a gym. Hmmm, perhaps I should get a financial consultant or start a online business." Why do we compulsively spin such stale thoughts again and again—unless they're a strategy to protect us from something that we don't want to see.

Skandha-mara (*skandha* means a heap, pile or collection in Sanskrit) is the temptation to spin the items in our personal inventory so that we don't allow neutral psychological space in our mind. The reason is that such well-ventilated space reveals our ego-self for what it is—a mind-made creation, a representational image or icon that doesn't reflect who we are at our depth. It's composed of layer after layer of selective memories that we weave together to create a convincing sense of being a solid and continuous entity, otherwise known as "me." The great spiritual secret is that this is not our true identity.

The seduction of Skandha-mara is that by holding onto this collection of ideas and images about ourselves, we avoid the shocking realization that our autobiographical identity is based on overlapping layers of memory or onion skins, at the center of which is space or openness, which is brilliant, clear, and wise. As our meditation practice deepens, we get little glimpses along the way of this deeper dimension of being. On the path of self-discovery we get repeated flickers of insight until we have unshakeable certainty that this is our true identity, *who* we are in essence. At that point, this Mara is much less of a seduction.

On a spiritual path we practice dis-identifying with our manufactured self-image, knowing that it distorts our perception of ourselves and our world. Through the meditative process we cut through layer after layer of our thoughts, images, feelings and sensations, until we experience a penetrating insight into the transparency of "me." Without the ego-self to protect or perpetuate, we have nothing to resist, and so we can relax into the immediacy of this arising moment. The idea of egolessness or selflessness can seem like too far a stretch, beyond the reach of ordinary people. Yet, we've all experienced these states, if only momentarily.

Imagine a delightful occasion when you watch a young child or an animal companion being completely themselves— playful, spontaneous, whimsical, and unself-conscious. You gaze wordlessly at this precious being who melts your heart on the spot. Now, where are *you* in all of this? You might notice that your *idea* or *image* of yourself does not stand out as separate or distinct from this scenario. Instead, your awareness spills over the edges of your so-called self to include the activity of the observed play. You're fully there, but without your idea or image of yourself. This is our natural egoless state. In each moment that we discover the inherent freshness and freedom of being fully present in our experience, we cut through the layers of our constructed ego-self.

Yama-mara: The Terror and Denial of Death

The fourth of the perilous seductions is *Yama-mara*. *Yama* means death in Sanskrit, and it's characterized by our underlying anxiety that time will run out on us. Most of us know that we're going to die, but we don't live with this fact as an ongoing realization. Instead, we tend to keep this ominous thought tucked safely away in the basement of our mind. Denying our necessary mortality creates enormous complications and hides the real motivation for our behaviors.

Since the ego-self cannot accept death, it goes about seeking transcendence in ways that actually prevent it. When we deny death we're demanding a future, as we imagine our separate self going forward in time. Time permits the illusion of continuing into an indefinite future. Paradoxically, by projecting ourselves in time, journeying back-and-forth between the past and our imagined future, not only do we repress death, but we deny the possibility of living timelessly—in the here and now.

The most expedient way to work with Yama-mara is to cultivate allegiance to the present moment. Maintaining awareness, moment by moment, is already a death of sorts because in order to be present we have to repeatedly "die" to one thought, memory, or fantasy after another. When we intentionally let go of thoughts, we starve with the ego-self which depends on a steady stream of thoughts and images to nourish it. These mini-deaths deliver us to the razor's edge of nowness, the best preparation for letting go of our body at the time of death. This is the further reach of where the spiritual path goes when we overcome the seduction of excessive pleasure, emotional reactivity, self importance, and the great unknown, death—the temptations of the four Maras.

(Although not traditionally taught as part of the teaching on the four Maras, historically, one of the ways we've tried to deny the fact of our impermanence is by projecting everything dark, inferior, or evil in ourselves onto others who become our scapegoats. In order to avoid contamination, which we believe would foreshorten our lives, we attempt to eliminate these unacknowledged aspects of ourselves through prejudice, persecution, aggression, or at worst, the murder of our designated scapegoats. There is a primitive, unconscious logic that if you "kill" your enemy, your life is affirmed because it demonstrates that the gods favor you. The anxiety around personal mortality seems to be temporarily pacified when our enemies are sacrificed on Yama-mara's altar.)

Second Threshold: The Siren's Call

The Siren's Call

You know that you've crossed the Second Threshold when....

You've begun to see that ego is your mind's creation, a nucleus of selective memories that enables you to create a self-image, an idea of yourself that you completely identify with. In meditative stillness and silence you get glimpses of ego's fear of psychological space, and notice how space undermines ego's solidity. You witness how ego compensates for its basic insecurity by spinning thoughts to create distraction and entertainment to fill its emptiness. Although they provide you with a comforting feeling of familiarity, they also reinforce the patterns that deprive you of freedom. You recognize that ego does not represent who you are in essence.

At the second threshold, you've begun to understand how most human beings repress awareness of death, as well as their intrinsic Buddha nature. You appreciate how meditation is an intentional act of dying, in the sense of refraining from confirming your ego or self-concept. As a result, you are more able to let go of the rope and fall into the open moment. This openness encourages you to do things for the sake of themselves and not for any ulterior motive. If you want to end your unnecessary suffering, you must be able to distinguish between your autobiographical self or ego, and your authentic identity—and know where your allegiance lies.

Contemplating the bureaucracy of ego, perhaps for the first time in your life, you begin to loosen your identification with your personality. This is significant. However, this increasing disidentification with the ego-self or personality can cause you to feel confused, stymied, or disheartened. It is here that the call of the sirens may tempt you to take refuge in various cocoons of comfort. You notice how the siren's seduction of pleasure and comfort sabotages progress on your spiritual path.

Through continuous mindfulness, you learn to identify the temptations of spiritual inflation, emotional reactivity, self-importance, and your subtle efforts to deny the threat of psychological space. When you're caught in the grip of Mara's seductions, you will not be able to rest in a state of simple *being*, but instead, these temptations will provoke you to struggle to survive psychologically.

The second threshold also marks your growing awareness of the shadow elements of your personality, unwanted aspects of yourself that hide from you. You are now more willing to communicate with these unacceptable or unlovable aspects of yourself, and also with the shadow aspects of the world. Now you must find a way to make visible what has been hiding in invisibility. This begins by recognizing how you project your denied aspects onto others. But you also need to learn how to love these unwanted aspects of yourself and the world. However, you also understand, at progressively deeper levels, that neither your ego nor your shadow is who you are at your depth. This wets your appetite to explore further.

To continue on your journey, you are now challenged to consider the nature of your motivation altogether. What is your real desire behind all your desires? Could the "me" that is seeking how to resolve suffering or neurosis be the same "me" that is the problem? Welcome to the labyrinth, the next threshold.

THIRD THRESHOLD: JOURNEY INTO THE LABYRINTH

The labyrinth is a maze of strange passages and chambers, an ancient symbol of the underworld and the unconscious psyche. It represents the journey to our inner depths, and back again to the world. The spiritual path involves methods for shifting our awareness from over-involvement in, and identification with our family and work roles—and towards our center. But there are pitfalls and traps lying in the labyrinth of our mind that can block our way.

As spiritual practitioners, we're inspired to travel this unpredictable, serpentine path towards the core of our being in order to reach our intrinsic wholeness—our Buddha nature. However, progress towards discovering our highest wisdom does not follow a straight line, but often involves obstacles and traveling roads that seem to meander aimlessly.

We must find a way out of our own labyrinth and back into a life of freedom. To do this we must place our spiritual quest above our misguided efforts to preserve our persona or self-image, and above our hope for divine rescue. The way out of the labyrinth begins by understanding the nature of our motivation.

We suffer because we do not remember our way back to our source and to our unique way of belonging to the world. We are obliged to understand how our thoughts, intentions, and actions have real consequences that often entrap us in a self-made labyrinth. Karmic cause and effect can lead us to destinations not of our conscious choosing, but they can also lead to the recovery of our true selfless self.

9.

Motivation, Desire, and Grasping

Ordinary desire is based on a sense of deficiency—that this immediate moment or experience is not enough. Feeling vaguely dissatisfied, we're provoked to reach for anything that eases our feelings of emptiness. This is what entraps us in an endless cycle of grasping.

We might feel that our first experience of abandonment was when someone near and dear died when we were very young, perhaps a beloved grandparent. Or we may think it was that special someone whom we loved hopelessly, who, without warning, left and devastated us. Some individuals remember their first experience of abandonment as the time when one of their parents became chronically depressed or bedridden with illness.

Yet, from a spiritual perspective, the first abandonment was when *we* separated from our indescribable totality and became identified with the voice in our head, which marked our feeling of separation from everyone and everything else. That separation created a psychological chasm between our intrinsic wholeness and our idea of ourself. This is what most spiritual traditions regard as the birth of ego, or "I." It is the part of our mind with which we're most identified, but which does not speak for our total being.

There is great unrest in that abyss, a subliminal feeling that something is not quite right. This primordial insecurity gives rise to the unconscious motivation to fill that aching void with any substance, relationship, or preoccupation that eases our feelings of emptiness. Most of us don't realize that we've separated out from our totality until we serendipitously find ourselves "in the flow," where *all* of us is in a particular experience. In the aftermath of such an experience, the contrast between that total immersion and our ordinary state of consciousness is stark.

What causes us to step out of the flow experience, where all of our parts seem to be synchronized and working optimally? We've all had unselfconscious moments where our head and heart, belly and soul were embodied in an experience—as when we're walking hand-in-hand with our beloved, or delighting in the spontaneous play of a young child, or walking an enchanting trail in a forest. When we're totally immersed in such an experience, we're awake and aware, and there seems to be nothing outside of that experience. We're "all in," so to speak. Ego—our identification with the interior "me"—is not at all prominent in those precious moments. Afterwards, our self-conscious ego-self reappears to reflect upon what just occurred, to savor the experience, as if to saturate ourselves with its delicious sensations. Although remembering events during periods of tranquility allows us to savor them again, more often than not, it is desire reacting to the threat of the bare moment— the neutral psychological space that doesn't yet have content.

Third Threshold: Journey into the Labyrinth

Desire is very interesting to watch from a meditator's point of view. When we sit in stillness and silence there's nothing to do except breathe and be awake. No one is making demands upon or has expectations of us. Yet, there's often an inner battle going on, as we struggle to remain present without being seduced by endless distractions. It's here in this experiential moment that most people get to witness their compulsive desire to find greener grass elsewhere.

If we want to escape from the labyrinth of mind, there is a Buddhist teaching that offers a very straightforward method. The doctrine of codependent origination describes twelve experiential links, an inescapable sequence or chain reaction of thoughts, feelings, desires and habitual tendencies that create our experience of ourselves and the world. The two links that meditators pay particular attention to are desire and grasping, *trishna* and *upadana* in Sanskrit.

Trishna is translated as desire, craving, thirsting, hungering for something or someone. It implies dissatisfaction with the present moment or situation, the feeling that "this is not enough." And so we look elsewhere for a better moment, one that is more gratifying or distracting. Upadana means grasping, clutching, or mentally taking possession of someone or something and pulling it back to "central headquarters" where it becomes part of our psychological territory. Desire is not the primary problem because wanting and wishing is simply human and unavoidable. Grasping, on the other hand, is when we energetically reach for the object of desire (internal or external) in an effort to *possess* it, but the moment that we do, it possesses *us* in turn. This is when we plant a karmic seed.

For instance, while meditating we have a narrative that we're running in our mind about going away for the weekend. We see it in our mind's eye, but we let it go. It appears and disappears. No problem, just a ripple on the surface of mind's waters, grist for the meditator's mill. But then we have a thought about our partner with whom we had an argument just this morning. This thought is compelling, and arouses anxiety and sadness, hooking our attention so that we can't let it go. Grasping it energetically, we get some perverse pleasure from taking hold of it, but the problem is that it now owns us—infiltrating our mind, and shaping our mood and perception for any number of succeeding moments, depending upon its emotional charge.

Desire connects our present experience with an imagined state of either satisfaction or dissatisfaction, but either way, it promises another moment of experience. It's like looking at a succulent slice of cheesecake while knowing that you're at risk for coronary disease. You're fantasizing how good it would taste if only you could have just a little slice, just a wee smidgen. Having given in to imaginatively tasting it, you now want it badly. That's desire! It's a pivotal moment. If you refrain from reaching for the cheesecake, you weaken the power of desire by starving the pattern. On the other hand, you might tell yourself that you're just going to take just a tiny slice, and surely that wouldn't hurt. At that crucial moment, you give yourself permission to cross a line. You go for it, and savor your spoonful of cheesecake! That's the upadana—grasping, possession, ownership—which feeds this pattern by insisting on momentary gratification for the separate self-sense.

Third Threshold: Journey into the Labyrinth

We plant karmic seeds (*bija* in Sanskrit) in our psychic garden when we fulfill three conditions: a desire or wish for something (trishna), acting on that desire (upadana), and finally deriving gratification from fulfilling that desire, which could bring pleasure or pain. We can be addicted to either. When there is only desire but no energetic grasping, the thought or feeling arises and falls, appears and disappears. By disidentifying with it, watching it come and go, we weaken the karmic pattern, and refrain from nourishing these seeds. When we take possession of something, but don't experience gratification, due to heightened awareness of what we're doing, such an experience decreases motivation to repeat it because of the absence of pleasure. Again we weaken the electrical charge of the pattern, leaving these seeds malnourished.

When we identify with a desirable thought, image, or sensory experience and then energetically grasp it, deriving gratification from it, that inclines us to travel that same path again and again, so that we tend to behave in an habitual way. This is what imprisons us. On the other hand, we might notice that when we finish doing the dishes after dinner, and before we're about to do something else, there's a *gap*, a slice of time and space before the next thing. In that moment we can listen to the hissing sound of the tea kettle on the stove top, or momentarily notice the pleasant aftertaste of garlic and basil from our fish dinner, or feel the fullness in our belly. Mindfulness of sensory phenomena is a way of interrupting the endless circular loops of thought, so that we're returned to the here and now, where we're less likely to plant karmic seeds.

There's so much acceleration as we go from one thing to the next, but we might be surprised to discover that at *this* moment there is no motivation to be anywhere other than where we are. That's the entrance into *nowness* . Meditation in action is the practice of waking up in this moment, this precious moment of listening to the wind blowing, as the tree outside our window brushes up against our house, connecting us to wind and earth and the season of spring. We feel joyful for no reason other than that. In a twenty-four-hour period we have a whole series of entrance or exit points. Entering any one of those moments during ordinary activities, we can get off the wheel of karma by stepping into *presence*, being there all at once. And then we get on with whatever activity we need to handle.

Perhaps at a red light, or waiting in line at the ATM, or at the social security department, we find moments when we can bring awareness to our body and our senses and land in the situation at hand. The result of doing this practice is that we starve the habit of seeking distraction, where the grass promises to always be greener on the other side of the fence. We make such seductions obsolete by not feeding them, so that they eventually lose their hypnotic power to kidnap our attention. We get a taste of what emotional nakedness feels like, that sense of openness and vulnerability.

However, sometimes we might indulge in an after-dinner cigar, another glass of wine, or stay up until 2:30 in the morning because we are enjoying a great movie, even though we have to go to work the following morning. Avoiding desire altogether is a tall order. The point is to convert automatic, blind, habitual behavior into intentional action. Understanding our motivation is the key to working with the karmic force, so that we choose intentionally rather than react compulsively to whatever glitters with promise, distracting us from ourselves. If

Third Threshold: Journey into the Labyrinth

we can move gently, lovingly, playfully without grasping, without trying to capture who or what we love, then we can enjoy our human life regardless of what conditions we find ourselves in.

10.

Karmic Entrapment and Liberation

Karma, action that leads to reaction, is our effort to convince ourselves of "I's" or the ego-self's continuous existence into an indefinite future. This is what traps us in patterns of predictable thoughts and behaviors because they reinforce the ego-self's identity. But when we do things for their own sake, we enter a timeless moment, where we're liberated from the karmic chain of cause-and-effect.

There's a well-known and often-quoted statement that is likely a paraphrase or a composite from several of the Buddha's teachings:

> The thought manifests as the word;
> The word manifests as the deed;
> The deed develops into habit;
> And habit hardens into character.
> So watch the thought and its ways with care...

When we think repeatedly about things in a characteristic way, they eventually find their way into our speech patterns; and as we speak about these things in our unique way, they often incarnate themselves in our behaviors. These behaviors, repeated over time, become habitual and harden into character. We might also say that character becomes destiny. That is, we magnetize to ourselves or we are drawn to situations or relationships that conform with our idea of ourselves. Over time, the pattern of our life displays a certain consistency and coherence that lends distinctiveness to our character.

The Sanskrit term *karma* comes from the root *kr*, which means volitional action, but it specifically refers to action on the part of an independent self, an inner "I" or "me," who feels separate and different from everything else. Being independent can feel powerful as when we feel that we're the master of our destiny, but it is also a precarious condition because we stand alone. This spurs the motivation to both protect ourselves from threat and to seek strategies for continued life. We usually set about achieving these ends by becoming attached to who or what we like, rejecting who or what we dislike, and ignoring what falls into neither category. Ignoring is when we deny or avoid situations that confuse or perplex us, not knowing what to do with them.

As humans, we're particularly aware that our life comes to an end. As a result we've unconsciously devised a deceptive way to convince ourselves of our immortality—by creating an inner subject, an "I" that appears to transcend the body's mortality. This ego-self doesn't accept the reality of death and so it continually struggles to further its own existence. As a result, we search for power, recognition, pleasure, wealth and knowledge to prop ourselves up, but these are substitute gratifications for what we really want—to return home to the experience of wholeness or Buddha nature. Substitutes for our intrinsic wholeness leave us feeling frustrated and vulnerable. Yet, to experience ourselves in our totality would require the death of the inner ego-self, but this is what we strenuously resist. And so, the karmic wheel spins endlessly as we blindly hunger for more substitute gratifications to satisfy the illusory needs of the substitute subject—"me."

Because of the undeniable truth of impermanence, ego's strategies are constantly undermined, causing it to re-double its efforts for continuity. This sets in motion a counter reaction from the larger environment from which we're never truly separate. Every action creates a reaction, and that reaction conditions the next moment, so that it's inclined to flow in a characteristic way. This is how we reinforce the karmic chain of action and reaction, cause and effect, as we inadvertently plant seeds that eventually mature.

In the nontheistic tradition of Buddhism, it's understood that we're not punished or rewarded by a cosmic agent or deity, but rather that we alone are responsible for our lives. Understanding how karma works clarifies our life as either one of endless repetition or transformation, either feeling stuck or feeling freedom. By cultivating a meditative state of mind we're able to recognize the particular pattern of how we are, what we are, and who we are—and thereby witness how we plant karmic seeds.

When we sit in silence and stillness with the intention to simply be present, we discover that as each naked moment arises, we tend to decorate it with our assumptions and expectations, hopes and fears. The open space of nowness emerges again and again, yet most of us find it incredibly challenging to be with that bare moment without compulsively filling it with our personal inventory.

Moment by moment, we all have the opportunity to just *be*, which does not mean motionless or thoughtless, but rather being all of one piece. Even when we're in the midst of activities, we can be awake, aware, and sensitive—in a state of *knowingness* without anything specific being known. *Being* is a state of radical openness, readiness, and relaxation. It's the absence of the reflex to compulsively fill in the space of openness, as when there's a lull in a conversation and we try to keep the momentum going, as if to dispel the silence and quell our discomfort.

I think it's safe to say that for most of us, whether we're happy or sad, agitated or relaxed, at work or on vacation, we're spinning our wheels, talking to ourselves in the privacy of our mind. That ongoing internal dialogue lubricates the wheel of karmic action and reaction. It does not stop spinning until there's a punctuation in the midst of our usual acceleration—when we behold something exquisitely beautiful, or we're feeling tenderness and affection for a loved one, or we experience a delightful pause while meditating, where one thought ends but the next thought hasn't yet emerged. These are the timeless moments when the wheel is not spinning, when *all* of us is just there and not extended beyond the immediate moment.

The karmic force can best be experienced when we slow down enough to relax into a natural state of stillness and silence. From this neutral place we can recognize that there's a maddening impulse to *do* something with our experience, rather than simply be with it. When we're having a very enjoyable experience, fearful that it may decrease in intensity or duration, we often try to prolong it. We try to hold onto that precious moment of connection with a cherished friend, or that moment of exhilaration as we gaze into the Grand Canyon. When

Third Threshold: Journey into the Labyrinth

experiencing pleasure we often want to capture it, to freeze-frame the moment, instilling it in our memory so that we always have access to it. We often try to amplify or embellish a special moment, making the flames of delight burn brighter. On the other hand, we might hold ourselves back from fully experiencing the magnetic desire for another person, fearing that such intimacy and emotional vulnerability will make us dependent and needy, and cause us to lose our self-contained independence.

The unconscious motivation behind all such efforts is that we're trying to shape or organize our experience so that we can *do* something with it, rather than experience things on their own merit. Feeling that we're a separate or isolated center of feeling and thought, we confront people and things, with an attitude of self protection and control. When we act as if we're a fragment rather than the whole, it puts us out of sync with the larger atmosphere with which we're always connected. Consequently, we create some kind of whiplash, some kind of ripple effect, and this is how karma cause and effect operates.

When we consider the power of karmic cause-and-effect, it's helpful to consider how we plant seeds by repeatedly enacting certain patterns of thought, feeling and behavior, which have unforeseen consequences. Witnessing is the first step. We observe how mechanical and predictable our personality can be —from the way that we bathe, prepare our meals, clean our house, how we relate with our family and friends, to the way that we deal with pain, loneliness, and boredom.

The second step in working with karmic cause-and-effect is to try to notice what imprisons us in and what liberates us from the karmic chain. To that end, the Buddhist tradition has provided numerous metaphors, each of which reveals a particular pattern of how we either mindlessly repeat ourselves or dare to step into the fresh territory of the unknown.

One of the metaphors that's used to illustrate the power of karma is that of a river that seasonally overflows its banks and creates temporary tributaries. When the river's waters return to their normal level the water in the tributaries recedes, leaving patterns etched into the landscape. When the river overflows again, its waters are naturally drawn to the shallow tributaries that were formed during the previous season. With each overflow those tributaries become deeper and eventually become rivers in their own right.

When we enact habitual patterns of thought, feeling, and behavior, we're creating neurological pathways that are analogous to the seasonal overflow of the river and its formation of tributaries. Once those neurological pathways are well-established, we tend to take the path of least resistance, moving in the same direction that we moved yesterday and the week before. Although such activities feel natural and organic, we limit our freedom of choice because of the blind magnetic pull of the familiar, tried-and-true way. The same principle applies to how we interact with others. Once we establish a comfortable and predictable pattern within relationships, we tend to not to step outside of the box in order to expand our repertoire of novel ways to engage each other. Over time, such relationships lose their crispness, freshness and vibrancy.

Every action creates a reaction, and that reaction conditions the next moment so that it's inclined to flow in a particular way. As human beings we are inclined to follow the road *most* traveled because it's familiar and predictable, even though some roads take us to places that cause us suffering. With ongoing mindfulness practice we can change our mind and our familiar way of doing things, and thereby change the direction and quality of our lives. We can recognize ego's blind push to create a sense of its own continuity.

Traditionally, the birth of karma is symbolized by a potter shaping a pot on a potting wheel. It represents the effort to mold the clay of fluid experience into something that feels convincingly solid. Solid things seduce us to hang onto them and to make them our personal territory. This in turn, convinces us of our own solidity. In meditation, when we let go of thoughts, we can momentarily experience the absence of solidity, and its almost immediate return—in the form of a thought, a memory, or a bodily sensation.

Karma is based on our unconscious effort to organize our experience so that it reinforces our idea of ourselves. Buddhist meditation challenges our cherished belief in an interior "me" who stands apart to witness and comment upon our experiences. The whole karmic project is an effort to convince ourselves that we're solid, separate, and continuous— when in fact we are fluid, interdependent, and discontinuous. To the extent that we witness the transparency of the autobiographical self by not giving it our obsessive attention, to that extent we lessen the compulsive force of karma to bind us to predictable patterns of thought and behavior.

A second metaphor involves the numbing effect of repeated thoughts, feelings, and actions. If you work in a garden, or do some kind of manual work, or play tennis you probably have developed calluses on your hands from the friction of your tool or tennis racket. Those calluses protect the epidermis from further injury by creating a thick wall of skin. The result is that we become insensitive in the area of the callous, which buffers us from pain but also minimizes our sensitivity.

In the same way, when we experience distressing feelings of grief, anger, anxiety, or insecurity, we might unconsciously create bodily and psychological calluses that prevent us from feeling sensitivity in this area. Once the buffer is in place, we're usually not aware to what degree we're blocking our sensations and feelings. When we continually deflect suffering through the use of defense mechanisms, they have this kind of numbing effect, blinding us, so that we don't notice the cause of our underlying distress.

The spiritual path involves daring to open to and experience the bright as well as the shadowy aspects of life. As long as we are present with our experiences, we have an opportunity to work creatively with our discomfort and insensitivity, and gradually transform them. We relate with the disowned, unacknowledged areas that we've been defended against in order to establish intimate communication with our emotional pain. By not resisting our conflicted areas, but by bringing our full attention to their energetic aspect, we avoid setting up karmic whiplash.

Communication with our emotional pain cuts through the reflex of action and reaction so that we bother to inspect and inquire how we're holding our emotional pain. Here we can witness whether we are blocking the pain or whether we are meeting the emotion with awareness and tenderness. This allows this to process our feelings. Incomplete experience leaves a residue, which takes the form of a karmic seed.

Third Threshold: Journey into the Labyrinth

A third metaphor of karmic causation is that of a waterfall that has been reduced to a drip that falls twenty feet onto a slab of granite. After many years that slow and steady drip of water carves out a pothole in that granite. The great yogis and yoginis have said that our continuous intentional effort is just like that drip of water that breaks through the seemingly solid slab of our habitual patterns. Our commitment to be inquisitive, to explore the boundaries of ourselves under *all* circumstances, bringing whatever life offers us onto our spiritual path, is how we harness the karmic force in the service of our personal transformation.

We use the force of karmic causation to produce favorable circumstances that are conducive to develop greater awareness, sensitivity, and understanding. We plant seeds that will enhance our spiritual path. For instance, we exercise discipline so that we get up 45 minutes before work in order to have time for meditation practice, or we're selective in what we allow our mind to feast upon, choosing to read or listen to material that clarifies our confusion and inspires us.

Positive circumstances are still within the chain of karmic cause-and-effect and will ultimately need to be cut through in order to be truly free. Ultimate liberation undoes even the strategy to create positive circumstances for ourselves, challenging us to be open and available to work with whatever life presents.

11.

The Karma of Personality

Our life emerges from the unique complex of family and culture, environment and genetics, but also from our past actions that tend to limit the range of our choices in the present. We can either operate out of our familiar patterns, the way that we've behaved in the past, or we can have a "fresh take" on the unfolding moment. In spite of the reality of karmic causation, we can still think and act without being bound to our past, that is, we can act creatively.

Consider the following scenario: You and a friend are walking leisurely through a neighborhood park and chance upon a table where a game of chess has been left unfinished. You both look at the intriguing configuration of black and white pieces and decide to continue the chess game with the pieces as they are. This could be a metaphor for karmic constraint, the result of past actions that shape or limit the range of choices in the present moment. It could also be a metaphor for the freedom of the open moment, the pregnant possibilities that wait for us to live into them.

The design of the chessboard, the configuration of the pieces, and the rules of the game represent the conditions of life that are given—being born into a particular family of a certain socioeconomic class and of a particular race and religion, and at a specific historical time and geographical place. At the same time, the always-present moment is open-ended and invites us to be creative within the parameters of the rules of chess. We can operate out of our familiar patterns, the way that we've behaved in the past, or we can have a "fresh take" on the arrangement of the pieces and play it forward, by moving spontaneously.

What follows is a series of personality types, each of which inclines us to think and act in habitual ways, reinforcing a karmic pattern that binds us to predictable and unsatisfactory ways of being. In each of the following scenarios, we witness some degree of self-rejection which separates us from our experience and robs us of the freedom to be ourselves. Such negative judgment is based on an idealization of who we should be. The separation between who we are at our depth and who we are trying to be, is another way of understanding what triggers the karmic mechanism of action and reaction.

We might be the kind of person who is very achievement-oriented, who plays with an attitude of fierce competition. This freezes an otherwise friendly game into one of winning or losing, succeeding or failing. Our attitude might have the effect of triggering our friend's competitive edge, which in turn reinforces our ambition to win. The initially open space now becomes small and confining. In our mind our friendly chess game has become highly polarized between friend and adversary.

If we think that we're losing the game, we feel that we have to retaliate with a deadly strategy. Our friend's casual remarks and engaging conversation feel like an infraction of the game's sober atmosphere, and trigger a suspicion that our friend is trying to distract us to gain advantage. If we lose the game,

Third Threshold: Journey into the Labyrinth

we'll probably become agitated and insist on playing a second game to even the score. If we do win, then our winning will reinforce our competitive drive, which will likely grow in strength and cause us to seek more occasions to prove our mastery. This compulsive tendency will shape our future thought and behavior, inclining us to "win" or to be "right" in various interactions with others, and will fuel the karmic force of our personality.

Alternatively, we could notice ourselves becoming rigid and tense, and recognize the signature of our competitive personality. At that pivotal moment, we could completely shift our focus and begin to play the game for enjoyment, while still pitting our skill, intelligence, and creativity against our opponent. Winning now becomes secondary to the spirit of play. We could transform our compulsive pattern into reflective clarity and precision, as we move along with the flow of the game, appreciating the rhythm of give-and-take between ourselves and our friend. Our sympathetic relationship with our friend and our openness to the playful atmosphere of our game invites enjoyment and relaxation. Because we're not trying to validate ourselves through success and achievement, we can enjoy the game for its own sake without necessarily planting karmic seeds.

If we happen to be the kind of person who's attached to peacefulness, comfort, and ease, then we might try to artificially buffer ourselves from the edge of challenge by ignoring the concentrated effort required for winning, as well as defending ourselves from the disappointment of losing. Compensating for our style of avoidance, we rationalize to ourselves that we can't be bothered by such pedestrian concerns. We justify our false immunity by reinterpreting possible loss with the thought that we were merely playing and wouldn't take any game seriously.

The more that we disconnect from the edge of unpleasant feelings, the more that we lose touch both with our secret wish to win or succeed in life, and our own underlying feelings of vulnerability. Such unwillingness to pay attention to these details dissociates us from our interior world, our relationship with others, and from the immediate environment. This invites karmic whiplash, which eventually catches us completely by surprise. We might find ourselves working at the same unfulfilling job, or living in the same tiny rent-controlled apartment, or remaining in a dead-end relationship after many years, feeling bewildered at how we've missed the opportunity to step into a larger life.

Alternatively, instead of being overly avoidant of conflict and chaos, we might relish the excitement of having innumerable possibilities of choice. Instead of standing back in our bubble of superficial immunity, we could fully participate in what life presents to us. In any moment we might notice that there are flowers blooming in a small triangular garden adjacent to our chess table, as a spider weaves a complex web between the flower stems, while in the distance children are laughing with abandon. We're also feeling the thrill and slight anxiety of challenge. These perceptions are not conditioned by a thousand yesterdays, and so they arise with refreshing simplicity.

With this quality of presence we can momentarily step out of our cocoon of safety and into uncertainty and unpredictability to risk the excitement of winning or the disappointment of losing. In Buddhism, such uncontaminated perception is called *thatness, or suchness*. It has no name, no explanation, and no story attached to it, but rather a quality of startling freshness, spaciousness, and innocence. In such living moments, we don't plant karmic seeds because we haven't separated ourselves out from the immediate environment as an inner witness, and so we're not resisting the flow of the situation. Nothing is the left undone.

We might have a personality that continually feels inner impoverishment, and regardless of the circumstances, we seem to suffer from poverty mentality. Driven by an overwhelming desire to consume things, experiences, or people in order to fill our aching void, we can't seem to find lasting gratification with anyone or anything. Bringing this mentality to our chess game, we try a little too hard to satisfy our need for friendship and our hunger to relish the playing of the game, but soon discover that our friend and the chess game have become part of our poverty mentality.

If we appear to be getting the upper hand in the game, we begin to feel troubled that we might be deflating our friend's self-esteem and thereby risk losing his or her friendship. Or if our strategy happens to be successful, we might regard it as just dumb luck, as we anticipate our imminent fall from grace by getting caught in a surprising checkmate. No matter what experience we have, it only temporarily fills our void, and we're left impoverished yet again. This sets into motion a ruthless karmic pattern of hope and fear, each alternation reinforcing our feeling of deficiency and pattern of craving.

On the other hand, we could relax our grasping mentality and encourage ourselves to feel gratitude for our loyal friend and the richness of our immediate experience. We could "feel into" the reassuring substance of our sensory experience without trying to consume it. We take notice of the late afternoon sun as it casts long shafts of light on the chessboard, while squirrels leap from branch to branch, rustling the leaves on the branches above us. There's the fragrance of damp earth, the vivid colors of autumn, and a feeling of sweet melancholy, all of which are reminiscent of the carefree quality of our childhood.

Such simple experiences communicate something precious to us, but ineffable. We could discover that any ordinary situation can have many layers, aspects, and dimensions, all of which are worthy of appreciation. If we open ourselves to our inner emptiness without negatively judging ourselves, such feelings can carve out places inside of us that enlarge our sense of self, where we don't experience a craving to fill our emptiness. We can starve this karmic pattern of poverty mentality.

We could have the kind of personality that has blind adherence to an habitual way of being. We take refuge in the comfort of fixed routines and instinct-like behaviors. Our minimalist approach to life is based on fear of change and uncertainty. We play deaf, dumb, and blind in an effort to hide from ourselves, from the irritating demands of everyday life, and from the complexities of relationships. Rather than approaching the chess game with a sense of adventure and an exploratory spirit, we rely upon our familiar chess strategies that we learned in grade school. The thought of trying something new feels like stepping out on a precarious ledge.

We fail to take notice of our friend's obvious strategy. Moment by moment, we reinforce our pattern of inflexibility and plant seeds of future insensitivity and numbness. Our refusal to communicate with what feels threatening makes us blind to those very things. Our rigidity and defensiveness grows ever stronger, putting us out of touch with changes in our environment and with social cues that would help us navigate relationships with others. This pattern of blind adherence to fixed routines invites karmic repercussions.

Alternatively, we could take a chance and encourage ourselves to tune into the unfolding freshness of the moment. This would require our willingness to temporarily step out of the invisible cage of our rigid personality style, which is the frame through which we perceive our world. Without the need to cling to what is safe and familiar, we dare to step into the open moment to see what possibilities await us. By not feeding our pattern of disconnecting from what appears to be threatening, we refrain from solidifying the walls of our self imposed psychological prison. Paradoxically, we leap into the unfolding moment in which we're *already* immersed, to find delight in being surprised.

Lastly, we may be the kind of person who continually seeks pleasure and creative ways to enhance pleasure. We dimly suspect that we're trying to fill our inner emptiness and boredom, but our restless and creative imagination provokes us to seek ever more subtle and refined pleasures. We wind up making numerous suggestions to our friend for how to make the game more stimulating and entertaining, such as switching seats and playing the game from the opposing side. Later we suggest that we move the chess pieces to a different table in order to be in the shade, and that perhaps one of us could go to the nearby deli to bring back refreshments.

The freedom of choice biases us towards indulgence in endless pleasure, but when not feeling sufficiently entertained, we become bored and irritated. This provokes a search for further forms of distraction, which might cause us to lose interest in whatever or with whomever we're involved. Every effort to seek stimulation as a way of avoiding boredom and feelings of emptiness, nourishes this pattern, making us need increasingly intense pleasures to achieve the same stimulation.

Alternatively, we could use our sensitivity and refined intelligence to witness the alternation between excitement and boredom, the thrill of novelty and the feeling of claustrophobia whenever we experience repetition. Meditation cultivates heightened awareness and sensitivity, and this provides the golden opportunity to work with the karmic pattern of our personality. By not trying to enhance or elaborate what we're experiencing, or impulsively seek alternative possibilities, we can transform our neurotic desire for endless pleasure and stimulation into an acceptance of both the peaks and valleys of experience. Eventually we learn to communicate with boredom as simply the absence of entertainment. Encouraging ourselves to be okay with minimal stimulation, we find ourselves more embodied, anchored in the present moment without need of escape.

12.

Character and Meaningful Coincidence

Although we appear to be pushed from behind by our prior thoughts and actions, and shaped by heredity and our parental upbringing, we're also pulled forward by the total being that we are yet to become. Buddha nature is like a magnetic attractor that exerts a continuous evolutionary pull on all of us.

Most of us think that as long as we're not pressured to do something by outside forces or other people, our choices and decisions are our own. But upon closer observation we might notice that a great many of our choices are not really our own but are suggested to us from our culture, which lives invisibly within us. Our parents were local representatives of the culture into which we were born. They embodied a particular way of life, a style of emotional expression or inhibition, a manner of interpersonal relationship, and a moral code with injunctions and taboos. The values of good and bad, right and wrong, acceptable and unacceptable were imprinted on us very early in life, and these values became our inner authority. This inner authority is what Freud called the *superego*, the critical parent that sits in the director's chair within our interior.

From a spiritual perspective, if we genuinely wish to be free, at some point we have to cut the rope that ties us to the dictates of our inner parent and social conformity. Many of us live beholden to how we imagine our loved ones see us—whether they be spouses, children, parents, dear friends, or the community or corporation to which we belong. These significant others have expectations of us and hold an image of who they envision us to be. Whether that image is accurate or not, there's a charged energetic field between us and our loved ones that pulls on us. We unknowingly tend to shape ourselves in accordance with how we imagine they see us and what we think they want from us.

One of the challenges of being free is to seriously consider whether we're living a life that's truly of our own choosing, and not in conformity with what others expect of us. What does the deepest part of ourselves want from our life? In an earlier period of history we might've asked, "What do the gods want of me?"

The concept of freedom can be better understood when we consider "freedom from" as opposed to "freedom to." "Freedom from" is emancipation from what restricts, limits, or compromises our ability to express ourselves and to live our lives as we see fit. "Freedom to" is more complex. It implies intuitive understanding and creative imagination to envision a life that goes beyond limitation, to a life that inspires us to be *all* that we can be—to being authentic.

The previous chapters in this section have discussed karma as the law of cause-and-effect, action and reaction. Although not intended as such, this doctrine seems to convey the image of a human being as an *effect*, the result of being pushed from behind by prior thoughts and actions. Although we make choices in the present that will influence and shape our future condition, our present choices have been shaped by many prior causes and conditions.

Concerning our theme of freedom, we need a fresh way of regarding the importance of our lives so that we can view ourselves as more than the result of heredity, parental, and societal influences, and our prior choices. This raises a crucial question, the answer to which determines how we will travel through our lives. Are we cosmic flukes, random flashes of light between two forgetful worlds of darkness? If our parents made love on a different day, would our mother have given birth to someone *other* than ourselves or would we (if *"we"* existed in some immaterial form) wait for another occasion to enter her womb? Does the world actually want us to be here? And if so, do we possess a uniqueness, a particular character that is there before our birth that asks to be incarnated?

This is a somewhat speculative inquiry, but it goes to the heart of the question of freedom. As the oak is in the floor plan of every acorn, could it be that each of our unique characters was embedded in an archetypal form, a primordial image that holds the essence of our true identity? Is this really too great a stretch, when we consider that we're born with Buddha nature, the furthest reach of human potential—awakened consciousness? If this is so, then we're not only pushed from behind by prior causes and conditions, but we're also pulled forward, towards who we can ultimately be. Perhaps our autobiography is guided by an invisible intention, but not by a destiny that is predetermined.

It's instructive to compare the terms *personality* with *character*. The word personality comes from the Latin, *persona*, which means mask. Personality is, in large measure, shaped or created, a product of social conditioning. It's the sum of patterned habits, traits, attitudes, ideas, and values of an individual, the result of genetics, parental upbringing, cultural influences, as well as significant experiences and relationships that have shaped us. Consequently, personality is an effect of innumerable causes and conditions, something that is both created and composite.

By contrast, the term *character* comes from the Greek *charaxo*, which means distinctive quality, or engraved mark or imprint. The word *character* originally meant a marking instrument that cuts indelible lines and leaves traces, as in an engraving. In this sense, character is not socially created but something we are born with. The idea of an original or archetypal image that exists prior to the creation of personality gives value and significance to the events and occasions of our life. It regards our choices as having an intention, but without necessarily having a concrete destination. From this perspective, when we live in alignment with our character, it would lend a feeling of significance to the events of our biography. There would be no trivial moments, but only various expressions of our unique character. To assume this attitude would leave us with a feeling of rightness about our choices and a sense of freedom.

Conceived of in this way, our unique character would not be an unchanging, monolithic entity existing *apart* from the experiential person that we are, or impervious to our environment. Instead, it would be a dynamic intelligence and energy, in intimate relationship and communication with our environment. When we envision ourselves in this way, the seemingly random events of life now suggest meaningful coincidences that are occasions for our unique character to express itself. In other words, so-called chance situations now appear to reflect a deeper unfolding order. Such synchronicity implies that inner and outer events are meaningfully linked, so that both mind and nature, inner and outer are in continuous dialogue, and not separate.

Instead of thinking about the events and occasions of our life as solely a product of causes and conditions, we can also view them as manifestations of the creative energy of our character. Our life can be experienced as having meaning and direction, empowering us with confidence and courage to live the life we were meant to live. Although the doctrine of karmic cause-and-effect is an essential teaching in Buddhism, it is not absolute. It is superseded by the fruitional teachings of Buddhism, which hold that our experiences are spontaneous manifestations of the creative energy of mind, suggesting a meaningful coincidence or synchronicity of the events of our lives. It is here that we can liberate ourselves from the labyrinth and find freedom in our daily lives.

Journey into the Labyrinth

You know that you've crossed the third threshold when....

You discover that even when in a state of stillness and silence, you have a great difficulty just being with what is arising in your experience. Instead, you feel an irresistible urge to shape or manipulate your momentary experience. This observation, repeated over time, marks your understanding of how the karmic chain reaction works.

Through meditation practice you discover that karma, the cause-and-effect of your intentions, thoughts, and actions, is a very real power that binds you to a repetitious way of being in the world, entrapping you in a self-made labyrinth.

At the third threshold, you've begun to understand the complexities and deeper implications of the Buddhist teaching on karma. You see that almost all forms of desire spring from dissatisfaction with the moment or situation you are presently in. Grasping fulfills desire by mentally or physically taking possession of someone or something in order to make it your personal territory. The moment that you do, you plant a karmic seed.

The way out of the labyrinth appears when you begin to discriminate the kind and quality of "seeds" that you plant in your mind. You can plant positive seeds of kindness, generosity, and compassion, rather than negative seeds of anger, harsh judgment, envy, and jealousy. Positive seeds promote favorable conditions in which to further your spiritual path. However, this is an intermediary step. Every seed comes to some sort of unavoidable fruition, limiting your freedom to some extent. You begin to have an intuitive understanding that complete and total

Third Threshold: Journey into the Labyrinth

action, like a good bonfire, leaves no trace, where no seeds are planted, and where no karmic repercussions will follow.

At the third threshold, you see that character is a double-edged sword. Character can become destiny when you mindlessly draw to yourself situations that conform to your ego-identity. Karmic action and reaction is the mechanism of such reinforcement. At the same time, character can be a conscious and intentional embrace of the life that wants to live through you. You realize that who you are is not merely the result of prior choices that seem to push you from behind, but that from within your depth, Buddha nature exerts an irrepressible force that pulls you forward towards who you ultimately are. Beyond your ego-self, you recognize that you have a distinctive way of being who you are and of expressing that uniqueness.

At this stage of the path, you are increasingly able to view the seemingly random events of life as manifestations of meaningful coincidences, suggesting that whatever you've done in your life could not have been otherwise. You become increasingly confident that there have been no accidental occasions. In other words, so-called random situations now appear to reflect a deeper unfolding order, suggesting that that your inner world and the outer events in which you find yourself, are linked in ways that are meaningful for you. You discover again and again, that mind and nature are not separate. It is now time to take a deeper dive where you will be challenged by both the simplicity and complexity of meditation.

Fourth Threshold: Belly of the Whale

The image of being swallowed by a whale comes from the well-known biblical account of Jonah and the leviathan. The belly of the whale is a symbolic womb where we go inwards into the depths of our mind and heart to be born again. Our over-identification with our persona or social image has created an imbalance in our psyche and it's this imbalance that precipitates the descent into the belly of the whale.

We are swallowed into the inner temple or dark depths of our own unconscious where we are naked and alone. We lose the reference points of our worldly life and our former idea of ourselves begins to feel increasingly shallow. Once inside we go through a process of symbolically dying to our familiar idea of ourselves, and everything we know ceases to be meaningful or consoling. We are alone and without distraction, and these are the necessary prerequisites to undergo a gradual metamorphosis.

Finally, after a period of time, the whale coughs us up onto a distant shore where we find ourselves as a stranger in a strange land, as if newborn. We're returned to a world that no longer feels ordinary, but one that we now experience as refreshed and revitalized. The belly of the whale is the magical crucible that symbolizes the journey of psychological death and rebirth. In practical terms, meditation and the meditative state of mind become the trusted vehicles that initiate us into a new way of being in the world, opening us up to a sacred view of life.

13.

Trusting our Right to be Here

Trust is a growing confidence that life itself is basically good in spite of the enormity of suffering in the world. Trust is an intuitive understanding that in spite of our shortcomings, we're informed by an intelligence that holds and supports us, and that our being here is not an accident.

Based on the flexibility or rigidity of our family of origin, not all aspects of ourselves were held, honored, and nurtured. The parts of ourselves that were *not* acknowledged either remain at an immature level of development or they've become part of our disowned "shadow" self. These are the parts of ourselves that we usually don't trust and from which we've become disconnected. When we begin to do psychological or spiritual inner work, these unacknowledged split-off places eventually confront us, challenging us to communicate with them.

The problem is that if we live exclusively within the boundaries of our socially conditioned self and don't explore what's beyond it, we then continue to mistrust significant parts of ourselves, which often causes us to have irrational dislikes or fears. Our personal evolution depends on questioning any misplaced loyalty to family and tradition where it undermines our ability to be all that we are. Trusting ourselves means that we set ourselves free from the *authority* of family and society wherever they contradict or sabotage our spiritual path.

It's instructive that the word "heal" means "whole," that is, to make whole, to restore to one's original integrity. It suggests the re-assimilation of separate parts into an organic whole. The process of healing begins by recognizing the need for communication with our forgotten, rejected, or unexplored parts so that they stop feeling alien.

If we want our spiritual path to involve our whole being, then it's necessary to allow our immediate experiences, both pleasurable and painful, to speak to us, as an expression of the natural unfolding of our lives. It's having the confidence that our body, senses, and mind are perfectly suited to make good use of our experiences. Whatever we experience has some intimate relationship with our inner being, although we may not understand this at first. Nothing we experience is completely alien but corresponds to some dimension of ourselves that's ready to receive it, or else it would be incomprehensible.

As we're able to make this connection between inner and outer, we begin to experience a growing conviction that the unfolding of our life is not haphazard. Although we may be presented with circumstances that are conflictual, contradictory, and ambiguous, trust is the intuitive feeling that what is optimal will occur. It is the growing assurance that life provides us with what we need, but we have to be open to receive and work creatively with what is offered.

The practice of meditation is about tuning into ourselves, listening with our heart, and learning to make friends with ourselves, all of us—the good, the bad, the ugly, and the

Fourth Threshold: Belly of the Whale

beautiful. It's also learning to make friends with the circumstances in which we find ourselves. Although we may be very high functioning in many areas of our life, spiritually advanced, and even intellectually brilliant, we may also be hung up on addictions, sexual obsessions, abusive power dynamics, and other dysfunctional behaviors that our spiritual path has *bypassed*. If we're going to evolve on the path of both waking up and growing up, it's necessary to inquire whether there are parts of ourselves that we're reluctant to experience because they threaten who we think we are.

We may be resistant to experience sadness or grief, largely because those feelings were not modeled in our family of origin. Or perhaps we refuse to abandon ourselves to sexual or sensual pleasure because of early parental ethical or religious injunctions. If we unconsciously block ourselves from experiencing certain feelings because of shame or guilt, then they get channeled into our shadow and remain unconscious. As a result, parts of our body close down and we become numb. Over time, we're likely to impulsively act out those suppressed areas without understanding how and why these patterns control us.

Trust in ourselves is cultivated as we make a relationship with our strengths and our vulnerabilities, with the spiritual and the sexual, the stingy and the generous aspects of ourselves. Our personality is a mixture of polar opposites—of aggression and kindness, agitation and peacefulness, narcissism and compassion. The challenge of all painful or confusing experiences is how to resolve and integrate them within our totality, and not split off such experiences from awareness. If we dissociate from painful memories, they remain exiled from the larger being that we are. This undermines our foundation of trust and sabotages our confidence in our own worthiness.

From a Buddhist perspective, we develop a trust or confident expectation that something intrinsic within us is supporting and helping us. This larger something includes the surrounding phenomenal world of sun and wind, earth and rain, plants and animals, pollinators and scavengers. It's the intuitive realization of the basic goodness of both ourselves and the world. Even though people are suffering the world over, and there are atrocities and injustices being committed, we place our trust in the *essence* of this earthly existence, in life itself, and not always on its outer expression. We intuitively realize there's an implicit intelligence and an inherent value both in the nature of the cosmos and in our existence.

Although an infant was never taught how to nurse, it has the confident expectation that when it reaches for its mother's breast, a source of life will be there. It trusts that when it cries, the outer world will respond to its distress. A flower bulb dares to unfurl its delicate petals, trusting in its implicit relationship to the sun. Trust is like that.

We open because we have a direct relationship with our own light or Buddha nature. Trust is marked by the attitude that the good draws the good to itself. As we develop confidence in our inherent Buddha nature, we open to experiences of irritation, boredom, depression, passing anxiety, and loneliness, knowing that there's something of value for us.

Mature trust roots us in our body, in our connection with our family and ancestors, and in the natural world. It is the foundation of our existence. From it comes the conviction that we have a right to be here, to feel that we belong to this world.

Fourth Threshold: Belly of the Whale

Without this grounding we are unstable. Although we may develop in other areas, we will be unable to support those gains if there's a basic distrust of ourselves, of our connection with our body, and of the earth which supports us.

STEALING FIRE FROM THE GODS

14.

The Method and Essence of Meditation

The essence of meditation is the return of our attention to the immediate moment, whenever we catch ourselves getting distracted. Again and again, we cut through the seemingly endless stories that percolate in our mind and kidnap our attention, and we return to ground zero of meditation—here and now.

There are two fundamentally different but complementary states that we can be in—being or doing. We live in an action-oriented, "doing" culture, where efficiency and achievement are valued. "Being," on the other hand, is associated with idleness, having nothing to do, simple relaxation, or taking time out for reducing stress. "Being" is commonly regarded as a valueless interval between doing necessary things, and having no intrinsic meaning, value, or purpose in itself. However, from a meditator's perspective, "being" is the only time when we're without our agenda, where our mind and heart are unguarded, when we allow ourselves to experience the moment without manipulating what arises.

Meditation is like sitting by the bank of a great stream. The stream's relentless currents carry our many memories, our rich tapestry of experiences, both painful and pleasurable, as well as our anticipation of what's just yet to come. Our job as a meditators is to remain on the bank of the stream without falling into its turbulent currents. We simply observe the stream of psychic jetsam and flotsam with interest, but without becoming overly fascinated by its contents. If our attention gets hooked by a provocative thought or image, we immediately fall into the stream and become part of the swirling debris, instantly losing our capacity for unbiased observation.

Meditation is the practice of recognizing when we have fallen into the stream. That very noticing immediately brings us back to our position on the bank as an observer. There's no need to be discouraged if you find yourself spending more time *in* the stream than on its peaceful shore. Your attention will alternate between witnessing and falling into the stream. That's what Buddhists call the path.

A key point to understand is that there aren't two steps —one of recognizing that you've fallen into the stream, and the other of getting back to the shore. When you recognize that you've fallen into the stream, by having become distracted, you're *already* back. You've come back into presence—being here, now. It's likely that you will become distracted again, and so you repeat the process of returning to the immediacy of *now*, again and again.

The actual practice of meditation begins by assuming a good, upright posture, either on a meditation cushion or in a supportive chair. We initially anchor our attention by feeling into our body. Little by little, we come down from the cloud-realm of discursive thinking and land in our body. With that comes a sense of being settled. We feel our body, as our breath moves in and out like the rhythmic tides of the ocean. Our heart beats and circulates blood, as the ordinary miracles of sight, sound, smell,

Fourth Threshold: Belly of the Whale

taste, and feeling all take place effortlessly. No matter what thought, image, or memory arises in our mind, if we don't become involved with it, it momentarily appears and disappears of its own accord. We simply sit, breathe, and are aware. There's an unmistakable sense of simple presence, a foundation or home ground. With confidence we can inaudibly affirm, "I am here, now," as our awareness objectively reflects the random, free-associative thoughts and images that flash in our turbulent mind stream.

One of the powers of this practice is that it brings our mind and body together, in the same place and at the same time, so that we're synchronized. Most of the time, our body is in one place and our mind is elsewhere. Our body is sitting as we're having a cup of coffee, while our mind is preoccupied with the day's agenda or with an unresolved issue. Few of us realize the implications of this phenomenon. In the usual state of *mindlessness*, we're lost in space, fully identified with our rambling, free-associative thoughts. They continually trigger a chain reaction of further thoughts, images, and feelings, and these make up our compelling inner narratives, which kidnap our attention from the earthy quality of what's here, now.

The essence of mindfulness meditation is that flash of recognition that notices that we're distracted. This signals a complete reversal of direction, bringing us instantly back to our body or our breath. By interrupting our story lines, our compelling narratives of love and loss, the hope of success and the fear of failure, we're brought back to the immediacy of this moment. Like a magnifying glass that gathers the sun's rays into a laser-like beam of intense light, meditation intensifies our attention to reveal that only one thing is happening at a time.

The discipline of mindfulness is to be there with that one-shot perception of nowness from which there is no real escape. Even when we're fantasizing about the future or reminiscing about the past, we're doing it *now!* According to Buddhism, that dimensionless point of awareness is the key to our true identity.

The path of meditation cultivates basic trust in ourselves, as our mind finally catches up with our body, so that we feel like we're all of one piece. There's a feeling of empowerment in taking a seat on this good earth without being knocked off our "immovable spot" by distracting thoughts. An important aspect of meditation is the gesture of extending unconditional friendliness and lovingkindness to ourselves. We acknowledge that sitting attentively in silence and stillness, while trying to resist the mind's seductive distractions, is very challenging. It's a noble thing to do even if we spend most of the time carried away by our mindstream. Extending kindness and understanding to ourselves allows us to weather the storm of getting repeatedly buffeted by our thoughts and feelings.

We bring the meditative state of mind into everyday life by inviting an atmosphere of openness and gentleness. We allow random gaps or pauses in the midst of our activities and interchanges with others. It could be as simple as taking a deep breath or shifting your attention to momentarily gaze out the window at the blue sky. In such spacious moments, we can simply be *aware* without having to think about anything in particular. Awareness is a kind of cognitive radiance without content, and although it's always available, we invoke it by letting go of discursive thoughts.

Meditation invites inquisitiveness. We might begin to wonder who we really are when we're not identified as a man or

Fourth Threshold: Belly of the Whale

a woman, a husband or a wife, a father or a mother, or an office manager or a mechanic. If our social role and its associated script is not *all* that we are, then who or what are we in our totality? If we persist in the practice of meditation, we might discover that our conventional identity begins to feel hollow. The ongoing practice of *disidentifying* with what arises in our mind renders our personal narrative somewhat hollow. Many meditators experience a sense of personal transparency, where their thoughts, images, and inner dialogue begin to feel diaphanous or ghost-like.

Meditation eventually extends the boundary of our identity further and further to include more of the world on the other side of what Alan Watts referred to as our skin-encapsulated ego. This extended "self" experiences a sympathetic relationship with others as well as with the natural world and marks our ever-deepening intimacy with the non-human world of plants and animals. When we stop thinking of our mind as something apart from our body, and ourselves as separate from the body of the world, then the whole of the natural world becomes a living presence, not fundamentally separate or different from ourselves. The whole environment taken together with ourselves, makes up one living being, so that what we see, hear, or feel puts us in touch with the soul of life itself.

I took a walk today in the drizzling rain. I stopped by a pine tree and noticed that on the tips of the pine needles, drops of water were refracting sunlight into miniature rainbows, transforming them into perfect little jewels. It was so simple and ordinary but how marvelous. Suddenly there was just that—dew drops, pine needles, and the rain on my face—without any need to capture the moment. Meditative transparency allows for these extra-ordinary moments where there's unexpected joy and freedom for no good reason. And if you're happy for no reason, then happiness can't be taken away from you.

15.

Mindfulness and Awareness

Mindfulness focuses on individual thoughts, sensations, and feelings, while awareness is the more panoramic aspect of mind that tunes into the atmosphere in which those individual thoughts and feelings arise. When mindfulness is joined with awareness, like two wings of a bird that give rise to flight, our meditation really takes off, giving us both the content and context of any moment.

In the late '60s, Richard Alpert, aka Ram Dass, wrote a book entitled *Be Here Now*, which, for my generation, was everyone's bedside bible. It was very readable, hip, and chocked full of wisdom. Ram Dass had been to India, met his guru, had remarkable experiences, and brought back centuries of Indian religion and spirituality, distilled in the message—be here, now. However, this is a deceptively simple expression.

Being here, now, is both a method and an orientation for how to infiltrate our everyday lives with a meditative state of mind, which often results in a change of heart. When we begin meditating, the basic instruction is to be present, to repeatedly bring our attention back to the immediate moment instead of allowing it to wander. That's the *now* aspect of being here, now. The term "now" relates to time. It's the sense of presentness or immediacy. The term "here" is spatial, conveying the sense of location, being *here* on this spot. It's the sense of presence.

Mindfulness, or *shamatha* in Sanskrit, tunes into our individual thoughts and feelings, the *content* of meditation, without necessarily having any insight about them, that is, without recognizing their connection with the larger themes of your life. Panoramic awareness or *vipashyana* in Sanskrit, takes note of the overarching theme within which your thoughts and feelings are occurring, the *context* of your experience, and therefore vipashyana is often translated as insight.

In our meditation, if there's a tight focus of attention on each momentary event, we could inadvertently block our intuitive insight into the implications of our experiences. For instance, suddenly an image of a steaming plate of spaghetti and meatballs pops into our mind, followed by the enticing thought of a new car, and then the enchanting image of walking on the white sand beach of an exotic tropical island. Each of these discrete thoughts can be seen precisely, in moments of presentness, but without revealing any significance about them.

However, the intuitive aspect of mind recognizes that we're feeling empty and are hungry for a change, for something to lift us out of our emotional plateau. Awareness or presence is a deepening or an expansion of the space in which we're meditating. Presence can be experienced as an expanded field of sensitivity. Yet, if our meditation is too intuitive, we could lose our anchor and begin to drift, losing the precision and clarity of nowness. The *integration* of both mindfulness and awareness allows the content of our meditation to be witnessed with precision and clarity, but within the context of intuitive awareness.

Fourth Threshold: Belly of the Whale

Beginning meditators think that nowness only refers to a point-instant in time, meaning only the individual thoughts or sensations happening at this moment—just this micro-event. But nowness also includes the current period that we're in. Nowness is elastic and can extend back nine months or project forward into an anticipated future that's framed by a project or relationship in which we're immersed. This is not to suggest that our meditation is composed of a flashing kaleidoscope of memories and anticipations, but rather that nowness is not divorced from our life situation.

Without panoramic awareness we could naïvely use mindfulness to avoid that larger and deeper sense of our life by focusing only on individual thoughts and images, while failing to intuitively feel the connection with what came before or with what will likely follow. While nowness or *presentness* pays meticulous attention to our individual thoughts, *presence*, the intuitive aspect of mind, senses the atmospheric field in which we're sitting, the overarching tone and texture that frames our life.

From a psychological perspective, we could think of panoramic awareness as the intuitive sensing of the unique chapter of our life in which we currently find ourselves. For instance, six months ago you met someone new and the two of you have been falling in love with each other, and are now thinking of moving in together. That's the current chapter in which your mind, heart, and your belly are all involved. In your meditation, many of the thoughts, feelings, hopes, and fears that come up are most likely related to this new relationship. You sit with the unarticulated feeling that you're living through a delightful chapter of your life, as you wordlessly recognize that many of your thoughts, images, and feelings are related to this time of life.

On the other hand, if someone close to you has died recently, you're likely experiencing a period of grief, and many of your thoughts, feelings, and memories will occur within that frame. To know that in the background of your mind you're passing through a mournful season of life gives you an appreciation and a perspective for how to hold what arises in meditation. You don't have to think about that perspective. You have it as a perceptual frame within which your thoughts, feelings, and memories arise and fall. When sadness or feelings of loss and abandonment come up in meditation, rather than thinking that something's wrong with you, or that you should get over it and be peaceful, you honor the sadness and feelings of loss before releasing them. You don't struggle with that, neither minimizing your feelings, nor pushing them away.

The various passages of our life can be benign, like starting a new job or moving into a new apartment, or they could leave us betwixt and between, where one phase of a relationship seems to be ending, but the new phase hasn't yet begun. We could find ourselves floating around rudderless and uncertain how to be and what to do next. That's the chapter of our life we're in right now, and so in our meditation practice our thoughts, feelings, or memories will likely occur within that frame. To know this, clarifies the relationship between our individual thoughts and feelings, and where we are in our life.

Concerning the "here" aspect of "be here, now," where exactly is here? We're sitting here in this chair or on a support cushion. Meditation begins with mindfulness of body. We feel our body, our bottom supported by the chair or support cushion,

Fourth Threshold: Belly of the Whale

we feel our shoulders and our upright posture, and some tension in our lower back. Awareness might silently inquire, "Where exactly is here?" Here is our breath, the rise and fall our abdomen, our arms, our legs—and we relax with that. If we're practicing with a group, here is also the sight of all these lovely people sitting around us. Here is the piano in the far corner of the room, and the windows and lights, and soft pastel-colored walls. Here is the carpet and the ceiling and the soft overhead lights. Here is the garden that is adjacent to this meditation hall and the distant sound of traffic. "Here" begins to get larger as we relax more, and tune into the environment that surrounds our meditation.

We begin to get flashes of insight that "here" is not this little geographical area but the entire atmosphere in which we are meditating, which includes us. "Here" is an atmospheric presence, and the recognition that we are inseparable from this atmosphere. Eventually we experience "here" as an immeasurable space with elastic boundaries that stretches out beyond our skin encapsulated body.

The experience of being here, now, intuitively understands that the whole momentum of our life has brought us to this spot. Infinite causes and conditions came together to bring us to this present situation, at this moment. There's no mistake. We can afford to take a deep breath and relax. Each situation we find ourselves in is not only an accurate reflection of our present state of mind but also reflects the characteristic style of how we are living our life.

Contrary to conventional wisdom, anything that we experience is connected with the entirety of our lives and shouldn't be regarded as accidental or a mistake. Whether someone comes up to us in the middle of the street and yells, "Screw you, you're ugly and have no merit," or we win the lottery tomorrow morning, these momentary events are connected with the personal thread of our life. The realization that the immediate situation of "here" coincides with the totality of ourselves, reveals that any piece of our life is *all* of it. Everything is present all at once.

Mindfulness integrated with panoramic awareness allows us to experience the precision and clarity of our thoughts and feelings but also opens us to the realization that the immediate moment includes past, present, and the future. Mindfulness joined with awareness also conveys that here is inseparable from from the larger container that holds our life. This affords us a continuity of meaning, and gives us confidence to be here, and to open fully to whatever life has to offer us.

16.

Being All There

The immediate moment is dangerous. In order to be with what is unfolding right now, we can't bring along our accumulation of beliefs, assumptions, expectations, or our idea of ourselves. They must be left at the door or else we won't be able to enter the living moment as it is.

We're fed by two streams, two fundamentally complementary forces that meet at the magical juncture of being human. On one hand, there's the activity of *becoming*, which is when we're on our way towards a goal or destination, or in the process of completing an activity. It's a motivated journey between present and future, a movement from where we presently are, to where we hope to be, involving some change or development. *Becoming* is like a wave that gathers fresh water, both retaining its shape, yet changing moment by moment as it rolls towards the shore.

On the other hand, *being* is the quality or state of completeness and satisfaction, when our mind and body, heart and soul are all of one piece—integrated in a timeless moment of presence. When we're in the space of *being* there's no motivation to be elsewhere. Each moment of experience emerges out of the fullness of our being. When we're in love, or appreciating natural places of power and beauty, or in a deep state of solitude, such experiences join us seamlessly with the moment and completely saturate us.

When we're dancing with a partner who is sensitively attuned to us, the dancing can feel effortless. The feeling of being a dancer eventually dissipates and there's only the experience of dancing. The ancient Chinese Taoists referred to this kind of activity as *wei wu wei*, "to do without doing," meaning that the activity is not motivated by the need to reach a destination or produce a particular effect. It is activity for the sake of itself.

When we truly listen to a favorite piece of music, where is the "me" who experiences the sound? Are we truly separate from the music? When we split the experience into a listener "in here" who is listening to music "out there," our experience of the music changes from our immersion in the all-surround sound — to an experience now split between here and there. When we are savoring our favorite dinner dish with all of our senses in play, we're engaged in the sight, smell, and taste of our meal. There's mindless enjoyment of this dinner precisely because the notion of "I" is absent from the equation. Once we are already in the experience of tasting or smelling there's no need to choose to smell or taste because there is no separation or distance between subject and object.

Our life is made up of seeing and hearing, tasting and smelling, feeling and thinking. All through our days and weeks, we have the opportunity to be completely with our experiences, or we can separate ourselves and observe them from central headquarters, the internal tower of mind. This separation is the generic cause of neurotic desire. Yet in any moment that we notice that we're splitting our attention between "me" in here and the world of external objects, we can relax into the fullness of embodied experience. We could be present with our granola, our Calimyrna figs and yogurt, or for that matter, with our loneliness and boredom. There may be something in it for us.

The practice of meditation in action is being completely, wholeheartedly with the smell, sound, taste, or feeling of any experience. It's the remedy for our obsessive picking and choosing, all of which give birth to innumerable competing alternatives and fuel the endless karmic chain reaction of one thing leading to the next. The point of this practice is not to boycott choosing where to eat this evening, what color we should paint our living room, or whether to go out to a movie with friends or stay home this evening.

Expressing a preference from a place of wholeheartedness is not really choosing in the usual sense of the word, but is rather being in touch with our totality. Our ability to sense ourselves and our immediate environment becomes a direct and immediate knowing, so that whatever direction we take becomes optimal. At any one moment, there's usually that one thing to do or not do. And it changes throughout the day. Either we do the laundry, or we pack a lunch and take a walk in the woods. Either we service our car today, or we call up a friend and meet for coffee. Any given moment is most ripe for a particular gesture—the one best thing to do in that moment, even if it means doing absolutely nothing. This is what it means to open up to that deep sense of being, so that all of us is there.

Many years ago I was teaching at a Buddhist seminary. The late afternoon summer heat was oppressive, and no matter how much coffee I drank, I wasn't able to stay awake during the afternoon meditation session. One day, the heat felt so intolerable that I walked out of the meditation hall during walking meditation. Just then my spiritual teacher was approaching and he noticed me leaving the hall. He asked, "So, where are you going?" I felt completely embarrassed—busted on the spot. Before I could respond, he said with a mischievous grin, "Well, wherever you go, there you are!" Although I didn't return to my meditation seat, for the remainder of the afternoon I felt haunted by his words. Whenever I had the thought that I was escaping from meditation practice, at that very moment I found myself being with my feelings of guilt or doubt, or with my momentary feeling of confidence, that I stuck to my guns and didn't obediently return to the meditation hall.

It soon occurred to me that wherever or with whomever I found myself, if I couldn't be present where I happened to be, and exactly as I am, where would I look for myself? If I'm not completely there driving my car on the freeway, or fully present in the bathroom, or while taking a shower, or when feeling irritation with others, where will I escape to? Wherever you go, there you are!

When we're walking on ice and begin to slip, the slip itself becomes the corrective. The loss of balance causes our whole body to automatically move towards equilibrium, so that we regain our upright posture. In everyday life we experience a thousand slips, yet each instance can be a reminder of how to bring balance to our spiritual path. No matter how spaced out or reactive we find ourselves, there's always the alternative of coming back into presence. That's the most important thing.

A formal practice is very important, but once we're in the trenches of everyday life, it's necessary to use ordinary situations as reminders to create a gap in the momentum of our habitual patterns. It could be the speediness of our day, that sense of acceleration that becomes the reminder, or a sudden breeze blowing in through the window that sweeps loose papers off the table, or the horrendous roar of our neighbor's motorcycle that punctuates the silence at 5:30 in the morning. We are instantly reminded of our insistence that the world should be other than the way it is. With this recognition we could give in to the moment—just as it is.

Although our daily life is made up of going from one situation to another, we can fully land in the experience we're already having without resistance or judgment. From this place, we can relate more genuinely to what the moment brings us. Being is a natural state that exists without our effort to prop it up. We only have to open to it. It's not the result of our effort, nor do we have to perform spiritual rituals to make it appear. We only have to drop what we're holding and open up. Being is always already here, and can be found anywhere and at any time. The music has always been playing, and it's waiting for us to jump in and begin dancing. The challenge is to find it in the midst of becoming—within the events, situations, and occasions of everyday life that invite our participation. This is how we integrate being and becoming.

17.

Meditation as a Way of Life

If meditation were limited to the practice of sitting in silence and stillness, it would be removed from the challenges of everyday life. The Noble Eightfold path offers a map for how to bring the meditative state of mind into our workplace, our bedroom, and to the challenges both of our intimate and our conflictual relationships.

Buddha, as the cosmic physician, diagnosed the problem of human suffering and provided its remedy in his teaching on the Four Noble Truths, the fourth of which is the Eightfold Path. This path provides a map and guidance for how to revision ordinary situations as part of our spiritual practice. The Eightfold Path is divided into wisdom, ethics and meditation, or *prajna, shila,* and *samadhi* in Sanskrit.

Wisdom involves right view and right intention, while ethics relates with right speech, right conduct, and right livelihood, and meditation takes the form of right effort, right mindfulness and right samadhi. The word "right" in the context of the Eightfold Path comes from the Pali word, *samma,* which means complete, total, and wholehearted.

Wisdom

The wisdom aspect of the path begins with *right view*, which helps us establish an overall approach towards our life. Right view is based on an understanding of nontheism. Buddhism doesn't reject the sacred dimension of life, but it doesn't depend on a transcendental deity to rescue us or help us make sense of our lives. The nontheistic perspective cuts through wishful thinking for a magical intervention to relieve us of our complications and confusions. Instead, we assume ownership of and responsibility for our lives.

The Buddha epitomizes this perspective. After six years of continuous practice, the soon-to-be Buddha gave up all external methods, means, and intermediaries and sat down under the famed bodhi tree, where he made a commitment to not move until he understood why he was born a human being. When he finally arose after seven weeks from his immovable spot of profound meditation, he had awakened spiritually to become the Buddha, "the awakened one." He did it himself, as a human being and not as a god. We use that as an example of how we walk the path.

Right view also means that the journey itself *is* the goal. The unfolding of our ordinary life *is* the path, and the path itself *is* the goal. How we live our life, the manner in which we deal with our suffering, distress and upset, how we relate with joy and celebration, is the path. Right view delivers us to this precious moment, again and again, challenging us to stay present and work with what's immediately available. We don't give up on any aspect of our lives or lose faith in our own fundamental goodness and basic sanity.

Right intention follows from right view. Right view is the orientation we hold towards our life, while intention signifies a course of action that we commit ourselves to. From a Buddhist perspective, when we take refuge in the Dharma as the path, then our intention follows from that. We take refuge in what promotes our path of self-discovery and not in what reinforces our neurotic patterns.

The Buddha taught that there are three kinds of right intention. The intention of renunciation or letting go counters the acquisitive drive to possess things. We practice releasing our attachment to them. We're able to do this by contemplating that all phenomena are transient. We cultivate loving-kindness for all beings in order to overcome anger, ill will, and aversion. But the practice of compassion goes further in that it is a deep empathy, a willingness to work for the benefit of others.

If we take right intention personally, it inspires us to contemplate what our real desire is behind our many desires. If you did a ruthless inventory of yourself, what would be the throbbing heart of your deepest desire—what you really want in this lifetime? Right intention is to know that, and to act from that place of knowing. Then you have a basis by which you can assess whether you're in sync with your view or in conflict with it. Right intention gathers depth and momentum from deeply contemplating why we're here on this good earth, and what our human life is truly about.

Higher Ethics

Following right view and intention are the ethical recommendations, the second category in the Eightfold Path. *Right speech* traditionally means we don't indulge in idle talk or gossip, or speak in ways that promote conflict or disharmony among people. It is the willingness to tell the truth, both to ourselves and others, under all circumstances. We sometimes deceive ourselves when we subconsciously give ourselves permission to step over a boundary that we have created. Instead, we're willing to expose any private pockets that we're safekeeping in our mind. When we're about to do something that contradicts or sabotages our spiritual path, we don't manipulate our inner conversation to camouflage our hidden intention.

Right speech also means that we respect silence. Right silence encourages us to allow pauses in conversation, inviting others to find their own voice. By punctuating our own speed, others have time to digest our words, as well as discover what they would like to contribute. By intentionally allowing space, we can simply be with another without feeling compelled to fill in the periodic silences.

Right speech is also mindful of the tone of voice, facial expressions, and gestures of those with whom we're speaking. We practice briefly pausing to see if there's some nonverbal cue from the other person before we continue speaking. We try to listen from our heart as others speak, and we commit to tell the truth no matter what the occasion. At the same time, we don't assault another with a harsh truth if it's going to cause unnecessary pain and confusion. We try to tell the truth as sensitively as we can so that the other person can hear it.

Traditionally, *right conduct or action*, the second of the ethical practices, involves refraining from intentionally taking life, stealing, sexual misconduct, and refraining from intoxicants. In essence, right conduct means that we're concerned about the welfare of others rather than being motivated only by personal gain. Right action is the willingness to cut through the seduction of self-centeredness in everyday life affairs. This flips ego's agenda on its head. We consider the consequences of our actions and whether or not they follow from our right view and intention. As a result, our conduct becomes right action because it's motivated by compassion and care.

Sexual misconduct and refraining from intoxicants are timely topics. Their abuse has led to serious transgressions in numerous spiritual communities, which have fractured those respective organizations. Right action does not prohibit desire or sexual relations but asks us to inquire whether we're entering into relationships of mutuality, respect, care, and understanding, rather than impulsively satisfying a desire for immediate pleasure. We might seize the opportunity for sexual relations as a perk for having a position of power in an organization or community, or alternately, use sexuality to jockey for positions of power.

Any substance that clouds our mind, compromising our ability to think clearly and act mindfully is a problem. If the use or abuse of substance leads to intoxication, disorientation, and dysfunctionality, obviously it goes against right conduct. If under the influence of substance, we find ourselves driven by a blind urge to satisfy a desire or impulse, or retreat into a private spiritual cocoon in order to avoid dealing with the demands and responsibilities of our life, then this is obviously not skillful action.

On the other hand, certain substances can encourage us to feel stimulated, impassioned, or inspired. This is undoubtedly a slippery slope. If we're impassioned to have a greater intimacy with others or deeper connection with nature, or experience greater inspiration in our creative endeavors, then the use of certain substances could be right action, as long as it doesn't lead to addiction or block critical feedback from others.

At the time of the Buddha in sixth century BCE India, *right livelihood* meant not working for any industry that either slaughtered animals or produced weapons. In the twenty-first century, the idea of right livelihood is considerably more complicated due to the global overreach of multi-national corporations and their exploitation of cheap third-world labor and the destructive impact of their products on the environment. We're never quite sure of the negative impact of our livelihood upon the lives of others or the environment.

Work needs to be integrated into our spiritual path, since we spend the majority of our waking lives at work. To bring right livelihood into the context of our contemporary world, we could ask ourselves whether our company or shop is involved in the manufacture of products that are sustainable or whether it is performing services that are exploitive of its workers. Does our workplace tolerate sexism, racism, ageism, or homophobia? Does our livelihood compromise or support our values, our capacity to deepen our awareness and cultivate compassion? Is our work an accurate expression of who we are?

Our jobs often put us face-to-face with power hierarchies, issues of competition, territoriality, and occasionally, aggressive and obnoxious people. Livelihood can be a profound test of our integration of the dharma with life. Whatever work we do, we occasionally confronted with our colleague's pettiness, ruthless ambition, or negative judgments of others. We could easily get triggered, revealing how we handle our own issues around power and disempowerment, conflict and its avoidance. Right livelihood challenges us to bring mindfulness and compassion to our everyday work so that it becomes an expression of how we walk our spiritual path.

Meditation

The last three, right effort, right mindfulness, and right samadhi are related with the third category of the Eightfold Path —meditation. The usual form of effort is oriented towards achieving a result or a goal. *Right effort* is characterized by "not too tight, not too loose," where we work hard with whatever our life presents us, but with a sense of playfulness, light touch, and enjoyment. We allow space, so that there is a rhythmic alternation between effort and relaxation.

Usually we give a great deal of effort to those things that matter most to us—perhaps family and work being at the top of the list—but we might give little or no effort to many other areas of our life. Right effort, from a meditator's point of view, is like an elephant's walk, slow, steady, and even, affording an elevated perspective so that we can survey the larger landscape. Our effort is spread evenly throughout the day, so that we give attention and care to all aspects of our life. Whether we win the lottery or our toilet overflows, we don't become either wildly exhilarated or overwhelmed. When we view our lives and our world as sacred, where every detail is worthy of our attention and our appreciation, evenness of effort becomes a natural expression of our path.

Right mindfulness means that we practice dissolving the boundary between the formal sitting practice of meditation and meditation in action. We try to be wholehearted in whatever we're doing. Taking time to prepare a well-balanced dinner is as important as how we do our job or how we express love to our intimate other. Making a tossed salad, scrubbing the bathtub, polishing a piece of furniture, or watering our plants, dealing with ill children, as well as how we respond to a call from a telemarketer in the middle of dinner—can all be expressions of our mindful presence or its absence. Ordinary life can be the best meditator's cave or cloistered monastery.

For instance, you're walking with a friend in a neighborhood park, having a delightful conversation. You notice out of the corner of your eye that there's an elderly woman sitting alone and feeding pigeons. She looks forlorn and lonely, and this touches your heart. As you and your friend walk by her, you pause and say, "You know, it finally feels like spring. The sun feels warm and flowers are beginning to bloom. You sure picked a great spot on this beautiful afternoon." And she looks up at you and slowly begins to smile, nodding her head. Your awareness of the larger atmosphere beyond you and your friend allowed you to seize a precious opportunity. The warmth of your momentary connection with her was like a ray of light shining into an apparently lonely world. Right mindfulness is having the sensitivity to spontaneously respond to situations, to be there all at once with a sense of compassionate presence.

The last practice under the heading of meditation is *samadhi*, a Sanskrit word, which literally means "to collect" or "bring together," and thus it is often translated as "concentration" or "unification of mind." It also can mean one-pointedness, absorption, or complete involvement. Samadhi cuts through the constant percolation of our monkey mind, so that we can be fully here with a sense of presence and appreciation.

Fourth Threshold: Belly of the Whale

Meditation is analogous to a microscope that looks at the many elements of our mind, while samadhi is the sustained attention to continue looking with inquisitiveness, without getting distracted. This is what permits us to penetrate the many layers of our mind as well. The power of our samadhi is what allows us to grasp the more subtle meaning of the Buddha's Dharma on a level that words can't always convey.

There is a famous story of one of the Chinese Zen patriarchs who was present at his mother's cremation when he was a young boy. As his mother's body slowly vanished into the flames, his attention was arrested by plumes of incense smoke as they slowly swirled before the funeral pyre. He watched intently and suddenly felt that the incense smoke epitomized the evanescence of life. With that samadhi-like perception, he attained enlightenment.

The Eightfold Path can be thought of as a spiral, rather than a linear path of development. As our spiritual journey evolves, our understanding of wisdom, ethics, and meditation also evolves. Each time that we work with the challenges of right view, right speech, or right effort, we meet them with greater understanding. Although the theme may remain the same, our experience becomes more subtle, more complex, having deeper implications. Our continual cultivation of samadhi promotes a deeper and more profound realization of right view, which in turn, provides a further understanding of right intention, and so on. The noble Eightfold Path is more like a process of growth, like the unfolding of a living thing, rather than like someone going from one stage of a path to the next or from one rung of a ladder to the next.

In conclusion, right samadhi is being completely involved in your life situation, whatever that may be. In sitting meditation practice, you are not a separate individual distinct from the process of meditation. Because the affairs of daily life reflect your immediate state of mind, you and your living situation are no longer experienced as separate and different things. This is the world of non-duality.

Fourth Threshold: Belly of the Whale

Belly of the Whale

You know that you've crossed the Fourth Threshold when....

Meditation has become your trusted ally, an opening where your experiences can speak to you. This inspires you to make a deeper, more intimate relationship with your unknown or underdeveloped aspects. The fourth threshold is characterized by meditation that involves both presentness and presence, and a spirit of inquisitiveness that appreciates details of your daily life that were previously overlooked.

Whether you are doing sitting meditation or preparing dinner, you understand the essence of meditation is that flash of awareness that recognizes when you've been distracted, and that brings you back to the occasion at hand. You are now more able and willing to interrupt your compelling narratives in order to be completely with the sensory phenomena of any experience.

You realize that the way to integrate the spiritual path with your life is to make use of the most ordinary situations as reminders to come back into presence—whether that be the slamming of a car door, the ringing of a telephone, or the barking of a dog. You use those situations as triggers, as ways of interrupting your internal dialogue in order to return your attention to the moment—just as it is.

At the fourth threshold, you have learned how to integrate mindfulness with awareness, so that you can experience your thoughts with precision and clarity, and with intuitive awareness of their meaning. You've begun to appreciate how awareness tunes you into larger atmosphere or environment in which you are meditating, offering a larger perspective beyond the scope of mindfulness.

You are now challenged by the more profound dimensions of meditation, so that you have a deeper understanding of the difference between your autobiographical self and the selfless self of your Buddha nature. Being here, now, means more than focusing on this point instant in time and space. Instead, you realize that any piece of your life is all of it. Any moment of experience is never separate from the life you've already been living.

At the fourth threshold, the Noble Eightfold path becomes a trustworthy map and a source of guidance for how to apply meditation to the nitty-gritty situations of ordinary life. You realize how ethics is intimately related with wisdom, and how both of these aspects positively shape your meditation, which inspires you to be wholehearted in whatever or with whomever you are involved.

Because of the challenges at the fourth threshold, you recognize the importance of extending lovingkindness to yourself, or else you're likely to fall prey to negative judgments, for both real and imagined faults. Having become a genuine friend to yourself, you experience a positive expectancy about life.

You now have developed enough of a foundation to be challenged by the descent into the realm of the senses. Here the tantalizing pull of desire and the magnetism of sexual-romantic love will test your ability to keep your balance on the path.

FIFTH THRESHOLD: THE JOURNEY OF DESCENT

Love, Desire and Embodiment

The phenomenon of spiritual bypassing is when we try to avoid the sensuality of our living body with its desires and longings, by channeling our attention to our mind. Like the invisibility and invincibility of God or spirit, we feel consoled by imagining that we can sidestep our instinctual earthiness by residing in our untouchable invisible interior.

In the Indian Hindu tradition, the god Shiva represents cosmic consciousness. He remains unmoved, unaffected, and unrelated to anything until the goddess Shakti, the dynamic, energetic dimension of life, seduces him from his remote abode to join her in the act of creation. The archetypal image of the goddess symbolizes love and desire as well as the organic foundation of life. Through her we experience the ferocity of our instincts and the enticing sensuality of our feelings. As we return to our senses and become more embodied, we can rejoice in our body's natural eroticism and affirm our most basic human wish —to find a pleasure in simply being alive.

It is only through intimate relationship and fearless love that this most basic human wish is fulfilled. But for this to be accomplished, we must completely surrender. To truly know the goddess is to know that she is not only life, but she is also the death of everything that we're holding onto. The secret is that it is only by letting go that we return to the fertility of open space, where we can experience what is pulsing with life.

The fruitional teachings of the Buddha, sometimes known as tantra, invite us into the earthy world of color, texture, taste, and fragrance, as well as into the conflicts and turbulent emotions of ordinary life. In the tantric tradition, nirvana is found in the living energy of life, in sensual pleasure, and in romantic-erotic relationships. The very things that most religions try to escape from are understood to be the quickest path to our freedom. At the same time, this path is dangerous because we can succumb to addictive indulgence in sensory pleasure and completely lose our way. Therefore, the earlier teachings of impermanence, suffering, and egolessness as well as loving-kindness and compassion are essential to practice.

18.

The Wisdom of the Body

The spiritual process is about enlightening the whole body so that no domain of experience is excluded from our path. Nor can we separate ourselves from the surrounding landscape, of which we are an integral part. Spiritual bypassing is the attempt to find immunity from unpleasant sensations and feelings, as well as from our connection with our environment, by taking refuge in our mind. This leads to a disembodied form of spirituality.

In our overly digitized Western world, we tend to live from the neck up and have become increasingly disconnected from our bodily sensations and feelings. We no longer appreciate the sound of rain, or find delight in feeling the wind sweeping across our face and tussling our hair. Rarely do we pause to enjoy the fragrance of damp earth, or listen to the enchanting sound of birds in the early morning.

One of the historical problems with many spiritual traditions, East and West, is their unspoken belief that the fleshy part of our human nature needs to be controlled or suppressed, and that we should try to bypass or transcend our body. The body, reminiscent of our animal appetites, is seen as the source of both desire and entrapment, seducing us with pleasure and inflaming us with riotous emotions. From this perspective, embodiment presents itself as a problem and a complication, ensnaring us in the delights of the senses, while binding us to a decaying body that's sentenced to death.

Spiritual bypassing is where we take a detour from the living body and shift our attention to our mind, where we can keep a safe distance from our raw feelings and instinctual desires, and temporarily insulate ourselves from the threat of mortality. The problem with such bypassing is that our spiritual path becomes disembodied, disconnected from our sensations, feelings, and the energy of our body. We risk losing our earthy connection with both our physical existence and with the surrounding natural environment. As our mind and body drift further apart, we rupture their intimate bond and fracture our intrinsic wholeness.

By communicating with the intelligence of our psychophysical anatomy, we begin the process of integrating mind and body, heart and soul, thereby enlightening the entirety of ourselves. The body is alive in every respect, on every level—organismic, systemic, and cellular. When we bring our awareness to the body, we start to notice that there are energies that pulsate, enliven, and animate us. We can awaken the living body by regarding our inner domain as an exciting terrain, analogous to the exploration of back-country trails, tropical forests, craggy coastlines, intriguing caverns, and raging wildfires.

Our interior landscape speaks in the language of sensation, which invites us not only into our own territory, but also connects us with the surrounding environment in which we are immersed. To fully participate in the life of the body is to be aware *with* the body and not *of* the body. All too frequently in

Fifth Threshold: The Journey of Descent

meditation practice, awareness of the body often means observing the body from a distance and thereby objectifying it, rather than living in it.

Without our body there would be no possibility of experience. We're conditioned to believe that our real self is an invisible essence within our interior and separate from the body, but the mind-body or body-mind is the true subject of experience. The living body is the very possibility of contact, the very means of entering into relations not just with others, but with ourselves.

When a desirable other makes welcomed advances towards us, like animals in spring, we feel the irresistible pull of attraction, as our heart quivers, our face gets flushed, and our bodily temperature rises instantaneously. Walking at night down an unfamiliar street, as we hear the approach of footsteps behind us, adrenaline cascades through our body, readying us for a flight or fight response. The boundaries of the living body are open, more like membranes then barriers. Our body is carrying on a silent conversation with our immediate environment, a dialogue that often remains below our verbal awareness. It's difficult to determine exactly where this living body begins and where it ends.

Reawakening the body begins with noticing whether or not we're aware of our immediate bodily sensations. It's important that we not stand back in the observer's chair like a director watching a movie. The idea is to bring our awareness *into* the sensation so that we can feel it. Once we connect with the living quality of a particular sensation, the next step is to *be* with it. We drop into the sensation and move along with its energy, sensing its qualities. Does it have a rhythm, texture, or tone? Does it pulsate, quiver, intensify, expand, deepen or contract?

Usually our attention goes to the parts of our body that feel familiar, but the challenge is to go to the parts that are less traveled. Because of our idiosyncratic personal history and the cultural and familial injunctions that we've received, we may be blocking off many parts of ourselves that remain unknown to us.

In the original *Four Foundations of Mindfulness* taught by the Buddha, the first foundation—mindfulness of body, grounds practitioners in the sensory experience of embodiment and increases sensitivity to environmental stimuli. When we bring awareness into our interior to our various organs, we discover that those organs are already centers of feeling. Bringing attention to our belly, we might suddenly notice that there's a mild ache of hunger and an acidic sensation. Shifting our attention to our breathing, we might become aware that our breath is shallow. If we continue to be inquisitive, we could sense a heaviness pressing down on us, and soon realize that an upcoming medical procedure weighs heavily on us. We're bringing awareness to the sensitivity that already exists throughout our entire body. We know our world most directly by actually sensing it, feeling it as a body.

The spiritual process of enlightening the whole body involves envisioning our body as an organization of living entities. Our heart, stomach, spleen, large and small intestines, liver, pancreas, lungs, and the canals of our veins and arteries are all living entities with intelligence, living in a cooperative community. They are as much *us* as the thoughts in our head. We're a living landscape not merely an assortment of mechanically functioning organs.

Fifth Threshold: The Journey of Descent

Perceptions, sensations, and feelings are all interrelated. We perceive something and immediately sensations arise as movements of energy. We may not initially know why we're suddenly feeling either light and buoyant, paranoid and frightened, or heavy and foreboding. The sensations in our body crystallize around particular events—the anticipated phone call offering us a much-desired job, or the disappointing letter that we opened two hours ago. We didn't make the connection between psyche and soma because it happened at a nonverbal level.

One contemplative practice for reanimating our body is to think of someone or something you really love. As you imagine that someone or something, immediately bring your awareness to your body. What is your body doing in response to that image? Are there sensations you can feel that are associated with that image or thought? If you lose the image of the person or the experience, resurrect it again and again, and then immediately return your awareness to your body and notice what you are feeling, if anything.

When doing such experiential practices, we may inadvertently tap into suppressed desires or painfully unresolved areas that we'd like to heal. Yet we might find ourselves stuck and unable to move. This often indicates that "yes" and "no" exist at the same time with respect to an issue. We may want to explore new territory, but at the same time, we might not be ready to open and venture forth. Most of us try to bypass these emotional knots because it's difficult to hold the tension between yes and no, to remain both open and closed simultaneously. However, these stuck places, although painful, can be valuable, signaling a need for heightened awareness.

If we're willing to trust the wisdom of our body and to be inquisitive, then this tension of opposites invites a dialogue. As we go back and forth, alternating between opening and contracting, we can get in touch with the part of us that wants to "go for the gold" and the part that feels resistant, fearful, or inhibited. We have two conflicting feelings that are expressing opposite motivations. If we direct our awareness to that bodily knot and linger there with curiosity, something might shift, if we stay with the *energy* of being stuck, and not try to immediately remedy it.

We wake up the body by inquiring what it *feels* like when we're in a knot and our energy is not moving. By communicating with the knot, as if it were a troubled child struggling to find her voice, we could inquire, "Can you tell me what's troubling you? Why is it so difficult to speak about this?" (Being inquisitive in our meditation practice serves the same purpose as verbalizing a question). Watch with interest to see if you begin to open or if you're zipping up your Teflon suit to protect yourself from feeling discomfort. What does your Teflon suit prevent you from seeing?

At some point you might actually see that the numbness and insensitivity of being stuck is trying to protect you from pain. The defense mechanism has intelligence, but it's at the developmental level of a child or a teenager. The key to this process is that we relate to the *energetic* aspect of the stuck place and not the problematic narrative in our mind. If we persist in this process, the knot often opens of its own.

The further implications of working with the body in this way is that we begin to realize that our body is in communication with energies, not only internally, but with

Fifth Threshold: The Journey of Descent

energies all around us. Our body is much larger, deeper, and more vast than we ever thought. The distinction between inside and outside is blurry. In order to maintain our lives, we eat other life forms, absorb sunshine and drink rain, and distill oxygen from the vast ocean of air sweeping across the globe. Like all life on earth, we perpetuate ourselves through interdependence and interpenetration with what is *not us*.

As we contemplate the deep blue of the boundless sky, we gradually let go of ourselves and fall into its mystery. We momentarily become the cool, dispassionate, and infinite expanse of the blue sky, as it simultaneously finds a place within us. Perception is the nonverbal dance between ourselves and the natural world. As we enter into sympathetic relations with the sights, sounds, and fragrances of daily life, the vivid world of insects and trees, flocks of pigeons, and babies in strollers enter us through our senses to become living presences.

Through the depth of our perceptions of the natural world, we can discover a new depth within our own interior. Hugging this great sequoia tree, we're in communion with an ancient presence that is perhaps looking back at us. To touch its rough bark is to experience our own tactile sensation, but also to feel ourselves touched by the tree. Walking along the beach as the tide rolls in, the crashing of the surf invigorates us, as an unmistakable aliveness also flows throughout our body. When we're anchored in our living body with our senses wide open, such perceptions join us to our world as participants, and not as isolated observers.

Through embodiment we invite spirit to incarnate evermore fully, even down to the cellular level. Because the energy of life is flowing through us at all times, as we return to our body and our senses, we can experience the inseparability of sensuality and spirituality, and our embeddedness in the surrounding landscape. We can perceive things only because we ourselves are part of the sensible world that we perceive. Perhaps we are the most sensitive organs of this world, and that world is perceiving itself through us.

19.

Pleasure: Problem or Promise

We experience primary pleasure when we allow life to tickle us, to penetrate us, so that we can find delight in the sensuality of touch, bathing, relaxation, or enjoy an aimless walk through a forest. The problem is that many of us have developed bodily armor to protect ourselves against feelings of vulnerability. This compromises our capacity to feel deeply and limits the range of what we allow ourselves to experience.

If a spiritual path is going to illuminate the entirety of a human being, it should shine a light into all aspects of our life. It's not enough to have one privileged area of our mind illuminated while our relationship with money, food, sexuality, and power remains opaque. In the twenty-first century, based on the findings of psychology and a feminist understanding of spirituality, spiritual awakening should involve a symmetrical development of the whole person.

In both Hindu and Buddhist traditions, the most evolved state of spiritual development has, as one of its indispensable features, *ananda,* translated as bliss, indescribable joy, or superlative pleasure. Such primary pleasure is euphoric because in the spiritually awakened state we don't experience ourselves subjectively inside "here" confronted by a world outside "there." Feeling neither threatened, nor in need of demonstrating our value, nor that what we're experiencing is not enough—we can finally afford to be where we are, as we are, and how we are.

When we open up to pleasure, we allow ourselves to be penetrated by the sensual world of sight, sound, smell, taste, and touch. We permit ourselves to feel deeply without having to make an internal commentary about what we're experiencing. Shamelessly enjoying the granola, fruit, and yogurt in our bowl so that its rich colors, fragrant aroma, varied textures, and juiciness completely infiltrate our system, we're simultaneously drawn out from our invisible center into the palpable world of form.

The chirping finch outside of our window suddenly resonates within us, momentarily dissolving the boundary between our sense of inner and outer, so that there's nothing *other* than the chirping melody in this moment—and *we are that!* When a loved one comes near to snuggle with us, we momentarily lose ourselves in the fragrance and feel of his or her body. The boundary between self and other melts, as touch and smell, image and sound magically arise in the transitional space between two bodies—as we find ourselves populated by our beloved. Opening ourselves to the unlimited nature of sensations not only fulfills us but mysteriously outshines our mortal fear of death.

The problem is that our relationship to sensuality and sexuality, sensation and feeling is largely based on our early familial conditioning. The criteria for what we allow to penetrate us and what we defend ourselves from has a very early history. As young children we learned about the sensual world by seeing

Fifth Threshold: The Journey of Descent

how our parents related to their bodies, how they related to food, music, touch, and bodily distance and nearness. If we experienced affectionate touch and bodily nearness that was not intrusive, we probably developed the capacity to trust and to be open to sensual experience. If our parents modeled bodily or emotional distance and avoided touching, it's likely that we developed a fear or mistrust of intimacy. It might not feel safe to let the world enter us and come in that close to where we are undefended.

If our parents freely hugged and kissed us and our siblings, and seized the moment to play with us and the family dog—such behaviors affirm love and pleasure as well as trust in the spontaneous expression of joy. Did your parents ever talk openly about difficult emotions and demonstrate how they handled such feelings, or did they put a lid on the expression of unpleasant feelings and suddenly get busy with other things? Did either parent enjoy preparing and cooking food, or take pleasure in a dinner's presentation, while commenting on the aroma, taste, and color of the meal? Such expressions or their inhibition communicate a trust or mistrust in embodiment, in one's feelings, as well as in life itself.

There are ancient beliefs and core fears that many of us have around pleasure. One of the biggest obstacles is the feeling that we need to control ourselves. I think for men this is more of an obstacle than for women. Men are given the cultural message that we're supposed to be in control of our feelings, in control of our body, in control of ourselves, and in control of our interpersonal relationships. This social script indoctrinates us to think that if we abandon ourselves to our whimsical and wayward emotions, we might lose our center of command or reveal our vulnerability to tenderness. There's often an unacknowledged war going on between being in control and surrendering to what we're really feeling. Such unremitting tension can harden into walls of defense, as we close of the valve to our life force.

Through the years many of us have developed defenses in a misguided effort to block emotional pain, which has compromised our capacity to experience sensual enjoyment. Defenses are not an intrinsically bad thing because they protect us from overwhelming emotional pain. However, after the immediate threat is gone, we no longer need to maintain them; yet out of fear of being hurt again, we tend to keep them in place. The irony is that the defenses that block pain also block pleasure. Our psychological armor limits our capacity to be soft, tender, and permeable.

Institutional religion has negatively impacted our capacity to experience sensual pleasure. Here in the Western world, which has been predominantly Judeo-Christian, the institution of religion has unfortunately taught a very negative view of the human body, pitting mind or spirit against body, man against woman, and humanity against nature. Institutional religion has given us the message that nature and the nature of this body, which is animal-like, must be controlled by the higher part of ourselves, that is, by our mind or spirit. There's a top dog/bottom dog conflict between those two polarities with the implication that nature should be subdued or controlled.

Another complicating factor that distorts our relationship with pleasure is that many of us have had experiences that we didn't fully digest because of our lack of maturity. We might not have known how to process painful

Fifth Threshold: The Journey of Descent

experiences. In many cases, our parents probably did not teach us how to work through emotions such as anxiety or depression, or how to make sense of our budding sexuality, or how to skillfully deal with conflict. As a result, many things happened that we never completely digested, which have accumulated in a body of undigested emotional experience that has become a barrier to feeling altogether.

When we take the attitude that our body is sacred, then eating, bathing, good conversation, hugging our children or frolicking with our animal companion become daily rituals that honor the sacredness of life. A primary pleasure means that it doesn't have a further purpose or goal other than itself. There's no ultimate endpoint or destination beyond its immediate enjoyment. Like snowflakes melting as they touch the surface of a pond, we take delight in lowering ourselves into the steamy warmth of a hot tub, or like ripe fruit falling from a branch, we effortlessly drop off into sleep after a day of hiking. There is an uncanny parallelism between us and the natural world.

Every ripple of water, every gust of wind, every clap of thunder, is a living power and has its own subtle influence upon us. Each thing, small and great, expresses its mystery in a unique way and provokes our senses into a reciprocal communication. The natural world is alive. Subatomic particles whirl inside of atoms, which dance within the molecules within the crystalline structure of seemingly inert rocks and stones. Everything is throbbing with life, moving, interconnecting, interpenetrating, an expression of the dance of energy. We're constantly being touched, caressed and penetrated by the phenomenal world.

Primary pleasure spontaneously emerges from our trust in life. It's about opening up to the natural circulation of life force and permitting ourselves to be penetrated and embraced by the phenomenal world. It's discovered in our natural drive to seek relationship, connection, communion—the urge to merge with the luscious sensory world. It is feeling invigorated by the charged atmosphere of an outdoor concert, thoroughly enjoying a walk along the shore, luxuriating in the sun bathing our face. But only by making ourselves vulnerable to it can we experience the world as alive and sensual. The essence of primary pleasure is that it's free. We can open to it, but it emerges spontaneously like love. We have to allow pleasure its freedom to come and go as it will.

20.

The Two Faces of Desire

When the Buddha taught that desire was the cause of suffering, he was addressing deficiency desire—the desire that is trying to remedy a feeling of lack. Healthy desire is an expression of our intimacy with life, fulfilled in our love of others and in our passionate engagement in activities for their own sake.

The whole world comes into being and sustains itself because of desire. Without desire, nothing would happen. Yet at the same time, when not fulfilled, the driving force of desire can produce tremendous suffering. But not all desire is the same. There are two fundamentally different kinds of desire: one reveals our intimacy with life and is a natural expression of love and sexuality, and passionate involvement in cherished activities. The other is based on a sense of lack or deficiency.

Deficiency desire is based on our habitual reaction to boredom and restlessness, with it's hunger for stimulation and immediate gratification. It can take the form of the indiscriminate consumption of things or people that promises to fill our emptiness and relieve us of our malaise or lack of enthusiasm. It depersonalizes our relationships with everyone and everything by reducing people and things to pleasurable objects to to conceal our emptiness.

The primary kind of desire is when we unself-consciously move towards someone or something with our totality—with our head, heart, and belly. It's based on our feeling of implicit interrelationship with life. This desire draws the world close to us, allowing us to feel at home. We're naturally moved to connect and communicate with who or what speaks to the greater part of us. Primary desire heightens our sensitivity to beauty, to what truly holds value for us. It is the catalyst that opens us up to love and is the source of passion and sensual pleasure, the urge to merge with another in erotic-romantic love. When we feel desire or sexual attraction for another, there's electricity in the air as we suspend inhibition, cross boundaries, and seek intimacy with our idealized beloved.

This desire is similar to Eros, the wish to extend ourselves into our surroundings or to draw others or other things toward us, as we yearn for fusion with whomever or whatever is desirable. Unless this primordial desire is joined with discrimination, judgment, and insight, it runs the risk of becoming ordinary or neurotic desire—the impulse to fill what feels like a deficient emptiness. Ironically, this neurotic desire is a reaction to our true condition of being without a solid, continuous inner self or ego. It causes us to feel that something is missing, that our immediate experience is neither complete nor sufficiently fulfilling, as if we don't properly exist as we are.

The problem is that long ago beyond memory, we separated from our intrinsic wholeness or Buddha nature, and as a result, we continue to feel estranged from the total being that we are. This feeling of estrangement is the motive behind deficiency desire, which tries to fill in the psychic whole created by our original disconnection from our naturally existing

Fifth Threshold: The Journey of Descent

wholeness. This neurotic desire wants something that would make us forget our dissatisfaction or confusion, and it motivates us to constantly move on to the next thing. Impulsively we reach for a stick of gum, a cigarette, a piece of chocolate, or feel that we need to repeatedly check our cell phone for the latest text or email—anything to get through this moment that may feel flat and uneventful. A good deal of suffering has to do with this kind of reaching.

Primary desire is informed by wisdom and not based on a sense of deficiency. It is an expression of wholeheartedness, where *all* of us is in our gesture of desire. One of the contemplative methods used to clarify the nature of desire is to inquire whether anything is lacking in any given moment of experience. The following series of contemplative exercises are an invitation to tune into your immediate experience of sound, smell, taste, or feeling in order to observe the distinction between the two forms of desire.

Choose a favorite piece of music to play. Begin by sitting in silence and stillness for five to ten minutes in order to settle. Then play the piece of music you have selected. Give your full attention to the resonant and melodious sound. Silently ask yourself whether anything is missing in your experience of listening. Are you wanting anything more or anything else right now? If so, what is that? Inquire whether your wanting is based on the evaluation that the music is not completely fulfilling. If that's the case, notice how your yearning for something *other* than the piece of music you've chosen compromises the quality of your enjoyment. If the experience of the music is sufficient, leaving you with nothing more to want, notice how that state of mind affects both yourself and the quality of the music.

Sit in silence and stillness for five to ten minutes as you did before, and then choose a preferred food to sample, perhaps a cookie or some dessert. Chew it slowly, savoring its taste, staying focused as much as possible. Give yourself to the moment by moment experience of tasting, smelling, and feeling the texture of this dessert. Is anything lacking in this gustatory experience? Could you stay with the experience of taste, fragrance, and texture, bite after bite, swallow after swallow? Was the cookie or dessert interesting enough to hold your attention? Did you make judgments, evaluations, or comparisons? If you did, how did that affect your experience of taste and your state of mind?

When you can make the time, go for an aimless walk in a neighborhood park or a non-urban area that you're familiar with. Keeping your senses wide open, take in the sights, sounds, smells, and whatever stimulates your bodily sensations. You can caress a branch, embrace the trunk of a tree, hold a leaf in your hand, or smell the fragrance of wild fennel. Then inquire whether all of this is enough. If it is, then your mind and your senses will remain open and appreciative as you amble along the path on which you're walking. The boundary between yourself "in here" and the world on the other side of your skin, may become quite thin as you find yourself *in* the surrounding landscape rather than observing it from your interior.

If your aimless walking was not fulfilling, then inquire about the quality of your experience. Did your mind journey elsewhere to things that were not immediately present. Did you yearn for something more interesting to capture your attention? Notice the effect of wanting something other than what you were presently experiencing. This secondary form of desire

Fifth Threshold: The Journey of Descent

causes suffering, although we may not be aware of its impact on us. The essence of meditation in action is to catch your attention the moment it leaves the immediate situation of sight, sound, or smell and to gently bring it back to *nowness*—the moment before you had thoughts about fixing the washing machine, ruminations about why your daughter hasn't called you this week, or images of your upcoming vacation in the Hamptons.

Deficiency desire is the subtle perceptual shift we make when we want the present moment to be other than the way it is. There's a world of delightful fragrances and foul odors, feelings that are flowing or foreboding, effervescent or ominous, as well as sounds that are cacophonous or melodious, soothing or uplifting. There are textures that are smooth as silk, bumpy like gooseflesh, or grainy like a tree trunk. The point is to discover whether we're open to, impatient with, or oblivious of the diverse sensations of everyday life—the sound of the BMW motorcycle starting up in the morning, the melodious song of a sparrow, the fragrance of freshly cut grass, or the unpleasant sight of a recent roadkill. Gazing at a beautiful California sunset and then noticing how your mind abruptly superimposes your memory of a glorious Florida sunset onto the immediate experience allows you to see how such shifts dilute the moment in which you were immersed.

We occasionally get glimpses of how we flee from experience even when it's positive. When we're totally immersed in an experience, there's no contrast, no conflict, just an open field of sensitivity. This is threatening to our ego, which needs conflict, contrast, and comparison, so that it knows what it is not, in order to know what it is!

Desire that comes from our depth is an expression of relatedness and relationship. It's the magnetizing energy that draws desired qualities toward ourselves, from loyal friendships to sexual fusion, from artistic and aesthetic experience to spiritual union. Because of our tenderhearted willingness to love our world, we incarnate the visible, audible, and palpable forms of the natural world. Enjoying the sound of children playing in a pile of leaves, or a sudden spring shower that ignites a frenzy of movement, or holding the hand of an ill parent, the natural world arises within and comes to life through us. By cherishing the tangible forms of everyday life, desire alchemically transforms the beings and things of everyday life into living presences who now live within us.

When we give our undivided attention to the hummingbird at our feeder, the fragrance of wood burning in a fireplace, the distant sound of the surf, our sense of isolation diminishes, and our sense of community widens. However, before we can experience intimacy with our everyday world and find lasting value in our relationships with others, we first need to love ourselves with the warmth of our own loving-kindness. The deeper form of primary desire encourages us to honor the individuality of every part of ourselves, both the small and the great, the light and the dark. This deep desire is the magnetic loving energy that draws our forgotten parts into a larger sense of personhood.

Desire from our depths is boundless and can enrich us by taking us into the depth of life itself, where we are brought to the magical interface between ourselves and the world, where the natural world penetrates and communicate its mysteries to us.

21.

Fearless Love

The practice of fearless love puts a spiritual practitioner on the spot all the time, because it requires openness to who or what we might find unlovable. We must make peace with the imperfections of intimate others, as well as our own, and welcome the disappointments that life inevitably brings to us. We couldn't have a real life without its so-called blemishes.

The ideals at the heart of Buddhism are known as the Three Jewels or Three Treasures. They are the Buddha or awakened teacher, the Dharma or the teachings, and the sangha or community. A community of practitioners is challenged to live a Dharmic relationship with each other, practicing generosity, discipline, patience, loving-kindness and compassion. At the same time, their understanding and spiritual maturity is tested and authenticated in relationship with others who are walking the path.

As a Buddhist practitioner, if we're not relating with some form of a sangha or community, then our relationship to the other two jewels, the Buddha and the Dharma, may be eccentric, off-center. Whether in a secular or spiritual setting, intimate relationships and committed friendships are the mirror from which we cannot escape our own reflection. They are the crucible in which we transform our neuroses into sane expressions of our spiritual practice.

Intimate relationships are not safe. In the meeting between lover and beloved, we confront the "mysterious other" who seems to hold the key to our heart. This creates excitement and desire but also fear, because we come face-to-face with the unknown, and there's no guarantee what will happen next. Tremendous energy is aroused that sparks eager communication with our partners but also with the different parts of ourselves that are now aroused by the dance of love.

The magnetic pull of love often triggers the wish to possess our beloved, but if we succeed, then he or she is no longer the "mysterious other" because love has been captured. Love requires that we relinquish our efforts to control our partners and that we not colonize our relationships as a way of maintaining our safety and security. Intimate relationships present us with a difficult challenge. The exalted ideal of romantic-erotic love must struggle to find a home in the ordinariness of everyday life. We bring a whole host of expectations and unfulfilled needs that our partners rarely can fulfill. Marriage or committed relationships have a way of deflating our dreams of romantic love and domesticating our fantasies of freedom. Even a deeply loving relationship will not protect us from anger, boredom, and ambivalence, both our own and our partners.

Our idealized connection with our beloved may be neurotic or healthy, a retreat from the world, or an expansion and deepening of ourselves. We and our intimate others will not always be loyal, truthful, and willing to make sacrifices for each other, nor will we always be willing to accept each other's

Fifth Threshold: The Journey of Descent

imperfections. We will have to make peace with the disappointing disparity between our idealized version of our partners and the reality of who they actually are. Many of us may be attempting to satisfy ancient desires only to grow disillusioned by our partner's inability to fill our emptiness or completely mirror us.

The partnered state will not always feel like a sanctuary as we realize that our loved ones will never meet all of our needs, or be there for us all the time, or complete us. We may wind up hating those we love because they're unable to satisfy our impossible yearnings. The willingness to love is to open to the truth of life's uncertainty and lack of guarantees.

Intimate relationships bring us face to face with our core issues: the tension between commitment and freedom, self-preservation and self-sacrifice. Those of us who suffered invasive parents will fear engulfment and being emotionally controlled by an intimate partner. Those who struggled to secure love and affection from unavailable or emotionally distant parents usually fear neglect and abandonment. Those who were the victims of physically or emotionally abusive parents will be on guard against emotional intensity, fearing that they could escalate into renewed abuse. The danger is that these themes may get activated in our intimate relationships, provoking us to either dramatize them or to shut down completely.

Intimate relationships expose our fears and hangups, and our fantasies and obsessions. They challenge us to look at both our light and our darkness, our beauty and our ugliness, our compassion and our pettiness. Our partners or loyal friends may uncover parts of ourselves that we most strenuously deny, but these are the very aspects of ourselves that most need our love and acceptance. When shared with our partner or friend, they strengthen the bond of our relationship.

Genuine relationship is our growing capacity to surrender our hidden corners, the willingness to be fully visible before ourselves and our intimate others. We cannot find intimacy with lovers, family or friends if we haven't cultivated intimacy with ourselves. Many of us may not have healed and reconciled the hurts that we've suffered from the disappointments and failures of previous relationships. Consequently, we may feel justified in keeping our defenses up and our heart guarded. Such defensiveness limits the degree to which we can actually feel tenderness, sweetness, and beauty.

Before we can establish a healthy outer marriage or relationship, we will first need an inner marriage. This means becoming completely intimate with ourselves in order to confront and communicate with our shadow, or else we will not be able to tolerate the "darkness" in our significant others. On our spiritual path, as we weave the many parts of our life into an integrated personality, we're also challenged to embrace our masculine and feminine energies. C.G. Jung referred to the female within every male as "anima" and the male within every female as "animus." The anima/animus is the strange "other" within each of us who holds the hidden potential to complete us. In order to protect our gender identity, we may try to defend ourselves from either the masculine or feminine principles within us, yet we're irresistibly drawn to our complementary opposite, for without it we cannot be whole.

There's a strong human tendency to repeat our ancient patterns of relationship. Men tend to deny their dependency on others by being emotionally cool and unavailable with women.

Fifth Threshold: The Journey of Descent

Men favor individual achievement over attachment while the socialization of women encourages attachment, caring, and communication. Many women seek emotional bonding and intimate communication with their partners and their children, and can become bitterly disappointed when their loved ones are not available in the way they had wished.

In their quest for independence and self-reliance, males run the risk of disowning the feminine parts of themselves. In particular, they may struggle with the fear of intimacy because it threatens their sense of hard-won independence. In their desire for relationship and emotional attachment, women are more threatened by separation. With either gender, intimate relationships can also threaten us with the possibility of engulfment and loss of independence, or rejection and abandonment.

In loving fearlessly we offer to our partner what is most precious and alive in ourselves—our passions and pains, our fantasies and enthusiasm, our silliness and sadness. In a spirit of natural generosity, we're concerned with the life, well-being, and growth of our partners and trusted friends, even if such growth doesn't meet our personal needs. We're willing to respond to the needs and preferences of the other, even when it is inconvenient to do so. To keep the connection alive and growing, we're challenged to be more present to the subtle nuances and inner promptings of both our intimate others and ourselves. By walking a razor's edge between separateness and surrender, we stay both sensitively attuned to ourselves and related to our significant other.

Fearless love is naked and unashamed. It exposes our unguarded wish to love and be loved, to know and to be known by our beloved. We radiate our heart's warmth without limitation and welcome the idiosyncrasies and imperfections of our beloved's personality. Whether with lovers or loyal friends, if our committed relationships are to continue growing, then conflicts must be welcomed. If we're empathically attuned to the changing needs of the relationship, we and our partner will deepen our capacity for compromise and compassion, sacrifice and surrender.

Fearless love requires openness to and patience with confusion, conflict, and painful disappointments in our significant relationships. The complications and contradictions of our everyday life bring the idealism of romantic love down to earth. Our relationships become an expression of our spiritual path when we surrender our fixed ideas about how we or our partners are supposed to be. By cultivating a taste for uncertainty, ambiguity, and complexity, we're able to let go of what's no longer alive and growing.

As with our spiritual practice, genuine love encourages us to understand that painful experiences, hidden fantasies, unresolved conflicts, and broken promises need our acceptance and not our judgment. This requires courage, patience, and humor in order to find value in the shadows of love. At the same time, we enjoy the playful side of life because play lightens the tedium of everyday existence. In sexual play and fantasy, we release our self-consciousness and dare to be transparent, both to ourselves and our partners.

When we make love with our partners, the life force beyond our skin-encapsulated body surges between our beloved and ourselves, as the polarities of life dance together in a marvelous ebb and flow of opposites. In such moments we are not individual personalities, but we become gods and goddesses, universal principles that take us to the deepest dimension of ourselves.

The ever-deepening intimacy between two individuals can instill a longing to dissolve all boundaries, all forms of separation, and open us to a greater embrace of life. In the act of loving, of giving ourselves to the other, we discover something more than our partner or ourselves. What began as a cherishing of our significant other can mature into a deeper intimacy with life itself. Intimate relationship is a metaphor for life itself, calling us to open to what both holds us and transcends us, and to appreciate the auspicious coincidence that brought us together. Fearless love is the capacity and willingness to communicate with the whole of life.

The Journey of Descent: Love, Desire, and Embodiment

You know that you've crossed the Fifth Threshold when....

You realize that spirituality is not opposed to your body and it's desires. You understand that maturity on the spiritual path is found in embodiment, in discovering the pleasure of simply being alive, and being able to appreciate the sensory pleasures of watching a bird in flight, or walking barefoot through a grassy meadow. Your willing embrace of your desires and feelings speaks to your trust of life.

At the fifth threshold, you've become increasingly suspicious of the seduction of spiritual bypassing, where you shift your attention from your living body to your mind. Your practice of meditation in action discourages you from boycotting sensual pleasure and erotic relationships, even when they threaten your meditative equanimity. You've discovered that through your living body and its sensory perceptions, you know the world most directly by sensing it and not by thinking about it.

At this stage of the path, you have developed the increasing capacity to discriminate between deficiency desire based on feelings of emptiness, and healthy desire, where all of you is in your desire. You discover that healthy desire intensifies your sensitivity to beauty and brings the world closer to you so that you can appreciate its magic. Neurotic desire seeks to fill an inner emptiness, wanting the moment to be other than the way it is. Healthy or primary desire is an expression of wholeheartedness that can take you into your own depths as well as the depths of life itself.

Fifth Threshold: The Journey of Descent

Your spiritual journey now challenges you with the practice of fearless love. Here, you meet your wish to love and be loved. Your interpersonal relationships become an expression of your spiritual path. In genuine loving, you learn to make friends with fear as well as with the ambivalence inherent in all relationships. Even when feeling ungratified or distressed, you do not hold back your gesture of compassion to others.

At the same time, to love fearlessly is to accept the uncertainty and insecurity inherent in an impermanent universe. You understand that intimate relationships expose your light and darkness, your unresolved conflicts and wounds, your willingness to commit and your need for freedom. You also recognize the tension between abandoning yourself to strong feelings and the opposite impulse of controlling yourself from feeling too deeply. These all will need your love and acceptance. For this to be accomplished, you must establish an inner marriage by becoming completely intimate with these polarities within yourself.

At the fifth threshold, your relationship to your body and the body of the world has been shaped by an attitude that views both as sacred. You've discovered that when you give your undivided attention to someone or something, without evaluation or judgment, you experience the pure perception of sacred world." There is no purpose or goal beyond the aesthetic immediacy of that moment. When you meet the world with such tender openness and inquisitiveness, the world meets you with its living energy. Having had a taste of the journey of the descent down into your roots, you are now ready to be challenged by the journey of ascent where you are challenged to make the seeds of Budddhahood grow upwards towards the heavens.

SIXTH THRESHOLD: THE JOURNEY OF ASCENT
Wisdom, Virtue, and Transcendence

In our Western culture the polarities of order and disorder, human and nature, man and woman, and God and the devil have been set apart as antagonistic opposites. In mystical religion they are recognized as the two aspects of the One. This truth is commonly hidden and reserved only for those who have matured on an inner path of transformation, for they can be trusted to not spoil the divine play.

In Indian religion, this play is known by the Sanskrit term *lila*, which refers to the cosmic game of hide and seek. The formless One incarnates as the multitude of worldly entities and beings in order to eventually have the ecstatic discovery of waking up to His/Her true identity. In human terms, this is what we refer to as spiritual enlightenment.

As spiritual practitioners, when we realize the hidden aspect of our own nature, we live our lives in a spirit of creative play or playful seriousness, rather than one of burden and struggle with life's seeming opposites. Realizing the link between time and eternity, samsara and nirvana, neurosis and sanity, we step through the secret gate to experience the inseparability of our human nature with our ultimate nature. As we mature on our spiritual path as bodhisattvas, or big helpers, we are of immeasurable service to suffering sentient beings, for we demonstrate the futility of continuing the life-and-death struggle between the "two hands of God." Paradoxically, we are in the world but not of it.

22.

The Life We've Been Missing

Meditation opens up our perceptual frame so that familiar things lose their solidity and fixed definitions. We're introduced into a landscape beyond the edges of our known world, where we might experience something entirely new and fresh about ourselves and the ordinary things in our world.

The Buddhist path is about how to cultivate a love affair with our life. We do this by embracing ourselves wholly—both the good and the bad, the broken and beautiful, our wounds and our virtues. The love affair with ourselves calls us into deeper intimacy with all of our aspects, the obvious and hidden. For some of us, it's the wounded or broken parts that are hardest to connect with, but for others it is the beauty and power within them that they are most reluctant to embrace. In either case, when we eventually explore what is hidden and integrate our missing parts, our fixed idea of ourselves and our world completely changes.

We have to find a way to make peace with the gnarly aspects of both ourselves and life by recognizing that they are an intrinsic part of our spiritual path. We often think that when illness is over, when the divorce is finalized, when we finally figure out how to care for our aging parents, when the house is paid off, or when we manage to finally get out of debt, *then* we'll be able to live and dance and play and sing.

This is the dualistic frame of mind that Buddhism cautions us against. We must widen and deepen our being to include endings, divorces, deaths, unexpected reversals—and have the courage to lean into what has the appearance of "otherness." Although it seems like a tall order, we can practice making friends with these shadowy aspects of our life by appreciating that, in spite of our best intentions, some things will remain thorny and unresolved. There aren't answers or remedies for everything, yet we could still practice loving the imperfection of life.

The love affair with life begins as we learn to appreciate that our experiences are far more open-ended than we imagined. Meditation practice helps us realize that moment by moment, we're actually stepping into a landscape where we could have multiple perspectives about any one thing, none of which are final. When we come face-to-face with the depth and expanse of the moment, we tend to make a limited gesture. It's tempting to reduce vastness into the familiar image of the world we already know but by doing so, we inadvertently imprison ourselves within its limited boundaries.

Perhaps an example will be helpful. Sitting along the secluded shore of Twin Lakes, I'm enjoying the early morning sun, as long shafts of light bathe the surrounding alpine forest in soft pastel colors. Little by little, as the sun continues its arc across the sky, the wind picks up, igniting the surface of the lake into twirling circles of sparkling light. Without my noticing it, a large bald eagle has perched itself on a branch not more than fifteen feet from where I'm sitting. Dragonflies mate in mid-air,

Sixth Threshold: The Journey of Ascent

while ravens perched in tall evergreens call to one another, and seemingly out of nowhere, a red-tailed hawk swoops down to snatch its prey. The air is redolent with the rich fragrance of pine needles that have matted the forest floor, reminding me of every every alpine forest I've hiked through and filling me with deep appreciation. As I reach for my daypack, my slight movement is immediately detected by the now-ascending eagle, and for several timeless moments there's only the whoosh, whoosh of its enormous wings in the stillness and silence of Twin Lakes.

Later that evening after my campfire has burned down, I experience a heaviness weighing down on my heart as I remember someone very dear to me who is no longer in my life. Somehow, the unspoiled beauty of Twin Lakes and the feeling of safe containment that it offers allows me to open to this vulnerability and tenderness. Feeling simultaneously empty and full, I lay out my sleeping bag, gaze at the stars, and soon fall asleep. Within minutes I'm suddenly startled by the fierce growls of a family of raccoons, who let me know in no uncertain terms that I've encroached on their territory. I'm now forced to move to another location. Feeling inconvenienced and yet strangely amused, I again lay out my sleeping bag under the pines and soon fall asleep to the gentle lapping of the lake's waters.

What does Twin Lakes mean to me? How would I describe it to a friend? Is it this body of water and its geographical location in the forest? Is it a beautiful place to camp and swim and relax? Or might Twin Lakes be the occasion of my ever-changing and limitless sensory perceptions and feelings, each one revealing some new aspect of my surroundings and of myself—all of which we conveniently label—Twin Lakes?

What we call reality refers to the collective agreements we make that determine how we perceive and conceptualize our world. We format our experience of things, people, places, and situations in language, so that we can communicate with each other by virtue of the shared meanings we give to these entities. Experiences that lie outside of the frame of our known world often feel like foreign territory or are not perceived it all—but they may hold the key to the life we've been missing.

Beyond our thoughts and random labeling of things and events lies an uncharted world yet to be discovered. The unknown holds a peculiar fascination and terror. It is uncertain and ambiguous and yet can open us to new experiences, to unusual sensations, subtle feelings, and intuitive insights. We might experience colors, tastes, textures, and feelings we've never had before. We might notice patterns between events that previously had no connection for us—how the unspoiled simplicity of nature spontaneously delivers us to a child-like innocence within ourselves. We now can experience the unfolding moment in a refreshing new light. There are innumerable aspects, facets, and perspectives, and in fact, inexhaustible dimensions to any one thing or person. This leads to the realization that what we call home, work, mother or daughter, Bob or Sharon, or "me," are truly open-ended, beyond their conventional labels.

Through the meditative process we begin to see the transparency of our conventional labels so that we're free to discover the naked truth of ordinary things. The Buddhist term for this is *emptiness,* or *shunyata* in Sanskrit, the experience of stepping into a world that we haven't yet mapped out. Emptiness is the absence of everything that obscures the rugged,

Sixth Threshold: The Journey of Ascent

colorful, and vivid qualities of ordinary things—so that we can perceive their *suchness,* their brilliance beyond our descriptions of them. It could be the way icicles hang from branches, or the sweet smell of cherry blossoms, or the shocking rawness of a dilapidated ghetto. Our evaluations, judgments, and interpretations of the cherry blossoms, the icicles, or the ghetto appear only *after* our initial awareness of just what is there. If we do not place cherry blossoms and ghettos in conceptual categories, then they remain simply as they are, free from our superimpositions, free from the filter of memory, and liberated from how we imagine they're supposed to be.

When mindfulness and awareness work together, our meditation gives birth to a heightened cognitive faculty known as *prajna,* which "sees" shunyata, or emptiness. In the Western world, when people hear the word "emptiness," they immediately think of existential emptiness, feelings of desolateness, scarcity, or deficiency. Shunyata does not mean that. The experience of emptiness reveals that no one perspective is final or permanent. Emptiness points to a world that has no bottom or limitation, a world that is shifting moment by moment, as we ourselves are.

Although the countless forms of the phenomenal world are empty, emptiness displays itself as the vividness of things seen, heard, felt, and tasted—revealing a living, breathing, palpable world that exists with its own purpose, on its own merits. In the well-known *Heart Sutra,* which is chanted in Buddhist countries around the world, the Buddha is sitting in deep meditation while surrounded by his community of practitioners. Shariputra asks Avalokiteshvara how one should practice meditation in order to awaken transcendental wisdom like the Buddha. Avalokiteshvara offers a very detailed response, the essence of which is "Form is emptiness, emptiness is form. Emptiness is no other than form, and form is no other than emptiness." A very paradoxical and confusing statement for Western audiences. What does this mean?

Beyond our familiar ideas of things, people, and events, they remain who and what they are, even beyond the notions of emptiness. We don't have to see them in the light of some kind of spiritual understanding. After seeing the world as empty of our projections, the living colorful world of form comes back into view. Our bread-and-butter world arises, but now free from the familiar categories within which we've captured it. We can perceive ordinary things with extraordinary vividness—the exquisite blue-and-gold brocade box seen with uncommon clarity, the piquant taste and rich aroma of freshly brewed coffee that gives us a jolt, or the cringing of our abdomen as we dare to entertain a taboo thought.

The basic point of the statement "emptiness is also form" is that we don't use meditation to go to some rarified realm within ourselves where we can rest in emptiness in order to spiritually bypass the often compelling, seductive, fickle, and overwhelming world of form. The Buddhist path throws us back into the ordinariness of life where we're challenged to find freedom within our kitchens, bedrooms, and bathrooms. We accept the invitation to step more deeply into the complexity of our everyday life, so that we can now be surprised as we notice what was always there in full view but hidden by our thinking.

"Form is emptiness, emptiness is also form" also means that in the midst of suffering, we might discover pockets of freedom from suffering. Experiencing sadness or grief, we might find momentary joy, as light pours through the café window creating marvelous shadows on the walls. Things are constantly shifting, with unpredictable intervals of openness where something can happen that we weren't expecting. In the midst of our preoccupation with numerous issues, we could find momentary delight at how this hummingbird hovered in midair and then darted like a jet, or in the tiny finch that suddenly landed on a nearby branch to sing an enchanting melody. There are just vivid moments like that in the midst of the routine ordinariness of daily life.

This doesn't cancel out issues that need to be resolved but suggests that we can abruptly open up into experiences free of thought and free from our agenda, and see our world in a more innocent light. Emptiness is an unexpected clearing in the forest of thorny issues and weighty preoccupations—and by stepping through it, we create our unique path.

STEALING FIRE FROM THE GODS

23.

The Mystery of Being

*The Great Way is not difficult
for those who have no preferences.
When love and hate are both absent
everything becomes clear and undisguised,
Make the smallest distinction however,
and heaven and earth are set infinitely apart.
If you wish to see the truth
then hold no opinions for or against anything.
To set up what you like against what you dislike
is the disease of the mind.*
                              Hsin Hsin Ming

Zen Buddhism is a tradition that characterizes itself by its method of direct pointing, encouraging us to bring our attention to the immediacy of the moment unfolding right before our eyes. Zen takes its origin from a supposedly historical event that occurred in India during the sixth century BC, at the time of the Buddha.

The Buddha was seated before a large audience of nuns and monks, about to give a dharma talk or teaching. On this particular occasion, he sat motionless for a long time while the whole assembly of practitioners waited expectantly for the master to begin his discourse. However, he remained silent. At some point he reached for a flower from a bouquet that had been offered to him. He mindfully held it up, tenderly regarding that single flower, and then gracefully placed it back down. That was all.

The Buddha was transmitting his awakened mind, his entire state of being in that single gesture of holding up a flower, but in this large congregation, only one person got the message. Only Mahakashyapa was open and ripe enough to receive it by dropping everything that he might have been holding and simply opening his mind and heart. This is considered to be the origin of the Zen tradition of direct pointing—a simple gesture that reveals a whole universe.

We could be sitting in our garden in the early morning and suddenly notice that a dewdrop just rolled off a branch, splashed on the leaf below it, and then fell to the earth. For just one moment, everything stops as our mind also rolls and falls like the dewdrop. We could be sitting at our kitchen table having breakfast with our mind in knots. Everything that we are thinking feels like a complication. One insidious thought follows another and we find ourselves at a dead end with no resolution about anything. Suddenly, our attention is drawn to the steam rising from our cappuccino as it unfurls in provocative cloud-like plumes—as *we* arise out from our morning's dilemma—for just that moment. We have just entered into a vastness that outshines our usual monkey mind.

From the perspective of conventional truth, we are simply experiencing a temporary pause in our anguish, watching steam rising from a cup of coffee. Nothing more. However, from the perspective of our deep intuitive mind, we are experiencing wordless wonderment by this display of simplicity and beauty, as a seemingly inconsequential event reflects life's shape-shifting evanescence.

Zen points to these kinds of moments as concrete metaphors for how to pass through the secret gate to innocence to our original mind. For no obvious reason, we might suddenly find ourselves marveling at the obvious fact that spring follows winter, and summer follows spring, that plants grow upwards towards the sun, while their roots grow downwards into the dark earth. We can be struck by the mystery of how a single fertilized egg cell matures into a complex fetus, or be thrilled at the inconceivability that our cosmos exploded into existence from absolutely nothing—but we feel these phenomena with our whole body and mind.

This wisdom exists universally and has been articulated by philosophers, poets, and artists through the ages, but Zen emphasizes the method of direct pointing to bring about a genuine change of heart. The quote from the *Hsin Hsin Ming*, which appears as the epigraph of this chapter, was the only document left by the Third Zen Patriarch Sengtsan. His words are simple but subtle: "When love and hate are both absent everything becomes clear and undisguised....If you wish to see the truth, then hold no opinions for or against anything." These lines from the first stanza are at odds with ordinary life.

We might wonder, what's the point of not having opinions, or not loving or liking? This seems so anti-life, robbing us of any sense of autonomy and agency. Usually, what we mean by love is a kind of emotional attachment to someone or something. If a loved one doesn't meet our expectations, or a cherished thing or activity fails to deliver anticipated gratification, our love can change at the drop of a hat. This kind of love is not on solid ground. Of course, to love someone involves emotional bonding, shared intimacy, care, and understanding, inclining us to feel some degree of attachment to that special person. Yet once we have an emotional attachment to someone, we silently cast a net of expectations onto them, which exerts a psychological force. We inadvertently telegraph our preferences through subtle facial expressions, gestures, and tone of voice, hoping that they will remain connected to us in predictable and reassuring ways.

The *Hsin Hsin Ming* is not suggesting that we abandon loving others, but it is pointing out the blinding power of emotional attachment. What transforms our intimate relationships into forms of bondage is our expectation that others will always be there for us in a particular way. When they're not there for us in that predictably characteristic way, we can feel threatened and begin to suspect that they're moving away from us emotionally. This sets in motion a series of reactions and counter reactions, which often leads to complication and confusion.

Animosity is more complex. An adversary could be someone with whom we're having an issue, someone from whom we've become alienated, or perhaps someone who has hurt us in the past. We can't forgive them, and so we've ex-communicated them from our heart. When we've cast our adversaries into a dark dungeon, psychologically speaking, we've become their jailers. We now have to maintain a defensive posture and a narrative to justify our attitude. At some point, if we truly want to be free, we have to invite them back to the table and listen to them with an open mind, beyond notions of right and wrong, or victim and persecutor. Optimally, they will also soften to make the same open-hearted gesture to us.

Our habitual liking and disliking, pushing and pulling our world, reinforces the ongoing sameness and predictability of our everyday life, but it's what keeps us from waking up into a refreshed, revitalized world. On the surface, refraining from liking and disliking could seem highly undesirable, as we might fear being reduced to spineless jellyfish or hapless leaves blown by the winds of other's agendas. The challenge is to meet unpleasant experience *before* we react by grasping what we like or rejecting what we dislike. By allowing neutral psychological space we might discover something new, something revealing that we hadn't noticed before. Even the darkest thoughts, feelings, and experiences can shed light.

The *Hsin Hsin Ming* states, "Make the smallest distinction, however, and heaven and earth are set infinitely apart." Not taking either side of a dualistic situation is the kind of tightrope walk that describes the Buddhist middle path to enlightenment. In theistic language, it is said that God doesn't take sides. Life is not for or against us. Sometimes it is grotesque and destructive, and sometimes it is glorious and fills us with happiness and joy. When we practice relaxing our continual judgments of like and dislike, we might see that this immediate moment has its own reasons for being exactly as it is.

The moment could be your reading of the words on this page, the taste of rocky road ice cream, a tender embrace by a loved one, or the pain of being alone on a Friday night. If we open into the immediacy of this moment, without taking sides for or against, without grasping or rejecting, we might discover something of value here—qualities that were hidden from us because we were trying to shape the moment to fit our idea about how the world should be.

Many years ago I studied with an old Japanese Buddhist teacher who was my mentor in graduate school. After getting my graduate degrees, I continued to study with him at his home. We would eat sushi and drink *sake* while reading and discussing various Buddhist teachings. After many years of study, I was coming to the end of my apprenticeship with him but felt that my understanding of Buddhism was academic and that I was missing something crucial.

One evening I asked him, "Sensei, could you tell me in simple language, what am I supposed to realize from all this study and practice of the Buddha's Dharma?" He cracked up laughing and then became silent and still, and looked at me with an intense gaze. Very slowly he said, "Throw it all away." He then folded his hands and closed his eyes, indicating that was the end of our session. I bowed to him and walked out into the evening feeling perplexed and yet intrigued. Later in the evening, I dropped into a deep consideration of what I was just given.

The old master's enigmatic statement captured the essence of the entire Buddhist path—embrace life, but don't hold onto anything, because it will eventually be taken away. Love people, cherish who or what holds passion for you, throw yourself into creative works, make the world a better place than you found it, but don't hold anyone or anything in your clenched fist of possessiveness—including Buddhism. "Throw it all away" did not mean to cast anyone or anything aside in a reckless or indifferent manner, but rather to not grasp anyone or anything, as if to prevent it from moving in the stream of time and change.

Whether we are sitting in formal meditation, riding on public transportation, flossing our teeth, or talking to our aged grandmother on the phone, the meditative state of mind is the open space in which life happens *before* we superimpose our designs onto it. When we are not spinning our story, our assumptions, our beliefs, our preconceptions, or our expectations, then the meditative state of mind becomes the creative space in which just life occurs. To cling to our preference for beauty over ugliness, our ideas of right over wrong, or goodness over badness, usually means that we're subtly manipulating our experience, trying to make a tailor-made life for ourselves.

Our human life is such that painful circumstances will inevitably come. There will be old age, sickness, and death. People that we love will die and others who we don't like will enter our lives and become nuisances, bringing us conflict and distress. By refraining from judgments of love and hate, friend and enemy, and happy and sad, we just might discover freedom in the midst of any circumstance, precisely because we're neither resisting nor fleeing. A Zen practitioner might confront us with the paradoxical question, "If you can't find light in the midst of darkness, where will you look?" In the midst of a stressful or confusing situation, we just might notice that there's some unexpected brightness in the middle of our darkness.

We could be at a funeral feeling terribly heartbroken, yet we can't help but momentarily notice the stunning display of autumn foliage. It seems utterly contradictory, and even insulting to the recently deceased, that we should take delight in beauty, but light often breaks through the cracks of a broken heart. Just when we think our life is supposed to be one way, we discover that in the next moment, it points us in another direction that we didn't consciously choose.

Without any intervention on our part, rain falls from the heavens, flowers grow, the wind blows, and spring arrives after winter, whether we like it or not. In the same way, thoughts and feelings happen like a sudden spring shower. People talk in hall when we're trying to meditate, airport security personnel make us unpack our entire suitcase for no obvious reason, while a disagreeable neighbor helps us change a flat tire. Events happen because of causes and conditions beyond our comprehension.

If we don't fight with the moment that is given, or the life that we're living, this is the beginning of liberation. To walk through this secret gate requires a soft, open belly and a tender heart, a unique blend of intelligent relaxation and alertness. Meditation opens a door that invites a journey rather than offering a solution or an answer.

The paradox of the spiritual path involves stepping into the stream of life and surrendering to its currents, while simultaneously honoring the deepest wishes of our heart and soul. This is when our deepest desire coincides with what the world needs.

24.

Freedom

As we grow in sensitivity, we may stumble across the feeling that we are far from our true home. The refugee that lives within us all, is the feeling of our exile from wholeness. Out of dissatisfaction, we struggle to manipulate our experiences, but this separates us from the unfolding moment, and causes further suffering. We only discover freedom when we're not trying to be other than the way we are, or make the world other than the way it already is.

Years ago I read an article about a dramatic incident that occurred on the Paris Metro, the French subway system. A disheveled, apparently homeless man got on the Metro and began ranting and raving as he walked down the corridor of the train. He glared menacingly as he shrieked at the passengers, who sank into their seats trying to make themselves very small. At some point, this disturbed man walked by an elderly grey-haired woman, and his eyes met with hers. She held her gaze and slowly reached out her hand, beckoning him to come to her. He paused and then falteringly gave his hand to her. She gently drew him close to her and put his head on her chest, when he burst into tears and began sobbing uncontrollably.

In reading the account of this poignant incident, I was moved by the heartfelt response to human suffering—the spontaneous, benevolent energy of compassion that invisibly worked its way through the elderly woman to this forlorn man. That woman probably didn't say to herself, "It would be a good thing to caress this poor wretched man who probably doesn't have a mother, family or friends." Nor was it likely that she quickly rehearsed what to do by going through her inventory of skillful tactics for how to handle difficult people. The moment their eyes met, a doorway opened between her world and his—and she stepped through it. Something within her, deeper than her rational mind, came forward to respond to this man's intense pain and to touch his heart.

That alienated homeless man on the Metro lives in all of us. The yelling and screaming and ranting and raving is the refugee that lives in the jungle of our ego-self. It is the feeling of unrest, not being at peace, wanting to compensate for being far from home. It is the vague, unarticulated wish to return home to our source. This wish is sublimated in a thousand ways. It's often camouflaged by immersion in work and family, or by throwing ourselves into some endeavor that deflects our attention away from ourselves. But at stressful times when our defenses wear thin, we might suspect that this feeling is not situational but existential.

The avoided encounter with the deeper parts of ourselves reflect the tension between our yearning to step into our larger, unlived life, and our simultaneous fear of getting lost. The refugee within us is ultimately an expression of our exile from wholeness, where *all* of us is here at once—mind and body, heart and soul, and instinct and intuition. In moments when we feel in sympathetic alignment with what life presents us, we get a taste of our totality or Buddha nature. The great paradox is that

Sixth Threshold: The Journey of Ascent

we're never truly separate from our inherent Buddha nature, yet we live our lives as though there were an unbridgeable gulf between us and our enlightened nature.

The *Hsin Hsin Ming,* a document left by Sengtsan, the Third Zen Patriarch, that I referenced in the first chapter of this section, states that, "The Way is perfect like vast space where nothing is lacking and nothing is in excess. Indeed, it is due to our choosing to accept or reject, that we do not see the true nature things." The "Way" he is referring to is the spontaneous way of nature, life, and the cosmos. When we live in accord with it, its power, grace, and beauty lives through us.

When Sengtsan states that due to our choosing, we fail to see the true nature of things, he's drawing attention to the moment *before* we pick or choose. If we have a narrative running through our mind, explaining or justifying why it is good to do something, then our action will be bound by the frame of our preconceived ideas. Our gesture will likely come off as somewhat insincere or superficial. In the woman's response to the homeless man on the Metro, a well thought-out, polished gesture of compassion would probably have made him more enraged because he would have sensed that her effort to pacify or console him was made out of fear or pity.

The *Hsin Hsin Ming* goes right to the heart of the whole samsaric problem—our insistence that things or people should be different than the way they are. When confronted by life's slings and arrows, painful or problematic circumstances, we usually feel that such experiences shouldn't be happening to us. Secretly, we are disapproving of life as it is. Samsara is based upon *both* our failure to recognize that the present moment is not haphazard, and our misguided effort to manipulate it in order to get a better deal. If you had to remember all the steps that brought you to this present time and place, reading this very sentence, you would uncover an inconceivable network of causes, conditions, relationships, transactions, and experiences that moved you to this very point of being right here, now. The experience that you are having, for better or for worse, is not capricious or frivolous. On one hand, it arises out of a causal network, and on the other hand, it's a direct reflection of your immediate state of mind.

Freedom is the openness to and embrace of exactly where we find ourselves, so that we are fully *in* our experience rather than observing it from outside of it. Once we are in the experience we are already having, we discover that nowness is a fertile space with unlimited experiential possibilities. Freedom is not struggling with who we are or the way the world is. Whether we are having a lot of thoughts or a few thoughts, whether we are having an extraordinarily wonderful time or feel cornered and cramped by life's challenges, we allow situations to unfold without resisting what arises in our experience. This does not imply passively going along with events, but rather suggests that we step into the flow of situations and move along with their current while gently steering—honoring what holds meaning and value for ourselves. But we can only do this when we feel an intrinsic part of our experiences.

The coffee shop you just entered with its rich fragrant aroma, the patrons reading their news from laptops while sipping their morning java, the courteous smiles from those behind the counter—all of it is one the seamless experience. You are the focal point within which the whole scenario arises, the

Sixth Threshold: The Journey of Ascent

indispensable factor without which the experience could not be. Of course, the same holds true for each individual in the shop.

There are moments when our mind, heart, and body are in alignment, when we're "in the flow," and we move in tandem with unfolding situations—as did the grey-haired elderly lady on the Metro. Her gesture was probably not based on fear or conventional morality but was a spontaneous expression of her whole being. This kind of choosing is not coming from the logical, rational, or habitual mind but from a deeper place that exists within all of us.

In any moment that we have true intimacy with another, we step beyond the feeling that we are "inside here" confronted by an external other. Stepping beyond the dichotomies of like and dislike, inside and outside, here and there, is how we manifest our Buddha nature. Removing the barrier between us and the world, we're brought into intimate contact with reality, and there is no complaint with anyone or anything. This is a subtle point because most of us are not aware of how separate we feel from others and from ordinary situations.

Today, after my morning meditation, I took a walk along a meandering creek located behind my home. I came upon a beautiful snowy-white egret that was no more than fifteen feet in front of me. It was raining, and as I stood underneath my umbrella gazing at this lovely being, perched knee-deep in the creek, she suddenly spread her wings and quickly flapped them, ruffling her feathers to shake the water from her body. In the stillness of the morning, there was only the rhythmic beating of her snowy-white wings reflected in the blue waters of the creek. In the absence of picking and choosing, there was just that precious moment of intimacy, the all-surrounding experience of just *that*, from which not a thing was missing.

25.
Warriors of Virtue: The Bodhisattva Path

"Let us not think that because we are less brutal, less violent, less inhuman than our opponents, we will carry the day. Brutality, violence and inhumanity have an immense prestige..... For the opposite virtues to have as much prestige, they must be actively and constantly put into practice. Anyone who is merely incapable of being as brutal, as violent and as inhuman as someone else, but who does not practice the opposite virtues, is inferior to that person in both inner strength and prestige, and he will not hold out against such a confrontation."

Simone Weil

Buddhism distinguishes itself from the theistic religions by offering a map and methods for how to walk a spiritual path and wake up to our full human potential without proclaiming divinely-revealed truth. The nontheistic Buddhist path guides us how to transform a life of dissatisfaction and struggle to one of kindness, gentleness, and dignity.

At a certain point in our spiritual evolution we might feel that liberating ourselves from our own hangups is not enough. The enormity and pervasiveness of human suffering begins to make a claim upon us, tenderizing our heart, and spurring a response beyond logic and reason. At that point we step into the developmental stage that Buddhism designates as the *Mahayana*, literally "the big vehicle," which emphasizes cultivating compassion for all sentient beings. In effect, we make our lives a gift, an offering to others.

Compassion is not merely a sympathetic feeling but a deep state of consciousness where we experience our interconnection and interdependence with others, including the nonhuman world of plants and animals. We feel with others, sharing in their joys and sorrows, with the simultaneous aspiration to be of service. The nurturing quality of compassion has the power to transform others, like the sun's rays that crack open a seed's hardened shell so it can sprout with life.

At the Mahayana stage, we practice six virtues that transcend the ordinary idea of virtue, in that they go beyond conventional morality and logic. When practitioners on the Buddhist path feel inspired, they take the *bodhisattva vow*—making a commitment to forsake or delay their own enlightenment until all sentient beings realize their awakened nature. The Sanskrit term *bodhi* means to "spiritually awaken," and practitioners who take this vow are called *bodhisattvas*.

In taking the bodhisattva vow, we follow the example of the Buddha, who gave up his kingdom and dedicated himself to relieving the suffering of whomever he met on his travels. There is a feeling of celebration as we join the long lineage of bodhisattvas dating back to the time of the Buddha. Inspired by the lives of these bodhisattvas, we begin to develop greater friendliness towards the world, feeling that all circumstances are workable. We commit ourselves to completely participate in life and not be put off by the inconveniences that others provide for us.

Sixth Threshold: The Journey of Ascent

Taking this vow is already an expression of our awakened heart. We feel that our heart is blossoming and we want to share that. It has been said by the great enlightened ones that, although it is impossible to save all sentient beings, we still aspire to do so; although it is impossible to fully comprehend the entirety of the Buddha's teaching or dharma, we will never stop trying; although it seems impossible to become enlightened, we continue to walk the path with unswerving confidence in our Buddha nature. It is the spirit of the vow that is the essential thing. This aspiration completely changes our orientation because, by putting others' welfare before our own, we embody Buddha nature on the spot.

Although practiced simultaneously, the transcendental virtues are usually taught in a developmental sequence, which suggests that compassion does evolve. Each of the virtues remedies different areas where we get stuck on our spiritual path. The sequence of the transcendental virtues are: generosity, discipline, patience, joyous energy, meditation, and discriminating-awareness wisdom.

In order for our spiritual practice to be complete, it must involve compassionate relationship *and* wisdom. The first four transcendental virtues help us cultivate compassion, while the latter two virtues help us cultivate wisdom. Without wisdom, the bodhisattva's compassion runs the risk of becoming merely kind, indulgent, or sentimental. Compassion must be joined with courage and intelligence, so that our expression of virtue reflects the clarity and ruthless honesty of our meditation practice.

1. Generosity

Think of a flower bud in spring. As the season progresses, the bud softens and gradually unfurls its delicate petals, exposing the pistils and stamen within its center. Generosity is like that. It opens in response to the sun of our own awakened heart. When we begin to connect with our own basic goodness, our heart naturally opens. As our meditation practice matures, we feel an undeniable sense of sanity and worthiness that is beyond our personality. It is that refreshing feeling of health and wholeness that we may remember from childhood, before we divided the world between friend and enemy, and for and against.

Generosity could be a material or physical gesture, as when we donate to our favorite charities or when we give time, money, energy to a family member or friend who is in need. Transcendental generosity includes that, but it goes much further. It also means that we listen deeply both to ourselves and others, intuitively sensing what is needed in a given situation — and we spontaneously "deliver the goods." This kind of openness takes courage because it means that we are willing to step beyond our personal boundaries.

Generosity is also the courage to openly communicate with whom or what we usually avoid or reject. When we encounter a troubled person, burdened by unresolved issues — perhaps due to their divorce, or their mother's death, or because of losing their job — our compassionate presence can soften the knot in their heart or belly. Our generosity infuses the interpersonal space with loving-kindness so that they might feel safe enough to release whatever grief, guilt, or self-blame they've been holding onto.

What makes this a transcendental gesture is that we ourselves don't hold any idea of generosity. Our generosity is like a flower naturally opening to the sun. We give up the idea of being a "giver" of generosity, by surrendering the "me" who has extended a compassionate gesture to another, and then we move on.

We try to practice generosity under all circumstances—even when we are sleepy, tired, cold, or hungry, stepping over our irritation and defensiveness. Sometimes we are totally inconvenienced by life's demands or a friend's personal request. We would like to say, "You know, I'm in the middle of something right now. Could you come back later, or better yet, could you ask someone else?" The virtue of transcendental generosity challenges us right there.

It is not possible to entirely avoid obnoxious, irritating people who press our buttons. When we're about to get triggered, we remind ourselves of our vow. When dealing with frustrating people or adversarial situations, we encourage ourselves to allow space and to remain receptive. This is our gift to them. By offering a neutral psychological opening and unconditional positive regard, difficult situations or people might be able to settle. It is said that bodhisattvas do not have enemies because they give no one cause to take issue with them.

2. Discipline

In our practice of virtue, we could be expecting some kind of acknowledgement, wanting to be recognized as being a good human being or a seasoned spiritual practitioner. In the absence of such recognition, it's tempting to collapse our posture of openness and compassion. At that precise moment, we invoke the transcendental virtue of discipline, which reminds us to protect our *path* and not our ego. In the practice of compassion, the expectation to receive complimentary feedback reduces transcendental virtue to conventional morality.

Our bodhisattva path is like railroad tracks that trail off into the distance towards an infinite horizon, never wavering, neither moving closer together nor further apart, which would derail the locomotion of our journey. There are no detours and no divorces on this path—and yet we remain quite human, with desires, longings, and feelings that perhaps we aren't doing enough to alleviate the suffering of others.

The practice of transcendental discipline cuts through our nostalgia for samsara, the impulse to take a break from the practice of virtue. When our spiritual path is making demands on us that feel terribly inconvenient, transcendental discipline means that we don't withdraw from full participation in life and take a vacation from our practice. Our effort is always to keep others' welfare in mind, and to be suspicious of our wish for immunity from the challenges of our bodhisattva vow.

The essence of transcendental discipline is the notion of proper conduct, which can only come about through the delicate balance between self-restraint and self-expression. Self-restraint follows from our commitment to not retreat to our cocoon of comfort when things get tough. Self-expression is the creative way that we communicate and interact with others, putting their welfare before our own. This commitment shapes our mind so that our behavior begins to fall into healthy patterns rather than being governed by the egocentric nature of our personality.

Another way to put transcendental discipline into practice is by considering the complementary gestures of holding on and letting go, both their positive and negative aspects. We tend to hold onto our beliefs, opinions, perspectives, and our idiosyncratic way of doing things. This is often a sign of our inflexibility and resistance to change. We also hold onto a sense of self-importance, a feeling of being special as aspiring bodhisattvas. This puts us at a distance from others and prevents us from being effective helpers. At the same time, holding on can mean cultivating and cherishing what is precious to us, our commitment to our spiritual path, and our willingness to embrace difficulty. Holding on can also mean restraining our impulsiveness and hunger for entertainment and distraction.

Letting go can be our willingness to release our grip on who or what we're holding onto—to let be, let pass, as we move along with situations and relationships as they unfold. It is our ability to liberate ourselves from the human tendency to become fixated on either pleasure or pain. But letting go could also mean abandoning our bodhisattva commitment, letting go of our discipline, our decorum, and at times, letting go of all restraint, as we dramatize our irritation, impatience, and anger. Transcendental discipline is a delicate balance between letting go and holding on, and knowing when to apply either gesture to balance our path when it has become eccentric.

3. Patience

Perhaps the most challenging transcendental virtue to practice for us as Americans is patience. Living in a culture that is so efficiency-based and performance-oriented, we always seem to be on our way towards the next destination. Patience in the digital age is remarkably difficult. No sooner do we boot up our computer when tantalizing opportunities stream across our screen, inviting us to shift our attention to something more entertaining. It's challenging to fully land in *this* moment without the nagging hunger to migrate to a more entertaining or distracting moment.

The transcendental virtue of patience reminds us that we're on a journey without a particular goal. Although we may have a variety of ordinary goals and objectives—to finish college, to pay off the mortgage, to help a son or daughter in trouble, to go to the gym regularly—this virtue emphasizes that the path itself *is* the goal. The path is not leading up the mountain to a final destination, where upon arrival, we plunk down our flag of victory—"made it!" The notion of a journey without a goal redirects our attention to *how* we cruise through our day and evening, *how* we deal with failure as well as success, *how* we can conduct ourselves in a dignified and inspiring manner, as an expression of our awakened heart.

The virtue of patience is not looking at clock or calendar time to mark its journey but is the absence of a linear, sequential sense of time, the idea of minutes and hours ticking away as a measure of the unfolding of events. By contrast, we live in a very action-oriented culture with an accelerated sense of time. We seem to be driven by the need to see the results of our actions, as if to reassure ourselves that we're being productive. Patience challenges us to break the pattern of seeking a result from our actions so that we're not full of demand or expectation.

Transcendental patience means that we are willing to bear difficulties without becoming resentful from the hardships of the path. Our feathers do not get easily ruffled when confronted by irritating or frustrating interactions with others. We're able to maintain ourselves in a self-contained, dignified manner by bringing to mind the preciousness of our vow.

Cultivating the virtue of patience affords us the increasing ability to not give in to impulsiveness, to not spill our precious life force for the sake of stimulation. As bodhisattvas at this stage of the path, we still must be mindful for how we might be projecting our hunger for distraction and stimulation out into the social sphere, hoping to spark an interaction that would dispel our loneliness and boredom. Transcendental patience helps us to see that the basis of our passing irritations, resentments, or anger is our failure to produce a desired result from our actions.

Patience allows a big perspective so that we don't magnify the petty irritations and inconveniences of daily life, which can potentially contaminate our outlook on the day. We include frustration, irritation, and disappointment as part of our practice of transcendental patience, so that we create balance, stillness, and equanimity in our lives. Pausing in the midst of everyday activities—when we're having our morning coffee and *before* we're about to get on with the next thing, or as we get into our car and *before* we're about to drive off—we could allow a gap, and simply experience the moment.

Throughout the day we could punctuate our daily life with little intervals by interrupting our robotic routines by taking a breath and exhaling slowly, or by abruptly bringing our attention to our body. We pause, listen to ourselves, feel our energy, and we don't move for a moment, *before* we push on to the next destination. We shouldn't miss the opportunity to stop and listen to the rain, or pause in order to watch the fog rolling in over the hills. There are many dimensions within a moment of stillness, if we know how to relax into it.

The practice of patience inspires us to stay and not go, to not always have to anticipate what's next, or figure out a plan of action. We understand there are no other moments but the one that's unfolding right now. With patience can we connect and communicate with the deeper and more subtle layers of daily life. Such practice deepens us so that we can transmit to others the assurance that they are safe as long as they stay in their experience.

4. Joyous Exertion

Without the transcendental virtue of joyous exertion, there wouldn't be the necessary fuel to continuously arouse egoless compassion. This is what energizes the execution of all the previous virtues. The essence of joyous exertion is taking delight in spiritual practice rather than regarding it as a burden. This virtue not only prevents us from losing heart but encourages us to rejoice whenever we encounter an obstacle or feel bored by the repetition of daily activities.

Most importantly, this virtue cuts through our samsaric preoccupations, when we get fixated on petty things—shopping lists, unfinished projects, indecision about where to eat this evening, or where we should entertain ourselves this coming weekend. At the same time, as bodhisattvas, we do not feel the need to repress any experience, or deny any thought or feeling as unworthy of inspection. Instead, we use all experience as steppingstones to further the endless journey of offering ourselves to others. This is how the bodhisattva conserves energy.

Sixth Threshold: The Journey of Ascent

We all have psychological defenses to protect ourselves from being hurt emotionally or physically. The problem is that instead of mobilizing our defenses only when we need them, we tend to keep them in place, and thus maintain a very expensive defense budget. We siphon off an enormous amount of life force to maintain these defenses, which leaves us with limited energy. As our bodhisattva path matures, we cut through the need to maintain these defenses, which are usually to protect our spiritual persona or social face. By increasing our willingness to be vulnerable, we free up enormous energy to work for the benefit of others—which is quite joyous.

In every culture, there are cultural mores, restrictions, and inhibitions, and sanctioned forms of communication and behavior. This often creates tension between what our culture dictates as permissible and our impulse to act out our wishes and desires. One of the ways to work with the virtue of joyous energy is to actually use the tension between cultural inhibition and our own impulsiveness. We're able to hold that tension because we've learned to trust the creative potential that can emerge from holding opposite energies within ourselves, without identifying with either one. This is one expression of the Buddhist middle path.

Although we're fully aware of the mores of our culture, the rules of the game, we don't take the game so seriously that we forget to play. By seeing the arbitrary, relative nature of societal rules and regulations, we move through our lives without feeling restricted or victimized by them, nor do we feel the need to rebel by becoming maverick bodhisattvas. This permits us to see the total pattern of any situation. Such a holistic perception generates joyous energy because we become totally interested in the emerging creative patterns of life. As bodhisattvas, we're inspired by the tension between hesitation and impulse. Our exertion is fueled by the friction between the confused mentality of samsara and the clear awakened sanity of nirvana.

For example, most of us were not trained in our culture how to creatively handle the electricity of desire, especially erotic-romantic desire. We tend to either to suppress or dramatize this energy, either avoiding the seduction of such desire, or we're driven to impulsively fulfill our desires. But consider the possibility of just circulating the energy of attraction without shutting it down or acting it out. On occasion, what if we allowed the magnetism of desire for another person to course through our body and mind without having to fulfill it in relationship. Circulating the energy can serve as a source of animation and enhanced aliveness.

Our practice of joyous exertion inspires us to let go and move along with situations as they unfold, not overly restraining nor overly expressing ourselves, much like dancing effortlessly with a partner, or like a jazz musician who has practiced their art for decades. They now can spontaneously express themselves with complete confidence. Through increasing trust in ourselves, we no longer suffer from the burden of excessive conscience, nor do we feel compelled to strictly adhere to external rules and regulations. Instead we play the game of life with passionate commitment to respond to others' suffering and to further their process of awakening.

Sixth Threshold: The Journey of Ascent

5. Meditation

The transcendental virtue of meditation is similar to the previous discussion of meditation in the fourth threshold, "Belly of the Whale." Here, it does not refer to the formal seated practice of meditation, but to the ongoing state of awareness that attends our expressions of generosity, discipline, patience, and joyous energy. It is the state of total involvement throughout the day, guided by the motivation to be of service to others. The virtue of meditation is a round-the-clock effort to employ mindfulness and meditative insight in all circumstances, expanding the range and depth of our awareness in order to clarify how the bureaucracy of confused mind works, so that we can work skillfully with all manner of human beings.

Waking up to our enlightened nature happens most effectively in interpersonal relationships, where we're challenged to overcome the dualistic barrier that separates us from others, as well as from the world. Our heart is alive and tender, and we want to share this gift. This open heartedness is an expression of our compassion for all sentient beings and an acknowledgment of our interrelatedness and interconnection with all of life.

Yet even at this stage of the path, we're still susceptible to shaping our experiences according to ego's primitive agenda. Ego's strategies are notorious for being without end. According to Buddhism, the most profound delusion is the timeless belief in the "ghost in the machine"—that there's an interior "me" that is different and separate from our thoughts and actions. The virtue of transcendental meditation challenges us to gradually cut through the illusion of the thinker of our thoughts, so that we're not reinforcing this subtle interior witness.

In the sitting practice of meditation, we let go of our thoughts and images, memories and anticipations, hopes and fears, and return our attention to the immediacy of the open moment. This starves our ego of its usual source of nourishment. The practice of meditation is the process of continual letting go, cutting through the ego's underlying wish for continuity, which opens us up to a refreshing feeling of boundlessness and freedom.

The creativity that arises from transcendental meditation keeps our mind in a continual state of readiness and receptivity. Such a state of openness can give birth to fresh perceptions as well as skillful methods for working with others' suffering. Whenever we encounter an obstacle, a difficult interpersonal conflict, or an adversarial situation, we no longer regard these as separate from our spiritual path, but as further challenge to embrace our Buddha nature in all of its many manifestations.

6. Prajna: Discriminating Awareness

Prajna, the sixth transcendental virtue is translated as the wisdom of discriminating awareness. Although prajna is taught as the last of the six virtues, it is what makes all the other virtues transcendental. It is the ground as well as the fruition of the six transcendental virtues. Prajna emerges from the integration of mindfulness practice *(shamatha)* with insight meditation *(vipashyana)*, as discussed in the earlier section, "Belly of the Whale."

In translating "prajna" as "wisdom of discriminating awareness," the word "discriminating" does not imply judgment, comparison or evaluation, but indicates our ability to distinguish one thing or quality from another. It is a heightened

Sixth Threshold: The Journey of Ascent

sense of precision and clarity, directness and immediacy that is able to discern samsara from nirvana in all of their many subtle aspects. It is traditionally symbolized by a double-edged sword that personifies the sharp, penetrating quality of mind that cuts through our intellectual speculations and dogmatic beliefs.

Prajna first cuts through our conceptualized version of the world, so that our assumptions, beliefs, judgments, and expectations are made transparent. It then swings back to cut the perceiver so that we don't make personal territory out of our experiences. We're liberated from any solid and fixed notion of self, which gives us an undiluted perception of the world as *it* is, not as we imagine it to be.

Prajna invites inquiry into our unfolding experiences for the sheer joy of discovery. By seeing the transparency of the boundary between self and other, it makes intimate contact with the world around us. Prajna perceives the open dimension of things, seeing that the forms of sight, sound, texture, smell, and taste all reveal endless dimensions that can never be exhausted. The ordinary sensory world is experienced as stunningly beautiful in the living moment, whether that moment is visual, auditory, or tactile. We intuitively feel the "is-ness" quality of ordinary things, their aesthetic immediacy or virgin freshness, so that the ordinary is experienced with extraordinary sensitivity and clarity.

To perceive something as it is, in its intrinsic uniqueness, is to perceive it aesthetically, with great appreciation. Our world is not made up of cold facts, but every aspect of life is precious in its own right. Were it not for life's inherent worthiness, prajna's inquisitiveness would reveal a valueless and pointless world. From this compelling interest in life comes the bodhisattva's tireless capacity to execute the transcendental virtues to the utmost limit.

As bodhisattvas, we protect and further the transcendental virtues with an eye towards the traditions of our society. We understand that it is only through their transformation that the wisdom energy of the virtues may radiate across social strata, inspiring others to begin the great endless journey without a goal.

Sixth Threshold: The Journey of Ascent

The Journey of Ascent: Wisdom, Virtue, and Transcendence

You know that you've crossed the Sixth Threshold when....

You realize that liberating yourself from your own neuroses and hangups is not enough. Your awakened heart inspires you to commit yourself to alleviating others' suffering. An important shift occurs at the sixth threshold. This Mahayana stage of the path is distinguished by either taking the bodhisattva vow, or by living in the spirit of the vow, carrying its benevolent spirit in your heart. Your commitment is to work for the benefit of all sentient beings and to even forsake your own enlightenment until all beings realize their own authentic nature and are liberated from suffering.

Although this vow is impossible to achieve, you still make every effort to fulfill it. It is the spirit of the vow that is the essential thing. You are making your life a gift for others. You can do this because you recognize that your awakened heart is an inexhaustible treasure. The gesture of putting others' welfare before your own, further awakens your own Buddha nature, transforming the quality of your mind and heart, and shaping all of your actions.

At the sixth threshold your integration of mindfulness and awareness, which began at earlier stages of the path, has now ripened to give birth to *prajna*, the cognitive sharpness that cuts through your conceptualized version of the world. This offers you a perception of the world in its innocence or nakedness, beyond your ideas of it. This perception invites intuitive insight into the nature of life.

You discover that freedom is the openness to and embrace of exactly where you find yourself, so that you're fully *in* your experience rather than observing it. Once in the experience you are already having, you realize that nowness holds unlimited possibilities for how to help others help themselves.

You continue to walk your path with confidence in your Buddha nature, but you now begin to practice the transcendental virtues of generosity, ethics, patience, joy, and insight, so that your gestures of compassion are joined with wisdom and skillful communication. You are continually challenged to express compassion in creative ways without diminishing your newfound sense of freedom.

At this stage of the path you feel an unmistakable sense of confidence and celebration, knowing that you've joined the lineage of bodhisattvas dating back to the time of the Buddha. The bodhisattva vow, or the spirit of the vow, inspires you to not feel inconvenienced by others heavy-handed neuroses—and to never give up. Much to your delight you find that every step along the way of the bodhisattva path deepens your realization of the hidden jewel at the core of your own nature.

SEVENTH THRESHOLD:
HEAVEN, EARTH, AND HUMAN

The principle of heaven is symbolic of expansive vision that is vast and profound, beyond our contrived, self-centered way of thinking. It is the source of all potential creativity, but made manifest through the earth principle, the embodiment of heaven's vision. The earth principle is displayed in the elegance and beauty of the natural world, its self-regulating, self-organizing, and self-correcting intelligence that maintains a balance between order and chaos. Earth also symbolizes the tangible forms that we create and the practical measures we take to promote and support a good life. As human beings, we are obliged to hold the tension between heaven and earth, mind and body, and to ultimately integrate these principles or capacities within ourselves and our society.

These chapters explore the dynamic principles of heaven and earth, and how to integrate the corresponding vertical and horizontal paths of development within our personality and in our life. The vertical path, aligned with the principle of heaven, represents an evolutionary view of spirituality through expanded states of awareness. The horizontal path, aligned more with the earth principle, represents embodiment, how to manifest the more abstract principles of heaven into tangible forms that serve our personal development and the betterment of others.

When we develop either an overly conceptual approach to life, often in form of secular or spiritual ideologies, or become overly identified with material form, concerned with only what appears to our senses and valuing only what is functional, we upset the communication between heaven and earth. This brings conflict in our relationships with others, a distorted approach to our environment, and creates imbalance in both ourselves and our society.

In order to reconcile ourselves with the heaven and earth principles when they have gone out of balance, we need to come out of our thinking mind and back into our heart and our senses, so that we may understand the difference between what is imaginary and what it means to hold a sacred vision of all life.

26.

Not Knowing

We depend on the people and things in our life to remain solid, continuous, and predictable, but they are constantly shifting in the sands of time, leaving us with a sense of uncertainty. Yet, with a shift in attitude, uncertainty becomes openness, possibility, and surprise. From this openness, the potential of the heaven principle dawns.

We live in a world that is both ordinary and also mysterious. The unknown awaits us at our local market. As you walk in and reach for your favorite bottle of chardonnay, you realize the price has gone up $7.00 since last week, and you are shocked. You were having a perfectly good day up until that point, but you now feel outraged and are already on your way to complain to the manager. Without consulting you, your own mind has morphed into righteous indignation. The unknown can meet us like that.

Alternatively, you might reach for that bottle of overpriced chardonnay and another arm, three inches from yours, reaches for the same bottle. At first blush, this feels like an intrusion into your personal territory. Immediately turning your head, you look indignantly at this arm and notice that it's attached to a lovely body and face, whose eyes now meet yours.

Without warning, the unknown meets you at a most tender moment, and what happens next is unpredictable. You can't rehearse for these moments. There's just that bare uncharted space when you're free to move in surprising directions.

Buddhism teaches that we are surrounded by unknowingness. We live in an ever-changing, impermanent universe where seemingly solid situations are continually shape-shifting. During unexpected illness or sudden catastrophes, we get to witness this most vividly. Most of us live our lives within a web of predictable routines. We pay our bills, balance our checkbooks, make it to work on time, care for our children and our animal companions, try to remember birthdays and anniversaries, and call our parents, if only infrequently, to say that we still love them. In spite of being responsible and good people, we can be met by a frightening diagnosis at our next doctor's visit, or be confronted by a parent's need for institutionalization, or discover that our teenage son or daughter has become an addict—and suddenly life is turned upside down. What was seemingly solid a moment ago abruptly becomes a big open space, and we're in free fall.

The uncompromising truth is that we can't protect ourselves from uncertainty. Buddhism recommends that we establish a relationship with the radical openness of our human life. We could try to use psychology, philosophy, or religion to explain or interpret a confusing or painful situation, but we could also permit ourselves to experience the situation at hand, directly and immediately, without conceptual filters. In order to connect with "things as they are," we have to let go of whatever we're holding onto as a shield against uncertainty and be willing to "not know"—to allow life to catch us by surprise. Our

SEVENTH THRESHOLD: HEAVEN, EARTH, AND HUMAN

"holding on" usually takes the form of presumed certainty that we know ourselves, our children, our love ones, and what our life is about. But upon further investigation, this air-tight assurance begins to dissolve.

We can't exhaust everything there is to know about any single thing in our world, not our husband or wife, our children, or our best friend. There is no bottom to anything, and that's the ocean of mystery, the immeasurable depth within which we unknowingly swim. This moment that we're experiencing right now happens once and only once in its marvelously unique way, and never again. The experience that we're now having, how we feel, the thoughts going through our head, the energies that are moving through our body, how we're connected with each other, happens only once in this unrepeatable configuration, and nevermore. One precious moment at a time, and then never again in that exact same way—although we don't perceive our world in this way.

We can be moved by exquisite beauty, feel the exultation of success, and can love so deeply, and yet these most precious feelings do not endure. We enter into this world with such open, sensitive, and vulnerable hearts, and yet those loved ones for whom we feel most deeply pass through our lives and are soon gone. Our seemingly solid world is far more fluid than we'd care to admit. Recognizing that the truth of impermanence also applies to our internal watcher, we realize that our cherished "me" is also empty of solidity and continuity. Giving up the "ghost in the machine" deprives us of our constant companion, but it opens us up to our awakened nature. The marriage of emptiness and wisdom is freedom. If we approach our life with an open heart and an open mind, we might find that the whole drama of life is marvelously creative and playful.

Buddhism holds that everything comes out of emptiness. What does this mean? If you trace back why you are having the thought you are currently having right now, you would have to account for all of the previous causes and conditions that led to this present moment. If you try to find the origin of why you said or did or experienced anything, you will be caught in an infinite regress, back and back through an indeterminate series of actions and reactions—yet you will not arrive at an ultimate cause of why you said, did, or experienced anything.

Of course, there are immediate precursors to events. "Well, she said or did that, and so I said or did this." "I lost my job and I now feel frightened and depressed." Emptiness in the Buddhist context, signifies that there's no *ultimate* or singular cause to anything that we experience. Because we're interrelated and interpenetrated by everything else, our thoughts, words, feelings, and actions cannot be absolutely separated from the innumerable causes and conditions that gave rise to them. We emerge from an infinite web of conditions whose origin or ultimate cause is unknown.

In a similar vein, when we meditate we observe the thoughts, images, memories, and feelings that pass through our mind. If we turn our meditative gaze on the "watcher" of those thoughts and feelings, it then becomes an object to be viewed by a more subtle watcher. If we then turn our gaze on *that* more subtle watcher, we're left with an even more subtle internal witness. Who or what is that witness? As we attempt to get behind that more subtle subject, we're caught in another endless regress. Although we can't seem to find the origin of anything, yet we can still rest in the immediacy of awareness, where the distinction between our internal witness and what it witnesses, collapses. At that moment, the space in which we're meditating or the life we've been living becomes very large and brilliant. And so we're left with *this*—the sweet taste and fragrance of this scoop of rocky road ice cream, or feeling at a complete loss to answer our child's question why her friend had to die. This is the principle of heaven from which spontaneous images, visions, and intuitions originate.

To access the principle of heaven, we try to communicate with the depth aspect of our mind that is formless and nonconceptual. Nonconceptual awareness is synonymous with "not knowing" but should not be confused with stupidity or lack of education. In this deep dimension of our mind, we taste the quality of being, where we might get the hint of a direction, or perhaps something occurs to us in an unusual way. Such intimations, if they are meaningful, will need to be adapted to our actual life circumstances. This is the earth principle, the need for practicality.

The heaven and earth principles are most effective when they're brought into balance and integrated within the human personality. The Buddhist teaching is that as we learn to swim with chaos or uncertainty with open eyes and open heart, we might discover that chaos and confusion sort themselves out, eventually revealing hidden patterns. Chaos could give us unexpected options where something good might turn up.

Many years ago when my father died, we had a gathering at my parents' New York City apartment. Our neighbors brought food and flowers, and expressed their genuine sympathies. After a few drinks, the tone of the afternoon became animated. Several of my mother's friends were getting boisterous as they shared stories and told jokes. My sense of propriety was offended, and as my negative judgments intensified by the moment, the living room suddenly became very tight and claustrophobic. I was about to say something in a tone of voice that would have surely offended many of the guests, but suddenly, for no apparent reason, an uncharacteristic openness punctured my momentum. I dropped my judgments and "permitted" Carol to be as she was—boisterous and loud, and "allowed" Paul to have a third drink and light up his cigar in our living room, and I softened my belly, as my uncle Max performed an irreverent pantomime of one of our relatives. I just watched all of these characters, neighbors and relatives, being exactly who they were. Everyone was enacting themselves, and it was both touching and humorous. The whole thing suddenly dissolved into openness.

Just a moment before, it was so solidly one way and then the whole thing evaporated and morphed into something totally different. We're convinced that our world is so solid, but with a momentary shift in our perception, we realize that our image or idea of others is not as fixed, continuous or defined as we thought. From this vast openness, the magical potential of the heaven principle dawns.

27.

Integrating the Horizontal and Vertical Paths

A developmental or horizontal path is an expression of the earth principle. It offers practical methods for developing ourselves through progressive stages. It also shines a light into the dark areas of many spiritual traditions that tend to focus on absolute truth. The vertical path is an expression of the heaven principle. It offers us methods for waking up to our intrinsic wholeness or Buddha nature. It shines a light into the psychological tendency to pathologize our problems and conflicts. The integration of the vertical and horizontal paths, the heaven and earth principles, would include all the aspects that make up a human being.

The Need for a Developmental or Horizontal Path

Having come of age during the spiritual movement in America in the late sixties and seventies, my generation saw many reputedly enlightened teachers from the East get toppled because of improprieties of power, sexuality, and substance abuse. Our disillusionment was only deepened by the denial of those improprieties by these teachers and their devotees. It appeared that something was missing, either in the Eastern notion of enlightenment or in the proponents of those traditions.

The personality or character of these awakened ones didn't seem as perfected as their illuminated mind. This was not true of all the Asian spiritual teachers who came to the West.

One of the historical problems in numerous spiritual traditions has been that the attainment of enlightenment didn't necessarily liberate the awakened individual from the shadow aspects of personality nor from the collective biases of his or her culture. In other words, the realization of enlightenment did not always illuminate the entirety of the spiritually awakened human being.

In the twenty-first century, we now recognize that waking up to our most profound spiritual potential needs to be fully embodied, so that our awakened energy can infiltrate the shadowy corners of our personality to transform *all* aspects within us—especially those that have been ignored. The light of wisdom also needs to illuminate the blind spots embedded within a given culture, such as patriarchal bias, sexism, racism, and class privilege and power. A developmental or *horizontal* path would involve methods to smoke out the hidden pockets both of ourselves and our culture, so that they can meet with the light of awareness to be transmuted.

The developmental method of Western psychology shines a light into the dark areas of many spiritual traditions, which, due to their bias to transcend our earthly limitations, often neglect or suppress the bodily part of being human, and the thorny issues that come with incarnation. This horizontal approach would involve an exploration of what is at the core of our stuck places. It would challenge us to skillfully manage and process our feelings of rejection and self-doubt, abandonment and loneliness, without the effort to spiritually bypass these difficult feelings or misuse our power position as compensation for our unmet needs.

The horizontal path is a practical application of the earth principle. It is *not* about transcending but about relating with our body and its energies, and working through our confusion and our stuck places. Many sacred traditions do have a horizontal path but it is *implicit* in their teachings and not always made explicit in practice. Consequently, the issues around money, food, sexuality and intimacy, privilege and power, devotion and obedience can be sidestepped because they may be treated too generically. When specific guidelines and recommendations for dealing with such issues are not clearly spelled out, practitioners can hide behind dysfunctional behaviors in the name of spirituality.

The Vertical or Ascending Path

From the *vertical* perspective, which is an expression of the principle of heaven, the awakened or enlightened mind is who we are at our depth. When we're not blocking the natural flow of energy through our mind-body, and when we're not exclusively identified with our self-image and our social roles, (devoted mother, loyal brother, creative artist, talented teacher, etc.), our actions naturally express our inherent Buddha nature. The vertical path could be thought of as ascending, waking up to the highest state of consciousness available to us. Opening up to our original or essential nature has a sense of psychological transcendence, going beyond the limitations of our autobiographical self.

What the Developmental Path Exposes

Buddha nature or radical sanity does not need development or to be improved upon in any way. It is fully matured, always already complete. On the other hand, the progressive cutting through of obstacles that obscure our true nature *does* need cultivation. As human beings, we seem to be bound and limited by our habitual behavioral patterns. We're frequently seduced by irresistible passions and petty irritations, stirred up by turbulent emotions and deflated by depressive periods that wash the color out of our days— causing us to fall out from our profound nature. The temptation is to try to bypass the personality, but the horizontal path reminds us that our personality needs to be transformed, so that the whole human being is enlightened.

In order to embody our essential nature, we first need to know what we truly want, what our primary motivation is. We need to clarify and understand our cognitive distortions, our emotional complications, and our interpersonal strategies. The horizontal or developmental path, as in the practice of psychotherapy, works with our conflicts, problems, as well as past traumas. It gives us tools to work through our issues and how to deal with negative emotions without trying to prematurely transcend them. This eventually creates a container so that we can hold the electrical "charge" of higher states of awareness. When we walk a developmental path, we establish an inner "structure" or container to support our more expansive states of consciousness.

Seventh Threshold: Heaven, Earth, and Human

A Psycho-Social Model of Horizontal Development

A developmental path is stage-based. First we learn to crawl, then walk, run, use language and interact with others, develop skills to use utensils, tools, a keyboard, and only then can we function as good citizens. There are numerous developmental models. Erick Erickson developed a well-known psychosocial model that serves as a good illustration of the progressive stages that chart our horizontal evolution.

According to his model, initially as infants we are challenged with whether or not we can develop trust in our mother and our early environment. If we achieve a good enough level of trust, this becomes a milestone, permitting us to open to the challenge of autonomy. If we fail to achieve a good enough level of trust, this would compromise the degree to which we can trust ourselves and our immediate environment.

Challenged by autonomy, as children we begin to expand our radius of connections with others and the environment beyond our mother and father. If we fail to achieve a good enough level of autonomy, we will thereafter doubt our own sense of self-direction, and be overly dependent on others or on established rules and regulations. Achieving this milestone we move onto the challenges of initiative and industry, when we develop feelings of competence and confidence to launch our ambition and to work cooperatively with others. Failing to achieve adequate development in this milestone, we become vulnerable to inertia and feelings of inhibition and incompetence.

As teenagers we are challenged by the need to establish an adequate degree of personal identity, that sense of being true to ourselves, so that we can negotiate the challenges of peer competition and sexual relationships. Failing to develop a confident sense of selfhood, we experience identity or gender confusion. Succeeding in this psychosocial milestone, we move on to the challenge of intimacy with loved ones and friends, demonstrating our capacity to feel affinity or rapport with others. If we don't achieve a good enough level of development in this area, we tend to either feel isolated or experience ourselves emotionally distant from others.

In midlife we are challenged by the need for generativity, where we distill the best within ourselves to offer our unique gift to the world. This could take the form of raising children, developing a meaningful and gratifying livelihood, or some creative endeavor that both expresses who we are, and that brings benefit to many others. Failing to adequately respond to the challenge of generativity, we tend to suffer from feelings of stagnation.

Beyond midlife we are challenged by the need to develop integrity and wisdom, so that we can gratefully embrace our one and only life and feel assured that our life has had meaning and value. We can take pride in the uniqueness of our individual life, while at the same time, feel a kinship with people of other cultures and other historical periods—recognizing the commonality of our human spirit. According to Erickson, the gift of this milestone is that we cultivate faith in what survives us. This brings us full circle to the first psychosocial challenge of trust, but on a much deeper level—where we now can trust the whole human life cycle. Failing this last developmental challenge, we are left with feelings of despair, regret, and disdain.

Seventh Threshold: Heaven, Earth, and Human

The point of describing these developmental stages is that, even after many years of meditation, we may not recognize the developmental phase within which we are living our lives. We may not be clear what tasks are required of us in our current stage, nor the vulnerabilities to which we are particularly sensitive. These stages do not commonly show up in meditation, but without knowing it, we will most likely interpret our experiences from within these stages. These developmental stages highlight real needs whose fulfillment brings us to full emotional-relational maturity.

The Shadow Revisited

A massive blind spot in many spiritual traditions is the failure to take account of our shadow and the inner work necessary to expose it. This theme was introduced in the threshold of "The Siren's Call" but it is worth repeating in this particular context. The shadow is the unacknowledged or denied part of each of us that often feels like an inferior or deficient self. It could be the part of us that is emotionally or sexually immature, or the part of us that hungers for power and control, but hides behind the pretense of light and love. Beneath our spiritual persona, we might have ancient unresolved hurts, possibly a narcissistic sense of entitlement, and a need for uncritical attention, affection, and loyalty from others.

Our shadow could also contain our infantile obsessions and hostilities, repressed urges and needs that have been denied for a lifetime. Many spiritual practitioners prefer to leave their all-too-human self behind and soar to a more exalted place. The problem is that any part of us that is split off from our awareness can take on a life of its own. Such dissociated parts erupt when we get emotionally triggered, after which we feel that we were out of character, and not ourselves.

One of the least threatening ways to access one's shadow is to inquire what aspects of yourself your parents mirrored or nurtured, and which aspects they failed to mirror. Usually the aspects of ourselves that were not held emotionally, are the very parts of us that go underground and remain invisible to us. As a method of working with shadow material, dialogue is a very effective tool. The power of communicating with a trusted and compassionate friend or professional helper allows our shadowy corners to be witnessed and reflected in a nonjudgmental manner. Eventually we're able to take our shadow elements out of the dungeon of darkness and expose it to the light of understanding, so that we are less likely to act out these aspects of ourselves or project them onto others.

The Vertical Path's Critique

From the perspective of the vertical path, the blind spot in the developmental path is the relative absence of the sacred. This surfaces in our lack of confidence and guidance for how to embrace our formless nature, the depth of who we truly are. Perhaps we've been in therapy like Woody Allen for the last forty years, working on one issue after another, but we are still feeling crazy after all these years. We've worked through our parent issues, and our sexual insecurities and issues around failure, and we've even embraced the fact we're going to die. Yet we might still feel something significant is missing in our lives that we can't quite name, and so we are left with an aching existential emptiness.

SEVENTH THRESHOLD: HEAVEN, EARTH, AND HUMAN

Until recently, Western psychotherapy has been pathologically oriented, focusing on conflicts, problems, and issues, but seemingly ill-equipped when it comes to a client's spiritual potential. Such clients would benefit from being introduced to contemplation, prayer, and meditation, and offered guidance and encouragement to step beyond their inner dialogue to explore their non-conceptual depths. Of course, this would require therapists and mentors who have a spiritual practice and have reached a level of maturity to guide others.

The vertical path is state-based, opening us up to states of consciousness and a quality of experience that is not commonly part of psychotherapy. The vertical or ascending path moves us towards the largest possible frame of awareness, within which we can hold our everyday experiences. Rather than trying to bypass our issues and conflicts, they are experienced from within an expanded context. Instead of resurrecting ancient conflicts and traumas in an effort to work them through, we try to recognize our experiences as reflections of the creative energy of our big mind or Buddha nature. We open to this living moment, to allow it to communicate directly with us, *before* we have an idea, interpretation, or opinion about it. Such uncommon experiences go beyond our conflict and problems.

For instance, your wise mind or a big mind, of which you are unaware, draws experiences to you that confront you with issues that you've been ignoring. The confrontation could be a difficult conversation that you've been avoiding, or grief that you've been suppressing. If you assume the perspective of your big mind, you can recognize what purpose your defenses have served, and what they have prevented you from seeing, and how contending with the underlying issues are necessary and meaningful. You might even marvel how the deepest part of you moves you to exactly where you need to be.

Integration of Vertical and Horizontal Paths

The horizontal path is a necessary body of methods that help us to work through our unmet needs and conflicts around trust, sexuality, intimacy, power, and control, and our possible lack of integration around these particular issues. The vertical path involves a conscious and intentional embrace of what transcends our limited autobiographical self—our awakened or Buddha essence, which instills a sacred view of life in us. What tends to be overlooked in many psychological schools is the possibility of transcending the limitations of our conditioned personality, that is, getting beyond our personal story and conventional identity, in order to glimpse our "original face," our true self, which is no self at all.

In the twenty-first century, we are witnessing the beginnings of a concerted effort to integrate the vertical and horizontal paths, body and mind, heart and soul, psyche and culture, so that our conscious evolution includes all the domains that make up a human being. The horizontal and vertical paths shine a light into each other's blind spots and serve as correctives for the potential imbalance of either. They enable us to be in a better position to integrate the best of the Western psychological schools with the best of the Eastern paths of liberation. Before we can cultivate complete trust in our basic being and assume our most profound identity, we need to find our seat in the magical spot between heaven and earth.

28.

Imagination: Bridge Between Heaven & Earth

Although our senses perceive a three-dimensional world of concrete things, imagination opens up communication with what lies beyond our five senses. Imagination mediates between heaven and earth, so that the invisible side of phenomena reveal their secrets to us in forms that we can utilize. Imagination uncovers real qualities within ourselves and our world that lie waiting to be expressed.

Five friends are having dinner and discussing what they feel is the essence of life. The first person states that for her, life is a creative project to transform her existence into a work of art. The person sitting next to her states that for him, its all about intimate connection with his loved ones and his circle of close friends. The next person at the table states that for her, life would be nothing were it not for a quest for some kind of Holy Grail, something that would lend meaning, value and purpose to her life. A fourth friend states that he sees life more as a game to be skillfully played, to enjoy the element of novelty, discovery, and stimulation that such an approach offers. The fifth individual states that for her, life is like a classroom where she continually learns lessons that broaden her horizons and challenge her to be more of who she can ultimately be.

In the above hypothetical example we have a palette of five possibilities for how to live one's life, or what constitutes the "good life." How did each individual arrive at his or her perspective? If they each tried to persuade the others that their perspective was more true, valid, or valuable, do you think that any of the others would be convinced and would accept this alternative view? It's unlikely.

Hard facts and plausible reasons are not the major determinants that shape our lives. Rather, how we interpret those facts, how we feel about them, and what associations get stirred in us are what gives shape and color, meaning and value to our lives. On one hand, we're a combination of nature and nurture—genetic transmission, and the qualities, attitudes, and behaviors modeled by our parents, teachers, and extended family. Yet we are more than nature and nurture. As individuals we weave lessons learned from our life experiences into a unique vision of who we are and what our life is about—from relationships that both touched and broke our hearts, from struggles that humbled and ennobled us, and from ideas and stories that expanded our mind—all of which mixed with our unique talents and peculiar sensitivities.

This weaving is the creative gesture of imagination, which is not a separate category of mind or character. Imagination is an intimate partner in shaping our life experiences into the unique form and substance of our growing personality. It's what allows us to find parallels, correspondences, and complementarities among and between different events or things, enabling us to integrate all of our

Seventh Threshold: Heaven, Earth, and Human

experiences into a unique sense of personhood. The capacity to cross boundaries and step beyond the fixed categories that we've set up in our mind is imagination's doing. Imagination corrals all of our faculties to meet the concrete world in order to form proper images of it. At best, it gathers the separate images of life events and integrates them into the largest possible context. At worst, imagination can also throw us into a dungeon of delusional thinking, into psychological realms of torment that we inflict on ourselves and others.

Many years ago, I received a birthday card from a dear friend, with an image of a lone rustic cabin set in a snow-covered meadow. In the darkness of dusk, its one window was aglow with golden light, as if from a fireplace, and a plume of grayish-blue smoke unfurled from the chimney. A simple cabin in a forest at dusk during winter. It has been nearly a half century and I still have that card. It conveys many things to me, qualities that I cherish—evoking a sense of solitude, my love of simplicity, feelings of melancholy, and the purity of the still and silent moment untouched by time.

Our senses perceive a three-dimensional world of discrete entities, but it is imagination that smokes out the invisible aspect of what is not commonly available to our five senses, revealing the intangible, unseen, and the unheard, echoing some unfathomable yet real quality within ourselves and our world. Getting up from our meditation session and walking into our kitchen or out into our yard, we might notice a peculiar clarity and brilliance to our perceptions. Morning light pouring in the window might seem especially luminous, as it brightens our mood. The chirping of a bird might reverberate within us, melting our heart and evoking a sweetness, or the rich fragrance of the earth might convey to us everything pure and unspoiled in our life.

Instantly we are brought down from the abstract realm of thought, as we refresh our connection with the palpable, visceral, animate world. Direct sensory perception combined with imagination opens us up to colors, sounds, fragrances, and intuitions that perhaps we've long forgotten. Imagination mediates between the invisible and the visible, between heaven and earth, seducing phenomena to communicate with us, to speak their secrets to us. This doesn't mean that we're making it up in the sense of pure fantasy.

I was walking today in late morning as I always do after meditation practice. There's a trail near my home that runs along a natural canal that winds through hundreds of acres of salt marsh. At this time of year there are literally miles of wildflowers in bloom. As I walked along the path, I found myself delighted with this display of tiny pansy-like pink-and-white flowers. The wind suddenly picked up, sweeping over a large swath of the marsh, as the pansies danced in rhythmic undulating movements, as if waving to me. I was immediately gladdened by the unmistakable taste of spring and opened into a sense of new beginnings, the promise of more to come on the horizon of my life.

The pansies swaying in the wind, the seasonal cycles of nature, and the lightness that lifted my spirits, all seemed part of one tapestry on this brilliant morning. My experience was neither objectively true nor a purely subjective interior event having no relationship with the actual landscape. When I saw the pansies being swept by the wind, I didn't conjure up little Walt Disney flower-like characters waving to me, but my pulse

SEVENTH THRESHOLD: HEAVEN, EARTH, AND HUMAN

immediately quickened, my gaze sharpened, and my spirits were lifted. There's more to what the senses literally report to us.

There is a common belief that when we engage our imagination or do imaginative exercises, it is a private activity. This perspective assumes that reality or nature is externally located and that our imagination is "in here," but a real connection exists between our human nature and the nature of life itself. It is not only our inner activity that is involved, but we may be tapping into a common ground that transcends our dualistic notions of self and world.

There is natural symbolism that can be experienced, which is not imaginary. The setting sun, howling Siberian huskies, nursing infants, smiling pumpkins on porches, and the homeless man sitting on the pavement are symbols of themselves, suggesting more than their mere appearance. Such ordinary symbolism is a lens through which the world communicates something ineffable to us. Imagination is the interactive process between the environment and something deep within ourselves that moves us beyond the obvious tangible forms we commonly perceive.

Through the practice of meditation, we deepen our sense of being and open the bandwidth of subtle perception, eliciting the larger intuitive aspect of mind. As we step into our life, we have the potential to experience ordinary things with extraordinary vividness and sensitivity that elicit qualities not obvious to our thinking mind. Imagination can be used to draw on the wisdom of our deep psyche, the region of our mind that is the home of primordial or archetypal images, images that are not constructed, but which spontaneously erupt into consciousness.

One of the meditation methods used in Tibetan Buddhism and other esoteric spiritual traditions, is visualization or envisionment. Such active imagination is a method of stepping into our subterranean domains with the intention of becoming intimate with dormant aspects of ourselves. It initiates an inner dialogue where one part of ourselves speaks to another part. By holding a specific sacred image in mind, we live into the image, evoking visual, auditory, and somatic sensory experience. We and the image merge so that it becomes three-dimensional or atmospheric. We become the living, breathing, luminous, sacred entity, which awakens that depth dimension within us. By identifying with specific images, our imagination holds the potential to elicit capacities, qualities, and powers that are either undeveloped or that we've never developed at all.

For example, you could choose a person, historical or currently alive, mythological or fictional, who embodies for you the superlative qualities that demonstrate the further reaches of human potential. Sit quietly for about five to ten minutes in order to settle your mind and then visualize this person, trying to invoke their presence. At first, the image will appear separate and different from yourself, but then imagine yourself merging with this individual, actually becoming him or her, taking on their qualities. By doing this, you contact the psychological place within yourself that is identical in quality and substance with your visualized entity. You are activating capacities, qualities, and powers that have been dormant within you, thereby invoking the principle of heaven.

Although imagery is in constant movement at all levels of our mind, there seems to be a unifying principle directing this flow that is working towards our intrinsic wholeness. In other

Seventh Threshold: Heaven, Earth, and Human

words, already within our innermost being, lies a seed, a magnetic attractor that acts as an integrating force in our lives. Although our development as human beings is not fixed or destined, it appears to be guided by a principle present in our core and working towards its eventual unfoldment. This is the archetypal symbol of the completely realized human that lives within all us—the primordial image of the Buddha or Christ within, or any culturally meaningful individual who transcends our limited, separate, and conditioned personality.

The human capacity for imagination may be nature's way of revealing itself to itself, using the human mind for its own revelation. Through imagination or envisionment, we are eliciting the creative intelligence of life, without which, the world is in some sense, incomplete. Through our capacity to both form images and discover them, we may be contacting the soul of the world to give it conscious expression. Perhaps planet Earth gives birth to human beings so that it can know itself through us.

STEALING FIRE FROM THE GODS

29.

Soulfulness: Finding Heaven on Earth

Soulfulness, as it is used here, does not refer to a metaphysical entity, but has more to do with our capacity for depth, relatedness, and intimacy with life, where inanimate things surprisingly take on character. Soulfulness finds value in things and events that we usually disregard—when we notice that they too have a reason for being here.

I grew up in a home where my mother and father were uninhibited in showing their love for each other. On occasion, there would be a song on the radio that both my parents loved, and although our family was in the midst of dinner, my dad would reach for my mom's hand and lead her into the living room where they would start dancing. My brother and I would look on gleefully, marveling at how they found such enjoyment in dancing, and how unashamed they were to show their love and appreciation for one another. When the song ended, they simply returned to the kitchen and resumed dinner and the conversation we were having. It was very sweet to see. But something else was occurring that was not obvious. By such spontaneous abandonment to the energy of the moment, they not only expressed their love for each other but modeled for me and my brother how to celebrate life.

In the heaven, earth, and human triad, our human position plays a pivotal role. We are a midpoint between expansive vision and earthly embodiment. The success of the whole human enterprise depends upon honoring both principles and also maintaining a dynamic balance between them. Heaven and earth are neutral, but depending on how we relate with them, they could manifest either positively or negatively. It is our human intelligence and ingenuity that determines how they express themselves.

On the positive side, heaven is the capacity to think big and open to the mind's vastness and profundity, to its nonconceptual wisdom. However, if we are biased towards heaven, we may lose touch with our living body, our instinctual energy, and the sensual pleasures of smelling, tasting, and feeling our world. This attitude seems to presume that our incarnation is a mistake. The earth principle is the beauty of tangible forms, the delight of the senses, and the creative capacity to transform the abstract principles of heaven into the currency of daily life. On the other hand, if we are biased towards the earth principle, we might become overly practical and utilitarian, concerned only with what is functional and efficient, and as a result, lack vision —that promising potential of what lies beyond the tangible forms of our world.

One of the ways to remedy the distorted aspects of either principle is to give expression to the place within us that lies between our Buddha nature and our ordinary waking consciousness that is bound to consensus reality. This begins by having a relaxed and flexible attitude that allows our definitions of the world to be porous and open-ended. For instance, although divorce is supposed to be a nightmare, the end of a

Seventh Threshold: Heaven, Earth, and Human

relationship could lead to a new and exciting friendship. Unemployment is supposed to be a terrible misfortune, but we might find that it opens up time and space that inspires us to create an entirely new life.

When difficult life circumstances drop the bottom from under us, we might find there is a brilliant light shining there. Even in the midst of despair, we can find a reason to be okay with it all, perhaps discovering a new found sense of self-containment. We may have to give up our idea about happiness to be truly happy, to abandon our idea of success to be truly successful, and surrender our idea of an abundant life to truly experience abundance. Such freedom is the gift of our heavenly intuition to find light in darkness. It is the mystery we glimpse when we look deeply into situations without an effort to change anything.

Children are wonderful examples of what it is like when we don't have fixed meanings for things, as children can play in a world that is loose, flexible, and amorphous. Through imagination, they can step over boundaries and definitions to be anything they desire, endlessly expanding their sense of being. At some point in their development, moms and dads explain to their children, "Okay, that was fun, but it is only play. It's now time to do your homework, so put your toys away."

Little by little, children learn that there is an indelible border between imagination and "reality" as they internally hears their parents' voice, "Oh, that's what children do. You're a big boy or a big girl now. We don't do that anymore." Eventually children map out their fluid world into conceptual categories, framed by the dualities of good and bad, masculine and feminine, and acceptable and unacceptable. Their thought and language patterns gradually reflect a network of socially agreed-upon meanings. Although this is part of natural socialization, the more that we hold fixed meanings about things, the more imagination dies in stages. We begin to confuse the map for the territory of our multidimensional world.

For instance, in your home you may have a dining table with six wooden chairs that have been there for many years. From the point of view of fixed meanings, a chair's function is to accommodate sitting down. That's what a chair is for. But if we bring in the mind that doesn't have solid definitions, that hasn't fit the everyday world of people and things into a grid of categories, we might see the same chair in a different light. In a kind of kaleidoscopic overlapping of momentary images and flashes of recognition, we realize that the cedar wood of this chair comes from Alberta, Canada. It was growing in a forest and shared an ecological niche with other trees, plants, animals, and insects.

As we continue to relax and dissolve our image of the chair, we might recall that these chairs supported us while our family feasted on meal after meal, told stories, had raucous arguments, celebrated birthdays, and poked fun at our relatives. These chairs also held our body while we tutored our son or daughter with math, getting him or her through middle school, when we never thought he or she would make it. These chairs supported our body and the body of our spouse as we looked at each other wordlessly, feeling grateful that we had each other. But now he or she is no longer here. These chairs hold that history.

Through a shift in perspective this chair takes on soul. It is no longer inert but a living entity with character and subjectivity that shares a common life with us. We feel less alone knowing that our home is populated by things with presence or soulfulness. We can feel intimacy with this chair and feel its relationship with us, if we let go of our fixed idea that a chair is only a function, only for the purpose of sitting.

Much of the world that we live in is a world of culturally-learned descriptions. We've weaved those descriptions into the personal narrative that we continually spin through our mind. Most of the time we are not living in a world of direct and immediate experience of color, form, and texture but in the cultural descriptions we've inherited. When there are gaps in our story, ordinary things might radiate an uncommon light that reveals more than what is presented to our senses. It's as if we've fallen out from the clouds and landed back on earth— thump— as we bite into this tangy Granny Smith green apple, and its tangy taste explodes into ripples of sensations that water our mouth. It reveals its soul as an embodied presence that is here for us.

Or we suddenly land on the park bench we were already sitting on, to abruptly notice the play of sparkling light on a pond's surface, the amusing quacking of ducks as we breathe the crisp cold air and welcome the sun's warmth on our face. We luxuriate in a feeling of well-being. We're simply here, but "here" includes the ducks, the crisp air, and the play in sunlight on our warming body. When we drop down from the abstract cloud realm of thought, we experience the mindless sensory enjoyment that's not organized with me inside here viewing an external world. There's just this inclusive moment from which nothing is missing. All of these many aspects go together to make up our mysterious identity.

As we permit ourselves to be penetrated by ordinary phenomena, we grow in soulful substance, feeling more at home in our world. When we value both pleasurable and painful experiences, something novel may be revealed to us about the most common things, taking us deeper and wider into our interdependent relationship with nature.

Soulfulness is a way of permitting the world to move us to our depth, where we find value and significance in small things, and even in things that we dislike. We can approach both joy and suffering as opportunities for uncommon experiences, subtle feelings, forgotten memories, hidden strengths, or a secretly guarded vulnerability—all of which add to our character. Soulfulness doesn't accept our identity as a given but as a mystery that may take a lifetime to fully appreciate.

When our energy moves us, we could find ourselves crawling on the floor with our dog or cat without thinking whether this is a good thing to do or not. We do it because we trust our body's rhythms. Or maybe we howl at the moon with our dog, not because it's a cathartic thing to do but because the wild energy of our body propels us. The spirit of play is also the play of spirit. When the spirit moves us we feel something larger in ourselves, a shift in atmosphere where we suddenly become animated, enlivened, and activated.

Contrary to our usual way of thinking, perhaps our husband or wife is fine the way he or she is, and that maybe life is enough just the way it is. We don't have to change people to make them the way we want them to be. Freedom and delight come from letting people be as they are, and not manipulating situations to fit us. It takes courage to leap into the world and let it be as it is. First, we have to accept and appreciate things as

Seventh Threshold: Heaven, Earth, and Human

they are, which is the earth principle. Then we can recognize creative possibilities for upgrading the situations and relationships we're immersed in, which is the heavenly principle.

The Indian Hindu system holds that the divine is playing, giving birth to and dissolving the cosmos in an eternally creative dance. As we introduced in the sixth threshold, this creative play of life and death, known by the Sanskrit term lila, suggests cosmic artistry or divinely playful creativity. Momentarily dropping our idea of who we think we are, we open into a larger life to find that we may be much more than we think, and the present moment may hold more than we suspected. From a willingness to abruptly step out of our autobiographical self, we discover that we are a deeper, more expansive entity than we previously thought.

As spiritual practitioners, we are obliged to hold the tension between heaven and earth, between visionary possibility and practicality, so that through returning to our body and its senses, we can translate heaven's vision into tangible forms that give shape and substance to our creative imagination.

30.

The Web of Life: Earth Community & Culture

"... the individual if left alone from birth, would remain primitive and beast-like in his thoughts and feelings...The individual is what he is and has the significance that he has, not so much in virtue of his individuality, but rather as a member of a great human community, which directs his material and spiritual existence from the cradle to the grave."

Albert Einstein

One of the themes running through this book is how we can appreciate very simple experiences in order to discover the basic goodness of being alive. From appreciating the beauty of forests and rolling green pastures, marveling at a spider's geometrically spun web, feeling the exhilaration of the crashing surf, or delighting in the fragrance of dogwood or a lilac, we are drawn into an intimate relationship with the primordial intelligence of life. At such moments, the boundary that usually separates us from these phenomena temporarily dissolves, as our sense of self expands to become an open field of sensitivity.

As we evolve on our spiritual path, we awaken beyond our identity as an individualized self to discover that our body *is* the world, and that the world is our body. This requires a radical shift in perception. This shift can emerge by being present to ourselves, being true to what we are experiencing moment by moment. Natural phenomena can inspire us, but with our inspiration we can also keenly observe the surrounding world to learn from and apply its magical properties to our society.

The heaven, earth, and human trinity can be used as a model to guide us in establishing a good society. We are held between heaven and earth, and although we are obliged to communicate with both principles, heaven's mandate can be abstract. Earth, on the other hand, offers a more tangible expression of heaven's expansive vision. Biologist James Lovelock used the term *Gaia*, the Greek mythological personification of Earth, to describe our planet's self-organizing, self-regulating, self-balancing capacities. From this perspective, earth is fully alive and infused with meaning, awareness, and a creative evolutionary drive. We are woven into the living processes of earth, and our mind is embedded in the larger ecological system of which we are an integral part.

When we bring the meditative state of mind to the way in which nature works, we discover that ecological and human communities display many of the same basic principles of organization. Both are based on interdependence and networks of communication and cooperation. The success of a whole community or nation depends on the success of its individual members, and the individual members depend on the success of the whole community.

For example, individual development is initially supported by loving interactions with nurturing parents who model for their children the capacity for empathy, bonding, and self-direction. But such parents need to be supported and nurtured by the larger societal system of which they are a part, so that they can develop into loving, nurturing parents. It's an interdependent relationship.

One of the well-known metaphors that Buddhism uses to portray the interconnectedness of all life is the image of the god Indra and his mythological net of jewels. Indra's net symbolizes the universe as a web of interdependent connections among all of its members, stretching out infinitely in all directions. Each jewel both reflects and is reflected by all the others, illustrating the principles of interdependence and interpenetration of all, by all. Whatever affects one jewel, affects them all. Every jewel contains all the others, so that every thing or being is both itself and the entire whole.

In a conscious and intentional community, each individual and group functions as a whole system within a larger whole. Each is complete in itself and is part of the larger systems that contains it but is also dependent upon the smaller systems within it. One of Buddhism's foundational principles is that there is no underlying, solid, and continuous self that truly separates us from others or from the surrounding world. Our true condition is one of egolessness. This is a negative way to say that our essential identity includes all sentient beings as well as nature itself.

The global crises that threaten our planet are largely based on a distorted idea of self—the highly individualized self, our "skin-encapsulated ego." This view of self falsifies individuals, as well as corporations and nations, by inflating the importance and supremacy of the individual. It also alienates us from the greater systems of life of which we are a part. As a result, we can be insensitive or oblivious to the negative impact that we as a species have on the rest of the world. It is only through an expanded sense of identity with other peoples, other nations, other species, and with nature itself that we have the possibility of establishing an enlightened society.

Contemporary biology teaches that life exists only in cooperative relationships with other life and not in individualistic competition for survival. A conscious, intentional community or nation emphasizes cooperation and compassion in the service of life. It nurtures the capacity for self-direction in order to create a thriving democracy. Instead of hierarchies of domination, enlightened societies would nurture the well-being of each individual and the community as a whole. They would emphasize the cultivation of mutual trust, sharing, and the equal distribution of power and resources. A conscious community or society values its citizens' need for personal development and expression and would provide the resources necessary for individuals to reach their optimal potential.

Ecological systems are diverse and resilient because many species can replace one another's functions. The more complex the network, the more complex its patterns of interconnection, and the more resilient it will be. Ethnic and cultural diversity play the same role in human communities. The quality of flexibility enables systems to adapt to changing conditions based on the multiple feedback loops that bring the system back into balance when there is disturbance or conflict. Flexibility indicates an open mind, and multiple feedback loops reflect unlimited communication, both qualities cultivated in the practice of meditation.

Seventh Threshold: Heaven, Earth, and Human

One of the revolutions that Buddha initiated in his time was the suspension of the Indian caste system that placed individuals in specific social categories, keeping them inflexibly bound to these social structures intergenerationally. Buddha encouraged men and women from all walks of life, from all social castes, to be part of his community of practitioners. When more individuals speak from their minds and hearts, the greater the collective wisdom of the group, and the wiser each individual becomes. The greater the diversity of a community, the greater its resilience in times of crisis, and the greater is potential for creative innovation. A diversity of age, gender, culture, religion, and race contributes to the resilience and creative potential of human communities.

A further example of how the earth principle can guide us in forming self-organizing and self-correcting communities is the tripartite human brain. Our brain is a complex system made up of three parts, each with separate functions. The reptilian brain, which is the oldest, ensures survival by coordinating breathing, regulating the heart, digestion, reproducing, and the fight-or-flight reflex. The limbic brain is the center of emotional intelligence, which gives mammals the distinctive capacity to experience emotion, empathize with others, care for their young, and to form cooperative communities. The third layer and latest to be developed is the neocortical brain, which gives us our capacity for cognitive reasoning, symbolic thought, and self-awareness.

The limbic brain, the source of emotional intelligence, and the intellectual functions of the neocortical brain, are both only partially formed in humans at the time of birth. The limbic brain must be cultivated through emotional interactions with the infant's caretaker and family members, enabling them to emotionally bond with significant others. Achieving the greater potentials of consciousness depends on the balanced development of both the limbic and the neocortical brains. By supporting the development of the limbic brain through loving interactions, nurturing parents increase the potential of their children to function as self-regulating adults with the capacity for empathy, bonding, and humanistic ethics.

Adults who have been raised by parents who have modeled humanistic ethics will value the full development of every human being and support the institutions of their community or society that strive for the optimal development of each of its members.

A parallel phenomenon in Buddhism, which we described in chapter 21, is the Three Jewels—the Buddha, the Dharma, and the sangha. As we explained, the Buddha is the teacher, the source of inspiration; the Dharma is the map or the teachings that show us the way forward; and the sangha is the community of practitioners, which is often comprised of ethnically diverse individuals. The Buddha and the Dharma could be thought of as the embodiment of the neocortex, the sangha as the embodiment of the limbic brain, and the reptilian brain might be roughly equivalent to the *vinaya* or the rules of discipline that monks and nuns take to protect and maintain the integrity of the tradition, preventing it from becoming diluted so that it loses its distinctiveness.

The principle of the Three Jewels can be applied to a secular community as well. The idea of the Buddha could be the vision that a particular community holds dear, its very reason for being, to which all members feel allegiance. The Dharma could be the various rituals, ceremonies, observances, practices, and teachings that members find meaningful. And the sangha would be the emotional bonding among and between its members, the practice of humanistic ethics, and the protocols necessary to maintain the integrity of the community or society.

This human community thrives through self-directed, self-aware, loving human beings who have reverence for life and feel a deep communion with all beings. These qualities enable us to transform our anthropocentric mindset to a more biocentric consciousness. They open us up to the benevolent force, which runs through all life and the cosmos, that gives support to our continued existence.

Reconciling Heaven, Earth, and Human

You know that you've crossed the Seventh Threshold when...

You're not only waking up, but you're growing up. The seventh threshold marks your deepening personal development by working through issues and conflicts that have kept you at earlier levels of emotional and relational development. Your primary challenge is to integrate the vertical and horizontal aspects of your spiritual path—heaven's spacious vision with earthy practicality. The horizontal path is the practical application of the earth principle, where you relate with your body in greater depth, working through subtle places that have remained stuck, and cultivating areas that you've neglected. The vertical path, which is an expression of the heaven principle, challenges you to awaken greater confidence in your original or Buddha nature.

At the seventh threshold, you have developed a relaxed and flexible attitude that allows your definitions of the world to be porous and open-ended. You see how imagination shapes your life experiences, how it gathers the separate images of life events and integrates them into an expanded context. This permits you to find connections among and between different events or things, affording new insights into situations. You discover that you are a more expansive being than you previously thought, and that the present moment is deeper than you suspected.

At the seventh threshold, you discover greater relatedness and intimacy with your world, and discover how ordinary things share a life with you. With this shift in perspective, inanimate objects take on character or soul. You've

Seventh Threshold: Heaven, Earth, and Human

developed renewed appreciation for imagination, as you realize how it mediates between heaven and earth, opening up communication with what lies beyond your five senses, so that the invisible side of phenomena reveal their secrets to you.

At this stage of the path, your identity expands to include the surrounding environment of forests, mountains, and oceans, as well as the community of insects, bees, and the animals that inhabit these diverse regions—of which you are an integral part. You realize that you are woven into the living processes of earth, and that you are embedded in the larger ecological system. As a result, you see how the heaven, earth, and human trinity can be used as a model to guide humanity in establishing an enlightened society.

Eighth Threshold: Being Human

We finally come to realize that the gods are the forgotten dimension of our ordinary bread-and-butter world. The human and the divine, samsara and nirvana are inseparable, each secretly enclosed within the other. The gods are the luminous energies of life, imminent in all things and beings. They twinkle through our eyes when we're enthusiastic, dance in the blazing flames of our passion, radiate through the smile of our children, but they're also the darkness of melancholy and despair, and the unwanted descent into unexpected illnesses.

The spiritual perspective is that our mind and the world are not strangers to each other, but that our very human life is an expression of the world's own being. We best serve ourselves and others by celebrating daily life, finding beauty in simple things, and goodness in ordinary events, but also by learning to love what's wild, so that we recognize our kinship with darkness, chaos, and destruction. Being fully human is to trust that the seasons of our life, the progression from birth to maturity, the hope of love and fulfillment, and the fear of loss and death—is the creative cosmic dance that goes on without end. Our challenge is to hold the tension between the human and the divine within us, without negating or exclusively identifying with either.

31.

Redefining Leisure

Genuine leisure is an open, receptive state of mind and a tenderness of the heart. Leisure is without expectation or hurry, without judgment or comparison, allowing events to unfold according to their own timing. When we meet the world with this nakedness, it freely offers itself to us.

By the time we leave childhood most of us have lost that magical sense of wonder and awe, that innocent openness to the miraculous. Because our world in childhood was not clearly divided between inside and outside, we could open to what was offered to our senses. However, through normal socialization and formal education, we have been conditioned to live in the abstract world of thought and have gradually become separate from our surroundings, from others, and even from ourselves.

With the advent of the information revolution, we have become fully digitalized, spending hours on our computers, writing and responding to emails, making purchases and paying bills, doing business, getting information, visiting our favorite websites, and watching movies. Because we expect an immediate response to the click of our mouse or keypad, our attention span has become compromised, leaving most of us with an intolerance of boredom and a hunger for stimulation.

We are living in an era of reality TV that promises extreme sensation and excitement, which is only relevant to a culture that has become so numb that it takes something extraordinary to get us to feel that we're alive. When we need the exotic or sensational to make us wonder, we have lost the wonder of being. This is antithetical to leisure, which is the growing capacity to actually *be* for stretches of time without an agenda, without the compulsive need to be entertained or occupied. What characterizes leisure is that we're not hurrying to get to the next destination or preoccupied with matters unrelated to the present moment. Instead, there's time to appreciate the details of ordinary things and to explore their more subtle aspects.

Usually when we think of leisure, we think of taking time off, chilling out, a time when we can unwind. But genuine leisure is something more. It's a forgotten art. It suggests an open, receptive state of mind without time constraints or pressure, when we feel free to pursue what interests us. To do something at one's leisure suggests doing something without haste or deliberation for its own sake.

Leisure is a willingness to enter into the liminal spaces where nothing has yet been discovered, planned, or figured out. It is when we are willing to drop our need to *get* something from our experiences and aimlessly walk into a unexplored territory. We might begin to marvel at little things that rarely merit our attention. We could find ourselves looking at raindrops as they strike a puddle and delight in how each drop, upon impact, creates ever-widening concentric circles, reminding us of how our thoughts and actions do the same—rippling out from us to the shores of others' minds and bodies.

Eighth Threshold: Being Human

Leisure is without expectation, hurry, or a destination, inviting us to notice what's unfolding before us, so that our mind spills over the edges of our known world to discover what has always been in full view and yet hidden. Leisure encourages us to drop out from our thinking mind to actually *feel* again with our whole body, giving our contemplative attention to things as if tuning into their interior. Although we are about to head into a busy day, we could pause momentarily to regard the way morning light falls on our night table, casting a soft golden light on our alarm clock and the small hand-painted lamp. We simply open our eyes to whatever offers itself to our vision. Things that are seen in this way enter into us nakedly, without judgment, comparison, or comment.

Leisure implies an inward calm, a silence and stillness, allowing events to happen according to their own rhythm and tempo. We steep ourselves in the mysterious nature of the world, where ordinary things come to us like a gift, unveiling aspects of themselves that we have not bothered to notice. Leisure is "living into" these moments to savor what they have to offer, rather than impatiently moving beyond them to what we imagine will be a better moment. There's much more to otherwise insignificant things then we imagine.

This morning on a short walk, I could see Mount Tamalpais in the distance, as cumulus clouds slowly swept across its peak, alternately concealing and then revealing it once again. The damp earth was fragrant after a week of rain. As I turned my head towards the horizon, I could see an opaque moon, when suddenly the silence was pierced by the melodious mating call of a sparrow. There was nothing that was missing, nothing that could whet my desire for something more.

Leisure is the capacity to find contentment in the most ordinary areas of life— delighting in the rich taste and fragrant aroma of this cup of coffee without having to read email, or sitting on a park bench and just enjoying the sight of passersby, or relishing the sound of squirrels scrambling from branch to branch as they rummage for acorns. This unhurried state of mind punctuates our speed and can momentarily recapture that childlike sense of wonder and awe, which can only be discovered in *this* immediate moment.

Our self-preoccupation has made us insensitive to the larger world beyond our busy lives. We seem to have lost the incentive and eagerness to investigate that larger world for its own sake, perhaps because we no longer feel its mystery, its soul. But we pay a price for this by living with a smaller identity. Ironically, this larger world is a partner in every step of our lives and we draw life from it in every step of our lives.

On occasion you could drop the usual structure of your day and casually explore an unknown part of your city or town, wandering with no purpose other than to see what you see and feel what you feel. You might notice a mother pushing a baby carriage in your direction. As you pass each other, you peer into the carriage, and you are met by the immaculate blue eyes of her infant. This precious moment brings a tear to your eyes. The innocence and vulnerability of this infant triggers the very place in you that is also unguarded and tender.

Or perhaps you walk by a drunken man sprawled out on the pavement. The sight of this pathetic human being presses down on your heart, as you wonder where are the family and friends who once loved and cared for him. No matter how beautiful or grotesque, momentous or insignificant we think

Eighth Threshold: Being Human

something is—everything has a right to be here. There's nowhere to be but here. We don't have to get something for ourselves, manage situations, or make the world right. We only have to participate in it.

Leisure confronts us with the challenge to relax our boundaries. Because most of us want immunity from suffering, we don't easily let go of the rope that binds us our learned description of the world, to fall into its unfathomable mystery. We sabotage our connection both with the world's soulfulness and our own by ignoring that larger life that stretches beyond our autobiographical self. If we can't let go of the rope, at least on occasion, we will be strangers to genuine leisure.

Related to leisure is play. When we watch children play, we marvel at how they enter into a realm of magic, as they shape-shift in a world of "as if," incarnating as a gushing stream, or as a wicked witch or a princess. Children at play enter places inside their souls that we as adults don't ordinarily visit. We get stuck in the serious business of being adults.

Scientific discovery can also be play—a different form of play. Scientists sometimes step outside of the structures of their discipline, letting their minds spill over the margins where nothing is yet known. It's a cliche by now that many of the great discoveries were made when scientists were playing with their grandchildren, mowing the lawn, repotting a plant, or doing something menial around the house. They were at their ease, and something just occurred to them. In 1941, a Swiss engineer, while walking with his dog, noticed how cockleburs attached to his dog's fur. Upon closer observation he saw how tiny hooks in the cocklebur caught onto the fur. From this unintended event, he invented Velcro.

Leisure includes more than play. It is also a willingness to drop our defenses so that we can be emotionally naked with our hearts cracked open. If we occasionally slow down and are willing to break our stride towards our next destination, we might find that we are carrying unshed tears of grief. When we allow ourselves the time and space to tune into what we are feeling, there may be deep grief for dreams that never came true, for people who have left us, for whom we didn't give ourselves permission to grieve. With a leisurely state of mind, we let life have its way with us, moving us, lifting us, or dropping us into our core.

We might find that as we age, we realize that we didn't accomplish what we thought we would, that we are not where we wanted to be in the big checkerboard of life, and this may be a pain that we've secretly guarded ourselves from. But opening to such emotional vulnerability, surprisingly, we could suddenly feel tenderness for our imperfect parents and our eccentric friends who really matter to us. Recognizing that a light would go out of our world if they were no longer in it, we now make it a point to express our love for them during our next phone call or visit.

Leisure is a receptive opening to ordinary experience, a readiness to meet what presents itself to our senses, untouched by the intention to alter things. Cultivating an attitude of leisure can open up unexplored dimensions of our ordinary world, in the undefined space where one activity ends and before the next one begins. There are many moments where we could pause and take notice of what we rarely give a moment's thought to. The crucial question for spiritual practitioners is whether or not we

Eighth Threshold: Being Human

can allow a gap in the flow of our thoughts and activities, where we can ride the moment to wherever it takes us.

Our sensitive membranes are the portals or bridges through which the natural world incarnates through us. We have eyes and ears, and nose and mouth, a skin-encapsulated body, and imaginative minds. The poet Rilke reminded us that the ordinary things of the world—teapots and pine trees, bowls of fruit and raccoons scurrying across our lawns at dusk—want us to incarnate them through our senses. Leisure invites us to withdraw the commonly accepted meanings and values attached to things or events, so they may disclose their hidden side. This is how we bring the sacred into everyday life, where meditation becomes a way of life.

I grew up in New York City where summers could be brutally hot and humid. Every summer my father drove our family, including my grandmother and our two parakeets, to upper New York State, where we spent the summer in a rustic bungalow colony. He spent the weeks working in the city and weekends with the family. On one of his visits, we were all sitting and talking on the screened porch of our bungalow when, without warning, a dramatic thunderstorm broke out, pelting the tin roof with a fury. Spectacular bolts of jagged lightning lit up the whole sky, as thunder resounded off the surrounding mountains. My mother instantly began to herd the family into the cottage, but my father motioned to her to stay. He was grinning and had a look of childlike wonder on his face. "Listen to that. Just listen to it," he said, transfixed by this natural wonder.

When a parent takes delight in such natural occurrences, it sends a message to their children that, at times, it's okay to relax their ideas about safety, and to participate in the ordinary magic of the natural world. Without intending to do so, my father transmitted his sense of awe, wonder, and appreciation for the elemental naked beauty of life. Because he was at his leisure, he could see that the world was more mysterious and wonderful than he had been taught to believe.

32.
Celebrating Daily Life

Meditation sensitizes us to the goodness and beauty of life. We realize that life is here for us, and that we belong on this good earth to enjoy what it has to offer us. We celebrate by fully participating in the life we are given, when we learn to love the most ordinary of daily activities.

When we think of occasions of celebration, we might imagine the sound of corks bouncing off ceilings, champagne bubbling over bottle tops, the clinking of glasses, the joyous festivity of birthday parties, graduations, and the ceremony of marriage. These are commonly recognized forms of celebration set aside from the usual affairs of everyday life.

Historically, celebration found its home in the festival, which itself was an expression of divine worship. The festival was a celebration of the gods, an affirmation of the great chain of being, and humanity's place within it. The great mystery of the universe, elicited by the festival, evoked awe and wonder in our ancestors, weaving individuals into the fabric of their culture through the shared sentiment of life's sacredness.

We now live in a secular materialistic society where almost every aspect of life has been commodified and quantified. Scientific materialism has taken the place once held by the gods, and has attempted to literalize and explain both our interior life and the mystery of the cosmos. Science itself is good and necessary, but scientific materialism views the physical world as largely unintelligent, assuming that the most human of experiences—consciousness, love, loyalty, and compassion—are all the result of permutations of bio-chemistry and neural activity. This materialistic perspective leaves us with a conspicuous absence of the sanctity of everyday life.

As we mature on our spiritual path, we need to awaken something within us that can't be objectively explained or quantified. By giving ourselves wholly to everyday situations, we must find the time to communicate with the most ordinary things in a simple and direct way, and thereby participate in their existence. For instance, it may be one of those busy weeks when we didn't have a chance to do a food shop, and we're hungry now. We open the fridge, and there's only a meager assortment of vegetables. Seizing the moment, we take out one large ripened beefsteak tomato, a bunch of green onions and parsley, and some grated Romano cheese. We clear the kitchen table but the atmosphere feels a little to bare. We decide to light a candle, and play some soft music while we cut our tomato. Placing it on a plate, we then pour olive oil on it, sprinkle it with a dash of red pepper and some parsley. Then cutting several stalks of scallion to accompany our tomato, we top it off by lavishing the tomato with some grated cheese.

We could pause for several moments and reflect on all that was involved in bringing this tomato to our plate—sun, rain, the fertility of the soil, and the many men and women who harvested the land. Noticing the way light illuminates the tomato, glistening in olive oil, we silently express gratitude for

Eighth Threshold: Being Human

the enjoyment this will bring to our senses. Taking that first bite, we let it linger in our mouth, and savor its sweet succulence. Who can say that we are not honoring this moment and glorifying the modest bounty of the earth?

In the Japanese Zen monastery where I lived many years ago, we were offered the opportunity to study flower arrangement or *ikebana*. The ikebana teacher would pick flowers and branches that were in season from the area surrounding the temple. When she made an arrangement, it became a miniaturized version of the season. There was such meticulous attention to detail, as well as delight in the way she handled each branch and each flower. Her movements were both spontaneous and yet deliberate. The arrangements were usually asymmetrical, reflecting nature's orderly chaos. Upon completion, something wild and beautiful now adorned our temple, reflecting the patterns and qualities in the larger than human world.

From the very moment the flowers were picked, they began their inevitable journey towards their death, yet continued to radiate beauty. A simple flower arrangement, a celebration of life in the midst of dying, conveyed the feeling that we were all part of something mysterious that extended beyond the temple and our individual lives. Celebration germinates and blossoms in the ordinary, nurtured in the smallest of daily activities. If we don't love particular things, then we cannot love the world, because what is the world but a bewildering assembly of individual things?

When I returned to the United States four years later, our fast-paced contemporary world felt exciting but empty, lacking in the appreciation of simplicity and the enjoyment of simple things. My sense of time was now so accelerated that I found myself moving faster and faster with each succeeding year. With the advent of the internet, psychological space seemed to shrink, and the frequency of person-to-person conversations gradually diminished, giving way to increased digital communication. I had to remind myself of the lessons learned in the monastery, that celebration had to be discovered in daily life, regardless of the conditions in which I found myself. Zen practice taught me that small things are not only a piece of the universe, they *are* the universe in miniaturized form and can be a portal into freedom and beauty.

Celebration comes as a fruition of meditation practice because it allows us to not only cut through distractions, but to sense the sacredness of life. Activities as simple as taking a shower, luxuriating in the feeling of warm water on our flesh, or savoring this piquant chicken cacciatore dish while inhaling its intoxicating fragrance, or walking hand in hand with our lover, not only dispel our existential loneliness, but move us into intimate connection with the beauty of life.

By contrast, when we're sitting inside of our mind in the director's chair, we're already disconnected from that larger world, as we shape our experience from inside here looking at a beautiful experience that appears external to us. The materialistic perspective disengages us from the living energy that involves us in the life of ordinary things, leaving us with a pervasive feeling of incompleteness or emptiness.

From this emptiness, we hunger for spectacle because it relieves us of our vague disenchantment and emotional flatness. Ordinary things no longer speak to us because we see them only as serving a function, and not for having value in and of themselves. When we deprive ordinary things of their soulfulness, then it's understandable how we could justify quantifying and commodifying everything in order to give us a sense of control over our environment.

When we keep company with the ordinary things of daily life—wooden salad bowls, antique clocks, the framed photograph of our parent's wedding, treating them with appreciation, care, and gratitude, we cultivate a sense of genuine relatedness. We can actually feel the living quality or soul of inanimate things, where something indefinable is in the room with us. Celebration is honoring such experiences that can evoke a sense of mystery, and feelings of tenderness and joy.

Hiking a beautiful trail while preoccupied with all the things we have to resolve before we could feel happy, we miss a stand of beautiful eucalyptus trees, whose peeled skin-like bark is dancing in the wind, scraping against their trunks, as if to say, "Listen!" Just before dropping off to sleep, we hear the hooting of an owl or the yelping of a pack of coyotes in the distance, and we're gripped by a poignant sense of loneliness and melancholy. Something utterly enchanting dawns on us, something that children and mystics know about. This subtle experience reminds us that there's an inherent meaning, value and beauty in things without our having to add anything to them. In such moments, we're connected to the owl that's hooting and to the cry of the coyotes. We belong to this world and it is here for us. Celebration is rejoicing in our feeling of home, wherever we are.

During a visit to our aging mother who has very little time left, we find her sleeping upright in bed propped up to by several pillows. We pull up a chair to be closer to her. Her withered, wrinkled face is in stark contrast with our memory of the beautiful young mother she once was. She suddenly opens her eyes to notice us sitting beside her bed. She smiles and tries to speak, but her words falter. She reaches out her hand, as ours meets with hers—and we burst into tears. Our broken heart, our dying mother, the wordless communication of love in the late afternoon light, all come together in its own unique design. You can't help notice the strange beauty of this moment and your deep appreciation for being included in her dying here, now.

We can participate in the ordinary events of our lives with a sense of reverence. The way to put this sacred view into practice is to abruptly flash openness—momentarily dropping your preoccupations, your wants and needs, and your hopes and fears. It's as if you suddenly hit the pause button, and everything stops for a timeless moment. You come out of the sky realm of internal dialogue to drop down into your earthy body, your senses, and your tender heart— and into this immediate visceral moment.

Celebration is not just the embrace of what is pleasurable, but also the embrace of what is fierce, chaotic, messy. Many of us have not made peace with the wild, unpredictable part of ourselves or the world, which could be unsettling. Sometimes a depressed mood that lingers can take us to an interior depth that we would never go voluntarily. Celebration is the willingness to honor the world's unabashed rawness, without defenses or justifications. The further reaches of spiritual practice involves this kind of shedding.

Many years ago, I did a month-long solitary retreat in Hawaii, where a friend of mine owned land. I meditated in an open-air coffee shack that had only partial netting. One evening, hours after the sun had set, I lit a candle and continued practicing. Large moths periodically flew into the shack, instinctively drawn to the candle flame. Unfortunately, their wings got singed and they'd flap around on the wooden floor for several moments before dying. Within moments, large spiders would scramble down the wooden posts of the coffee shack, seize the moths, and climb back up to their webs with their catch. Every now and then, a bat would swoop through the shack and pick off one of the spiders, rounding out the cycle of life and death.

Initially, I felt this drama was completely gruesome, and so I decided to not burn any more candles in the evening. But then it occurred to me that this is the world I belong to. Life, in order to beget life, must take life. As surely as these moths became food for the spiders, and they in turn became food for the bats, I would eventually become food for tiny critters as well. A single perception drew down the wisdom of life in one moment. When we are really in our experience, we can celebrate the exquisite beauty and undisguised rawness of life.

The Buddhist version of celebration suggests that we could rejoice in difficult times, even in illness, and in full view of our necessary mortality. There's a wonderful Zen story of a monk who is being chased through the jungle by a tiger. He comes across a natural pit, and finding a sturdy vine, he quickly lowers himself to get out of harm's way, but discovers that there's a tiger at the bottom of the pit. While precariously dangling from the vine, with one tiger above him, the other below, eagerly waiting to devour him, several mice emerge from the thicket and begin chewing on the vine. One by one, the strands begin to snap. Just before the last strand is chewed that will send the monk falling to his certain death, he notices a patch of wild strawberries. Reaching for the most succulent one and putting it in his mouth, he exclaims, "What a delicious strawberry!" This story points to the further reaches of our human capacity for celebration, regardless of the circumstances.

Our life is like a brightly colored sailboat that has gone out to sea, sailing towards a distant horizon, but which will never return to shore. This is our human condition. When this becomes our realization rather than a philosophical thought, we develop an intense awareness of the preciousness of each moment. Celebration becomes a deep love of the mystery of life and death.

Celebration is meeting life with openness and trust, in the space that is already provided for us by the universe. We step through the cracks of our stale idea of the world and enter into those indeterminate spaces, as if we were explorers on a new continent. We practice celebrating everyday life by appreciating that we can see the color red in its tantalizing vividness, hear the thrilling sound of a clap of thunder as it reverberates through us, feel the wetness of rain on our face without concern about getting dry. When we open up mind and body, a sip of wine can get us intoxicated, and one mouthful of nourishing food is already fulfilling. Sitting down with a trusted friend, without a word being passed, we celebrate silence and stillness.

If we miss these ordinary miracles, we miss something priceless that cannot be redeemed. We can get through our days, weeks, and months, providing for our families and do the right things, but at the end of our days we might realize with deep sadness that we have missed something very precious.

33.

Loving What's Wild

What is wildness, but our inability to control life's unpredictable twists and turns, and so it is feared and resisted. But wildness serves our spiritual path because it exposes how tightly we hold onto ourselves, and to our notions of order and rationality.

We might think that if we meditate forty minutes a day, take our vitamins, do yoga or tai chi, contribute to charity, eat vegetarian, and do no harm—even to insects—that somehow life will go smoothly for us. But life conspires against that idea. An intrinsic part of life is disorder. There are some days when our meditation is clear as a bell, precise, and insightful. We might naively assume that we've reached the stage where, from here on in, it's going to be clear sailing. The next morning, expecting to resume the clarity and tranquility of your previous meditation session, you discover to your dismay that your mind is spinning like a top with the most nonsensical thoughts. It's easy to become discouraged and confused, as you wonder whether the fault lies with you or with the practice of meditation itself. But at that point, it's necessary to stay on the cushion and to contemplate wildness as part of the path. We can't have a life without it.

Even if we are successful in business and marriage and are a nurturing parent of three high-achieving children, we are confronted by all kinds of thorny situations that are hard to anticipate. For example, although we always knew that the day would come when our parents could no longer live independently, the ramifications of their aging can catch us by surprise, when one of them suddenly needs institutionalization —which they vehemently refuse. We are now confronted by the inconvenient challenge to make a place for them in our own home. At first blush, we're not willing to stretch that far, yet this intractable issue doesn't admit of an easy solution or fix, and so we are forced to reconsider.

Having worked very hard to create right livelihood that affords us a comfortable lifestyle, and having established a network of friends, and the free time to both entertain and enrich ourselves culturally, our life finally feels balanced and healthy. We've spent years making it all work efficiently, but we've become increasingly ambivalent. It all seems to require too much effort, too much doing to maintain that level of success and comfort. We no longer feel like working so hard, but we're also afraid that if we "let go of the line," our comfortable lifestyle may start to unravel. Do we continue to give it our best shot or let it go? We never anticipated it would come to this.

We may discover that although we truly love our partner, we dislike him or her with equal passion. We're not ready to leave this relationship, but secretly we're festering in negative judgments about their neuroses. How do we make peace with these contradictory feelings?

The Buddhist teachings do not come prepackaged with formulas or remedies for all problems and conflicts. Practitioners eventually stumble across a deeper, more troubling aspect of impermanence— not only is life impermanent, but it can be

Eighth Threshold: Being Human

wild, chaotic, unpredictable, and beyond our control. The further reaches of our path challenge us to not set ourselves against gritty situations and the gnarly feelings they trigger. To think that our life should be happening other than the way it is, is to find ourselves very alone and far from our true home.

The word *wild* refers to life that is untouched by civilization—undomesticated, uncultivated, as in elemental nature. Wild could be a life without restraint or regulation, conjuring up images of being untamed, turbulent, or even ferocious. But it can also mean to be uninhibited in our passions, to be exuberant, thrilled, or ecstatic. Wild could be out of control and destructive, or spontaneous and creative. Wild could be a teenager's impulse to steal dad's car keys and take it out for spin, and end up getting into a serious accident. Wild could be a lioness savagely attacking and devouring a gazelle, which seems savage and violent, yet from nature's perspective, simply a display of the uncanny harmony of sustained conflicts in the endless cycle of life and death.

In the Buddhist tradition, a *mandala* is a pictorial image of wholeness, a circular design of ourselves and the cosmos—both of which include order and chaos. Wildness is another way of talking about chaos, the countless occasions of disorder that confront us daily. Although we've watered our plants, vacuumed the rug, checked our email, and balanced our checkbook, we accidentally knock over one of the plants, spilling its wet earth all over the carpet that we just shampooed. And that happens all the time. The growing capacity to embrace life's wildness is a remarkable shift in attitude.

Buddhism holds that when we are fully immersed in the world, then whatever we see, hear, smell, or feel has "one taste."

What presents itself to our mind and our senses is our own unique mandala. To reject one part of life and embrace another part sets us at odds with how nature works. Wildness has a purity, a lack of contamination or contrivance, and like nature at its raw elemental level, is ruggedly beautiful in its own right. One of the ways to extend the meditative state of mind after formal sitting practice, is to notice that the world is already its own work of art, although it doesn't have to be beautiful by conventional standards. Although hard to define, beauty evokes a sense of "just so" or "as it is"—that indefinable quality that arrests our attention, stirs our emotions, and transports us out of our mundane mentality for timeless moments.

Sometimes when things fall apart, through the cracks in our best laid plans, a strange light illuminates things with heightened clarity. Wildness can mysteriously intensify the presence of the world, so that we feel things most vividly, and we're momentarily dropped into an unguarded depth. Something as simple as autumn leaves that we've raked into a neat pile, suddenly swept up by the wind into mini-cyclones, can momentarily halt every reaction within us but that perception.

As we mature on our spiritual path, we no longer take chaos personally. We realize that wildness is the continuous movement of life that upsets our fixed ideas and habitual patterns. It is the confounding shape-shifting life force that evades all definition, as it transforms one thing into another, and finally dissolves those entities into formlessness. Wildness is the all-pervading rhythm of the universe in which creation and destruction follow each other like the alternating tides of breathing. Although it is the source of endless fertility, growth,

Eighth Threshold: Being Human

and creativity, it is also the dark goddess Kali who devours all the beings to whom she gave birth.

Our plans and strategies are part of human life, but they can't protect us from life's vagaries, those unpredictable situations that confront us without regard for our need for order and control. Yet, we have no other home but this. A life without cracks, gaps, and inconsistencies is not an authentic life. A fair portion of our life can't be predicted or controlled, nor do our conflicts always admit of remedies. We can take all the necessary precautions for ourselves and our loved ones, but there's no protection from life's wildness. If we're on guard against chaos, then our life is filled with a great deal of unnecessary suffering. On the other hand, through our embrace of life's wiggly lines, its irregularities, inconsistencies, and discontinuities, everyday affairs become inseparable from the spiritual path itself.

If we lack an intimate, caring relationship with the unruly things of our world, or with things that don't have an obvious function for us, then we will suffer a particular kind of deprivation and emptiness. When we attend to small things and bother to notice their details, our awareness magnifies their palpable presence. Finding random moments throughout the day to pause, we allow these things to enter us, where they can find their abode in the space that meditation has opened. Our willingness to make a place for wildness in our lives allows us to see that we are not strangers in this world, and that everything that is here, is part of our extended family.

In ancient times, our ancestors lived in an enchanted world, where mountains, forests, rivers, and clouds were experienced as fully alive and animated with spirit. Humans felt at home in such a world and nature was a place of belonging. All the members of a village, tribe, or clan were directly involved in the cosmos' unfolding and this gave meaning to life and a benign acceptance of disorder and chaos.

Meditation involves cutting through layer after layer so that there are no longer barriers of defense keeping us safe from the rawness of the world or our own unspoiled nature. The further reaches of wildness might be turning away from conventional wisdom and stepping out where we haven't been before to meet our authentic self. Celebrating wildness is our courage to step beyond the inner parent who whispers, "But, what will the neighbors think?" There's a time to turn our back on what society thinks to face the deepest, most authentic aspect of ourselves for the sake of our psychospiritual growth. This is not a form of rebellion but rather our growing allegiance to what is most true for ourselves.

34.

The Seasons of Life

We are inseparable from nature, woven into her grand design. As we live through our weeks and months, the chapters of our life reflect the challenges and gifts of nature's seasons— from the dormancy of winter to autumn's fruition. As the progression of the seasons embodies nature's intelligence, so does the unfolding of our life.

We can envision our human life as a microcosm of the world. The rhythms of the natural world and our inner world unfold according to their own intelligence and timing. The earth's goodness and beauty is found not only in the natural elegance of her rhythms and cycles but also in the seasons of our human life. A season can be a particular time of life, a phase of a relationship, or a stage of a project marked by a specific theme, a pervasive quality, or an emotional tone. Perhaps a defining energy captures a relationship or project that we are moving through, as either percolating or promising, edgy or enriching. Embedded within our human seasons, there is usually a personal story or narrative about the chapters of our life that provides a context or rationale for what we are going through.

Our seasons have beginnings and endings, but like the colors of a rainbow merging into one another, it can be difficult to recognize when one season ends and another begins. For instance, a relationship with a significant other or a long-term friendship could be envisioned as having moved through various seasons of its cycle. If you remember back to its beginning, there might have been a time in your life when you were without a partner or a close friend. While at a conference or a party, or perhaps while shopping or having your car serviced, you crossed paths with someone who engaged you in conversation, and something bright and promising began to happen. You found yourself drawn to this other person, and so you exchanged emails and you both expressed an interest in meeting again. In parting company, you silently acknowledged that there was something bubbling under the surface, that unmistakable chemistry of attraction which made you feel excited and hopeful, but uncertain. Later that day, you began to fantasize about this individual. This is spring, the season of rebirth.

The beginning of spring is when we thaw out from the coldness and inactivity of winter, the frozenness and emotional barrenness of being alone. Spring is the time when new buds suddenly appear on branches with the promise of more. The snows have melted and the crocuses have thrust up through hard soil with the hint of life resurgent. Our mood is uplifted and we begin to look forward with anticipation. The days are also getting longer with greater light, as we feel the warmth and brilliance of the sun. In spite of how dark, cold, and barren winter has been, spring infallibly arrives with a feeling of rebirth.

Spring is when we experience periods of creativity, hope, or love, seemingly emerging out of the dormant landscape of our psychological winter. We find ourselves in movement with a renewed sense of energy, feeling optimistic and encouraged that now is the time to ride the currents of this season and launch ourselves into our life. Rather than becoming inflated or intoxicated with ourselves, we simply recognize that we are moving through a delightful cycle brought about by innumerable causes and conditions that have given momentum to this season.

When we meet someone special and we start a relationship, we are tasting the sweetness of spring and nature's promise. It is an invitation to face forward towards a hopeful future. As the relationship continues to progress, we do more things together with our new-found significant other, exchanging more of our personal history, meeting each other's family and friends. We're beginning to deeply appreciate each other, and one fateful day, one of us says to the other, "I love you." "Well, I love you, too," we respond to our new special other. What was previously potential is now actual. We acknowledge that we're in love.

Spring now leads to summer, where there is a quickening, an energetic activation, a feeling of high energy as we lean in full tilt. We are doing more and more things together and are more involved in each other's lives. Not a day goes by when one of us doesn't call the other to ask, "How's your day going?" or "Good night.... Love you." "Love you too." Or we remember to do something special for our cherished other. The relationship or friendship seems to be moving of its own momentum. In a more general sense, psychological summer isn't limited to a romantic relationship but could be a friendship, or an activity that we were sampling that suddenly morphs into a passionate endeavor, with a heightened sense of aliveness and total involvement.

Summer is a time when we're flourishing, as we find ourselves extended outward into the social network of our friends, family, and community. It could be a time of inspiration in love or creative work, as many pieces of our life come together to work synergistically. Inwardly, it could be a deepening or maturing of a personal passion or project. There might be a feeling of either high energy and effort, or its opposite—effortlessness, as if things are moving of their own accord.

Sometimes we would like to just linger in the hopefulness of spring. It's so delicious because we're not yet bound by any commitments, and it's so full of bright promise. We could imagine all kinds of wonderful scenarios: "We'll move in together, and tastefully decorate our home, and we'll invite our friends to a barbecue to celebrate with us." In spring nothing has been actualized yet, but we're stoking our fantasies about what could happen. It's very safe. By contrast, by summer we've already made the connection and it's real.

Summer is the principle of energetic force and activity, when all of nature's systems are moving towards fruition. All movement, change, and transformation are expressions of nature's intelligent rhythms, and when we align ourselves with this life force, we move through our life without neurotic struggle.

Autumn is a time of fruition. We either live together or get married, or we get involved in a mutual project, perhaps starting a business together. Something has happened that sealed the deal. We have given birth to a new level of commitment, marked by a feeling of fullness and richness.

Eighth Threshold: Being Human

Joining our worlds together has resulted in the emergence of something new that is a product of both of us, whether that's the birth of a child, the purchase of a house, the start of a joint business, or being together in a much deeper, more committed way. We've harvested something that feels bigger than the two of us, which represents a fruition—the distinguishing sign of autumn.

At the same time, there is something melancholy about autumn. Although foliage season can be spectacularly beautiful, that beauty is also a statement of death. The leaves on the deciduous trees are turning color and falling off, leaving the branches bare, while fruit drops effortlessly to the ground. There is a sense of a natural cycle coming full circle, and completing itself in the bounty of the harvest. It is both fruition and death, back to back.

Autumn is that time in our life when we reap the results of our efforts, as the seeds that we've been germinating reach fruition. Harvest is the willingness to embrace that unmistakable feeling of completion and fullness when a job is well done, having brought something full cycle to it's culmination. This season suggests a time for pause and reflection, before we launch into yet another project. Autumn challenges us to notice how we tend to flee the open space that follows the harvest, in order to ward off feelings of emptiness and boredom. Instead, we can take in the good, savor the well-deserved fruits of our labors, take time to pause, be with ourselves, and listen to our heart, body, and soul. This is the gift of autumn. Many factors beyond our individual efforts contributed to the maturation of our seeds, and so we are filled with gratitude and humility, knowing that such cycles don't last forever.

In human affairs, as one full cycle comes to an end, we often want to hold on to the promise of spring, or the intense energy of summer, or colorful foliage and richness of the autumnal harvest. We might be resistant to move into winter again, with its colder weather and shorter days. Winter is when the days grow shorter, and when we are thinking more about sitting by our fireplace with a glass of wine, as our energies naturally move inwards, inviting introspection.

In terms of our human situation, winter may mean that we put less energy into our significant relationship. It could be a time to pull ourselves in, and contemplate, introspect, and increase our sensitivity to our own path— separate from our significant other or family. It doesn't suggest alienation from or a dissolution of our meaningful relationships, but rather a deeper acknowledgment that we are separate. We are together, but we are separate, individual people with our own unique agreements with life. For many couples, this is very threatening. "Why do you need to take space? What's the matter, you don't love me?"

Winter is an inevitable and necessary part of any natural cycle. We might back off somewhat from outward activity to allow space for something new to emerge, for another spring to be born at a deeper level. Winter could be a time of inaction, where our projects may lie fallow. Perhaps it's an uneventful time when nothing much seems to be happening in our life, and we have more doubt than hope, more inertia than initiative, more melancholy than cheerfulness. Such a season invites us downward into our own depths, a place we wouldn't ordinarily go. Although such an experience may not be pleasant, there's often value in dropping down into the darker dimensions of our soul. By being willing to go there and experience our shadowy

Eighth Threshold: Being Human

depths, we metabolize its destructive aspect, carving out a place in our interior where such dark feelings can coexist on equal footing with our light and bright feelings.

Psychological winter does not mean depression but may be a time when, removed from the fray of external activities, we come in close to ourselves and make time to incubate what was not fully experienced or understood. We give ourselves time and space to experience the ending of a phase of our relationship with our children or our partner, or perhaps the final stage of a project we've been working on for many months or years. If we don't allow a time of backing off and drawing inward to experience a gap or pause in the trajectory of our relationships or our intense involvement in projects, then a refreshed sense of spring doesn't arrive. Psychologically, the death of winter could mean letting go of who we think we are and relaxing our definition of our significant relationship or our creative venture so that we clear the ground.

If we are going to have another spring in our relationship, in our livelihood, or in another creative undertaking, winter invites to re-examine, re-evaluate, and perhaps re-vision what is most meaningful. Such reflection can reanimate our enthusiasm but can also shake things up a bit. It could encourage a couple or two friends to work through relational "knots" so that they can have another growth spurt, another deepening of their connection.

The advantage of framing our human life as a progression of seasons is that it normalizes the possible qualities, strengths, challenges, and vulnerabilities of that phase of our life. We can give ourselves permission to feel what we're feeling. If we're in the introspective aloneness of winter, the hopeful anticipation of spring, or the intense involvement of summer's activities, so be it. We are woven into the fabric of nature and there is a sympathetic relationship between us and the natural world. We can remain stable and unshakable like the earth, and persevere through difficult experiences, reminding ourselves that all seasons of our life have their own intelligence and unique rhythms. We can embrace both beginnings and endings without anxiety and fear of failure. Little by little, we learn to allow all manner of experience to coexist—the good, the bad, the ugly, and the beautiful—intuitively grasping that they emerge from the same soil.

In spite of the body's gradual deterioration and loss of some capacities, we can continue to develop an intuitive understanding that whatever we experience has some intimate relationship with our inner being, although we may not understand this at first blush. Nothing that life brings us is completely alien. The challenge here is whether or not we can trust the natural unfolding of our life, and the events and circumstances that make up our world, as a lawful process and as a sign of life's intelligence.

Eighth Threshold: Being Human

Being Human

You know that you've crossed the Eighth Threshold when....

Your appreciation of the meditative state of mind has grown even further, as you witness the unusual openness, receptivity, and relaxation it cultivates. Disappointments, upsets, and chaotic events no longer provoke your need for defense, but instead intensify your full-bodied openness. The eighth threshold marks your increased trust in life, so that you no longer take samsara personally. The fruition of your meditation practice has enabled you to hold a sacred view of life, regardless of the circumstances. You realize that whatever you experience has some intimate relationship with your inner being. Nothing is regarded as alien.

At the eighth threshold, you've made peace with the wild, unpredictable side of life, the parts of life that are neither sanitized nor domesticated by culture, neither orderly nor rational. You even welcome the times when things fall apart, noticing how chaos can intensify your presence to events and reveal what was previously concealed. By being willing to face the deepest, most authentic aspect of yourself, you've developed the courage to communicate even further with the shadow aspect of life.

You have regained a sense of wonder and openness to the great mystery that is your human life, having discovered that there is a meaning and value inherent in things as they already are. You are able to confidently enter the undefined, intermediate spaces in life before anything has taken shape or is known. Inquisitiveness has become its own reward and you no longer have to gain something for yourself from experience.

Nevertheless, you realize that life is here for you, and that you belong to this Earth. You can afford to celebrate your life by participating in the existence of ordinary things, fully giving yourself to them, and enjoying what they have to offer you. From time to time, you feel a sense of unexplainable mystery and are filled with feelings of tenderness and joy.

At this stage of the path, you realize that your human life is a microcosm of the world, and that there is a sympathetic relationship between you and the natural world. You see that your life has its own intelligence and unique rhythms, parallel to the progression of the seasons. You recognize and benignly accept the strengths and vulnerabilities of each phase of your life, but unlike the natural seasons, your spiritual path has transformed your life into an evolving spiral of continual development.

Epilogue:

Enlightenment Wherever You Are

The question of how to recognize the awakened state of mind in the midst of our struggles underlies every step of our journey through the progressive stages of our spiritual path. In the Buddhist tradition, we don't have to reject our neurosis before we can realize our enlightened nature. Instead, we can revision or re-frame our imperfections and problematic patterns so that they reveal our authentic nature lying at the core of our neuroses. We can do this because Buddha nature is here right now, within each and every one of us. Confusion and enlightenment are secretly enclosed within one another.

With meditative awareness, we notice that ordinary situations have a way of revealing the most paradoxical qualities about life. When we begin to slip on ice, the slipping itself becomes the catalyst for regaining our balance. We get vaccines that inoculate us with the very poison that our immune system tries to protect us from, so that we can produce the antibodies to fight the disease. Poison becomes medicine. The seed of a butterfly lives mysteriously embedded within the caterpillar's invisible interior—until it can no longer wait. From within its cocoon, a terrestrial being dies and is reborn as an aerial being, ready to fly off on its new life. From this perspective, the outer form of our personality is a distorted expression or imperfect metaphor for our awakened essence.

There is an ancient story about a thief who wanted to know whether he had to give up stealing before he could become a student of the Buddha. According to this story, Buddha stated that he could continue stealing but only if he dedicated his efforts to stealing the awakened mind. The thief took the Buddha's suggestion to heart and eventually had a spiritual realization.

We might have a craving for sweets—pastries, cookies, honey and fruits—but this might be a camouflaged hunger for the sweetness of life or love in a mistaken, literal form. On the other hand, we may have an aggressive nature that gets us into conflict with our family, friends, or colleagues. Perhaps we are responding, in a distorted manner, to our need to engage the battlefield of samsara to fight for truth or justice. When we become conscious of our heart's deepest desire, the energy of aggression is transformed into the protection of others, defending those that are vulnerable or disadvantaged, so that we promote rather than attack others in need. With a change of perspective, we could view our aggression and negative judgments as misguided expressions of our disgust with samsara; that is, as an expression of our repugnance with the unnecessary suffering that we put ourselves and others through. And with this change of heart, we could use the fierce energy of aggression to fuel our bodhisattva path.

There are times when we experience restlessness and boredom, a hunger that can't seem to be satisfied, no matter how much food, drink, or stimulation we indulge in. During such times of unrest, when we are feeling in need of a remedy or rescue, perhaps our hunger is for the only thing that can truly fill our feeling of emptiness—that unmistakable sense of coming home to our authentic self, whoever that may be.

Epilogue: Enlightenment Wherever You Are

If samsara is inseparable from nirvana, then we can use our imperfections and complications as a way to penetrate to the deepest truth of the moment. We must make ourselves our own lover. We try to love every part of ourselves, especially the parts that we regard as inferior, weak, wounded, or broken. If these deficient parts of ourselves are not loved, we cannot bring the fire of awareness to our entirety, and we will not be able to become our own best friend.

Who else knows how to love us perfectly but we ourselves? However, in the process of loving our deficient parts, we might come up against fierce self-judgment. We could imagine that if we loved these inferior parts, it would be the same as giving ourselves a pass for our "sins" of weakness, ignorance, inertia, or lack of courage. Many of us might think that we still deserve to be punished, to continue to feel bad for past actions or inactions, when we didn't live up to our idealized image of ourselves.

The reason such aspects of ourselves feel deficient or lacking is because they originated from experiences that were never completed, and lack our acceptance and understanding, without which we cannot bring closure to these experiences. Whatever the original situation was, we were most likely acting out of confusion and immaturity at the time, and not from our wisdom mind. Those experiences got embedded in our psyche in incomplete and fragmented form. Our negative judgments can be transformed when we love these stunted aspects of ourselves as we would love a child with a developmental handicap.

By looking our demons in the eyes and still loving ourselves, we consent to being exactly who we are, and to feel exactly what we're feeling. When we lack self-acceptance, we are at odds with ourselves and divided against ourselves. Whatever situation or condition we are currently in, that's exactly where we should be. The secret "fire of the gods" is that our present state of awareness, our ordinary mind is the awakened state—when we're not judging or resisting it, or trying to seek a particular result.

The way that we establish this kind of freedom for ourselves is by not struggling with life. No matter what occurs, no matter what the occasion, we don't resist, thinking that it should be other than the way it is. Instead, we practice not by going up against reality, but rather by allowing it. Allowing means that we don't deny, suppress, or dramatize experience. We allow disturbing feelings and thoughts to arise, and we either let them dissolve on their own, or we let them set a direction for inquiry or action—and we mindfully follow where they lead.

The challenge is learning how to metabolize negative or distressful feelings. When we meet with what is emotionally charged or are confronted by painful memories, we metabolize such experience by dropping the narrative associated with such feelings and by feeling into their energetic aspect. We keep our feeling-attention open, flexible, and free to notice what spontaneously arises. When we are in full contact with the energy of such feelings, we discover that like the force of nature, energy has its own intelligence, rhythm, and direction, and is self-revealing.

If we simply allow the energy to circulate without manipulating it, it becomes much more workable and can eventually take us to Being itself, the deepest dimension within us which is beyond ego. Who we are in our depths cannot be easily defined. Any thought or image we have of ourselves, is not who we are and does not capture our inconceivable totality. Buddha nature transcends our superego, ego, our instinctual urges, and our lust for power, yet it does not exclude them either. When we realize that the world does not point to a meaning beyond itself, our search for an ultimate transcendental meaning is finally surrendered. We discover that our life can be fulfilling here and now, and couldn't be any way—other than the way it already is.

ABOUT THE AUTHOR

Ira Rechtshaffer holds a Ph.D. in Buddhist studies and has been a Buddhist practitioner for four decades. He practiced Zen Buddhism in Japan for four years and has been a practitioner of Tibetan Vajrayana Buddhism since 1976. He has taught Buddhism in various seminaries, contemplative centers, and graduate programs, and conducts workshops on mindfulness meditation and embodied presence. As a practicing psychotherapist he works with individuals and groups, integrating Buddhist and Western psychology. His two books are *Mindfulness and Madness: Money, Food, Sex, and the Sacred*, and *What Was in Buddha's Left Hand?: Tantric Teachings to Transform Neurosis into Sanity*.

His website is: http://www.wayofthemandala.com and he can be reached at irarex007@att.net.

www.ingramcontent.com/pod-product-compliance
Lightning Source LLC
Chambersburg PA
CBHW072144100526
44589CB00015B/2074